A

I

THE LAST DAYS

OF THE SIOUX NATION

by Robert M. Utley

New Haven and London, Yale University Press

Library of Congress catalog card number: 63–7950
ISBN: 0–300–01003–6 (cloth), 0–300–00245–9 (paper)

Published in Great Britain, Europe, and Africa by
Yale University Press, Ltd., London.
Distributed in Canada by McGill-Queen's University Press, Montreal;
in Latin America by Kaiman & Polon, Inc., New York City;
in India by UBS Publishers' Distributors Pvt., Ltd., Delhi;
in Japan by John Weatherhill, Inc., Tokyo.

Originally published as
Yale Western Americana Series, 3.

The Red man was the true American. They have almost all gone, but will never be forgotten. The history of how they faught for their country is written in blood, a stain that time cannot grinde out. Their God was the sun their church all out doors. Their only book was nature and they knew all the pages.

Charles M. Russell

Preface

ON JULY 12, 1893, the young historian Frederick Jackson Turner rose before a meeting of the American Historical Association in Chicago to deliver his since-famous and controversial paper "The Significance of the Frontier in American History." "The existence of an area of free land, its continuous recession, and the advance of American settlement westward," he asserted, "explain American development."

Turner had been led to explore the fruitful topic of the influence of the frontier by a statement in the report of the Superintendent of the Census for 1890. "At present," the report read, "the unsettled area has been so broken into by isolated bodies of settlement that there can hardly be said to be a frontier line." Ever since 1893, when Turner expounded his frontier thesis, the year 1890 has been considered to mark the passing of the frontier.

From the beginning, few influences exerted themselves more powerfully upon the frontier than the Indians who resisted the westward advance of the white man. The Indian barrier stretched from Mexico to Canada and often immobilized segments of the frontier for decades at a time. Only when the Indian barrier had been pierced, pushed back, and finally destroyed did the frontier of settlement spread farther into the wilderness.

In 1890 the tragic battle of Wounded Knee Creek and the resulting suppression of the Ghost Dance uprising of the Sioux ended the long history of warfare between the Indian and the white man. Thus, appropriately, and perhaps not entirely coincidentally, the Indian barrier collapsed during the very year in which the Superintendent of the Census found it no longer possible to trace a line of frontier settlement on the map of the West. Coinciding in time with the passing of the frontier, the Sioux troubles of 1890 loom large in the history of frontier America.

The Ghost Dance religion took root in practically every western tribe. The content of the religion and its practice by these tribes found an able chronicler in the Smithsonian Institution's distinguished ethnologist James Mooney, who published his *Ghost-Dance Religion* in 1896. Perhaps the measure of Mooney's work lies in the fact that no scholar has since tried to tell the story in so comprehensive and exhaustive a fashion. The present work is not intended to replace Mooney. That will never be done. But Mooney's approach was primarily ethnological; mine is primarily historical. Mooney dealt with the Ghost Dance religion among all the tribes of the West; I examine only the Sioux, among whom the consequences were most portentous. Finally, Mooney did not enjoy so great a body of source material as is now available; nor could he benefit from the perspective that, with the passage of seventy years, is now possible. *The Last Days of the Sioux Nation*, I believe, supplements Mooney's work in many respects and corrects him in others.

I wish to express my gratitude to the many people who gave so freely of their time and talents to help bring this work to a conclusion. To three fine scholars and stylists who read the entire manuscript my special thanks are due for saving me from many blunders and offering valuable suggestions for more effective organization and presentation: Dr. Norman Maclean, Professor of English at the University of Chicago; Lt. Col. Norman E. Cawse-Morgon, Professor of Air Science and Tactics at Union University, Schenectady, New York; and Dr. John Alexander

Carroll, Professor of History at the University of Arizona and Editor of *Arizona and the West*.

My appreciation is also extended to those who read and commented upon parts of the manuscript: John C. Ewers, United States National Museum; Roy E. Appleman, National Park Service, Washington, D.C.; Maj. E. S. Luce, San Diego, California; Maurice Frink, State Historical Society of Colorado; Don Rickey, Jr., National Park Service, Jefferson National Expansion Memorial, St. Louis, Missouri; Franklin G. Smith, National Park Service, Santa Fe, New Mexico; Casey Barthelmess, Miles City, Montana; James S. Hutchins, University of Arizona; and Lessing H. Nohl, Jr., University of New Mexico.

For help in research I thank the staffs of the National Archives, Library of Congress, and Bureau of American Ethnology; Donald Danker, Nebraska State Historical Society; Maurice Frink, State Historical Society of Colorado; Don Russell, Chicago Westerners; the late Col. Louis Brechemin; Maj. E. S. Luce; Merrill Mattes, National Park Service; and Col. W. W. Whitside of Front Royal, Virginia.

Finally, this volume would have been unintelligible indeed without the splendid maps executed by Walter T. Vitous of Olympia, Washington.

R.M.U.

Santa Fe, New Mexico
November 1961

Contents

List of Illustrations

Maps, by Walter T. Vitous   *page*

1. *THE FIELD OF WOUNDED KNEE*

ON NEW YEAR'S DAY OF 1891, a bright sun broke over the creeks that drained northward into White River. It glared on the three-inch blanket of snow and formed icicles on the scrub pines dotting the ridges that separated the valleys. Three days earlier, on December 29, 1890, the battle had been fought. The next day the first blizzard of the season had swept the Sioux reservations. It raged for two days before roaring southward into Nebraska and Kansas.

Residents of the cluster of dingy frame buildings in the valley of White Clay Creek cleared the snow from porches and walks. On the south, between rank upon rank of neatly aligned A-tents and Sibleys, 700 cavalrymen muffled in muskrat caps and heavy yellow-lined cape overcoats moved about in the snow preparing breakfast and tending horses. Nearby, four times as many Indians, brightly colored blankets drawn around their heads, kindled cookfires among hundreds of conical canvas tepees.

Soon after breakfast a long procession of people, some mounted, others in wagons, wound up the ridge east of Pine Ridge Agency. The road led to the valley of Wounded Knee Creek, eighteen miles distant. There were about seventy-five

Oglala Sioux led by the agency physician, Dr. Charles A. Eastman, a full-blooded Santee Sioux. They were anxious to learn if
any wounded kinsmen of the Miniconjou Sioux tribe had sur-
vived both the terrible conflict of December 29 and the howling
blizzard that followed. It seemed improbable. There were also in
the group about thirty white men under Paddy Starr, who had
negotiated a contract with the military authorities to bury the
dead Indians at two dollars a body. And there was a troop of the
Seventh United States Cavalry Regiment to see that the burial
detail suffered no harm from the hundreds of vengeful warriors
roaming the neighborhood.

Shortly after noon the cavalcade drew up at the Wounded
Knee battlefield. In silence the people stared at the scene. The
crescent of more than 100 tepees that had housed Chief Big
Foot's followers had been all but flattened. Strips of shredded
canvas and piles of splintered lodgepoles littered the campsite,
together with wrecked wagons and twisted pots, kettles, and
domestic utensils. Here and there the skeleton of a tepee rose
starkly from the wreckage, bits of charred canvas clinging to the
poles. Snow-covered mounds cluttered the ground from one end
of the camp to the other; beneath them lay the shattered bodies
of the victims of the battle. Other mounds dotted the floor and
sides of a deep ravine along the edge of the campsite; and beyond, where Colonel Forsyth had tried to parley with the Indian
men, the mounds lay thick and numerous.

The Indians with Dr. Eastman burst into cries of anguish,
the sharp wails of the men mingling with the sustained moaning of the women. Some sang death songs. "It took all of my nerve
to keep my composure in the face of this spectacle," recalled the
doctor, "and of the excitement and grief of my Indian companions."[1] The whites, worried lest the Indians lose control of
themselves, fidgeted with nervousness. Eastman sent them to examine the mounds for signs of life.

Each mound hid a human form, torn by shrapnel and carbine
bullets, caked with blood, frozen hard in the contortions of
violent death. They were of all ages and both sexes. The storm

1. Charles A. Eastman, *From Deep Woods to Civilization: Chapters in the
Autobiography of an Indian* (Boston, 1920), p. 112.

of shot and shell had spared none. Paddy Starr found three
pregnant women shot to pieces, another woman with her abdo-
men blown away, a ten-year-old boy with an arm, shoulder, and
breast mangled by an artillery shell.[2] Others made similar dis-
coveries.

In the council square, where the bodies lay thickest, one of
the mounds yielded the remains of Chief Big Foot. Bundled
against the chills of pneumonia in heavy clothes and head scarf,
he had died in the first fire. Frozen in a half-sitting position, he
now looked out over the snowy field as if surveying in horror
the disaster that had befallen his people. Nearby, with the
charred remains of a tent surrounding him, lay the burned and
swollen body of Yellow Bird, the fiery medicine man who had
incited the young men of Big Foot's band to fight rather than
give up their guns to the soldiers.

Not all were dead. Beneath a wagon, partly protected from
the storm, Eastman found a blind and helpless old woman who
had escaped injury and lived through three days of freezing
temperature. In Louis Mosseau's trading post, where the road
crossed the creek, the searchers found more sparks of life. Several
wounded people had dragged themselves into the store. Some
had died but others still lived. Beneath a mound of snow, Eastman discovered a little girl, about four months old, lying beside
her dead mother, who had been pierced by two bullets. The
infant was wrapped in a shawl, and on her head was a buckskin
cap bearing in embroidered beadwork the design of the American flag. She was mildly frostbitten but otherwise unharmed.[3]
In all, the searchers collected five adults and two children who
were still living. "All of this," observed the Indian doctor, "was
a severe ordeal for one who had so lately put all his faith in the
Christian love and lofty ideals of the white man."[4]

The wounded were eased into wagons and driven back to

2. Paddy Starr Interview, Ricker Collection, Nebraska State Historical Society.
See below, Bibliography, p. 288, for further information about this important
collection of source material.

3. James Mooney, *The Ghost-Dance Religion and the Sioux Outbreak of 1890,
14th Annual Report of the Bureau of American Ethnology, 1892–93*, Pt. II (Washington, 1896), p. 879.

4. Eastman, p. 114.

Pine Ridge Agency. There they joined the other wounded survivors brought in by the soldiers on the night of the battle in
the hospital improvised by Reverend Charles Cook (another
educated Indian) in his mission chapel. One old man, badly
wounded, was tearfully greeted by his wife and children, who
had supposed him dead. Two days later he died.[5]

Yellow Star

The infant in the buckskin cap, now an orphan, was adopted
by Brig. Gen. L. W. Colby, commander of the Nebraska militia
troops recently mobilized to protect the settlements, and was
reared in his home as Marguerite Colby. Some of the Indian
women called her Zintka Lanuni, "Lost Bird"; others named
her Ikicize-Wanji-Cinca, "Child of the Battlefield." Two other
children, also orphaned by the battle, had been saved on the
29th. They, too, found foster homes—one, a son of Yellow Bird,
with schoolteacher Lucy Arnold; the other, a girl of five, with
Capt. George Sword, head of the Pine Ridge Indian Police.[6]

Working at their grim task, the burial detail remained on the
field through the following day, January 2. On top of the hill
from which the artillery had raked the Indian camp, the men
dug a rectangular pit to serve as a mass grave. The bodies were
gathered up and stacked on the hill. In all, there were 146.
William Peano, member of the burial party, recorded 102 men
and women of adult age, 24 old men, 7 old women, 6 boys between five and eight years old, and 7 babies under two.[7]

Some whites stripped part of the corpses for Ghost Shirts and
other mementos of the occasion. Then, still frozen stiff, the
bodies were dumped unceremoniously into the hole. "It was a
thing to melt the heart of a man, if it was of stone," said one
observer, "to see those little children, with their bodies shot to
pieces, thrown naked into the pit."[8] When the last body had
been rolled into the grave, the whites lined up around it and
had their picture taken. Then they shoveled dirt into the pit
and rode back to the agency.

    5. Ibid., p. 113.
    6. Mooney, pp. 879–81. L. W. Colby, "The Sioux Indian War of 1890–'91,"
Transactions and Reports of the Nebraska State Historical Society, 3 (1892), 159.
    7. William Peano Interview, Ricker Collection.
    8. Quoted in Mooney, pp. 878–79.

Later, the missionaries built a church in front of the grave, and in 1903 the Indians erected a monument over it. The inscription reads:

> This monument is erected by surviving relatives and other Ogalalla and Cheyenne River Sioux Indians in memory of the Chief Big Foot Massacre Dec. 29, 1890. Col. Forsyth in command of U.S. troops. Big Foot was a great chief of the Sioux Indians. He often said, "I will stand in peace till my last day comes." He did many good and brave deeds for the white man and the red man. Many innocent women and children who knew no wrong died here.

It was true. Many innocent women and children died there. What is more, the Sioux Nation died there. Before Wounded Knee, despite more than ten years of reservation life, the Sioux had never really accepted the reality of their conquest by the United States Army. They still harbored illusions that the day of liberation would come, that somehow, someday, they would return to the way of life their fathers had known, to the time when no white men interfered with their religion, their economic system, their government, their society. Indeed, this was the meaning behind the Ghost Dance movement that culminated in Wounded Knee.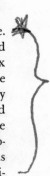

After Wounded Knee, even though only a tiny fraction of the Sioux Nation met death, the reality of the conquest descended upon the entire Nation with such overwhelming force that it shattered all illusions. Progressively, after December 29, 1890, the cohesion that bound the Teton Sioux tribes to one another grew looser. Progressively, the unity of tribes and bands weakened. Progressively, the individuals fitted into the mold of the reservation system.

The Sioux thus suffered two conquests: a military conquest and a psychological conquest. It was the latter that destroyed them as a nation and left emotional scars that persist today. But the road that ended in the second conquest began before the first. It began in the old life.

2. THE OLD LIFE

SIOUX OF THE 1880s recalled with nostalgia the way of life that the white man had set out to destroy after the military conquest. It was a way of life, they seemed to think, that had endured changeless since antiquity and that had no place in it for white men. Actually, as the life span of a people is reckoned, the old life was not so very old. Paradoxically, it had been made possible by the white man, and the white man had played a continuing, vital role in it.

There were many varieties of Sioux. This story is about the Teton Sioux, or Teton Dakota. "Dakota" and "Sioux" are the same people—"Dakota" meaning allies and "Sioux" a name given them by their enemies, meaning enemy. Originally the Sioux were forest people who dwelt in the lake region around the head of the Mississippi River. They lived in semipermanent houses of pole, earth, and bark and subsisted on berries, fish, and game, procured on foot. Then, during the first half of the eighteenth century, French traders moved up from the southeast, equipping the Chippewas, bitter enemies of the Sioux, with firearms. No longer could the Sioux hold their own against the Chippewas, and, with food growing increasingly scarce anyway, they drifted westward, up the Minnesota River Valley.

Some of the Sioux continued to the treeless prairies beyond and around 1760 began to reach the Missouri River in mounting numbers. These people who pushed westward to the Missouri, and later still farther west, became the Teton Sioux. By the opening of the nineteenth century they had evolved into one of seven well-defined divisions of the Sioux confederation. The Teton division was itself a loose confederation of seven tribes: Oglala, Brulé, Hunkpapa, Miniconjou, Sans Arc, Two Kettle, and Blackfeet. Each of the seven tribes in turn subdivided itself into numerous bands of changing size and composition.

The Teton division, like the parent Sioux confederation, had no form of central government, and the tribe and band thus commanded the largest share of the allegiance and affection of the people. But kinship and similar customs, history, and danger forged strong bonds among the Teton tribes. Even though they rarely achieved unity of action, there was a unity of spirit that more or less justified the label applied to the Tetons in later years by the white man—the Sioux Nation.[1]

Two significant gifts of the white man, combined with and applied to the economic imperatives of the land in which they had now chosen to live, dramatically changed the life of the Tetons from that of the lake and forest country. In the decades of the migration they at last began to acquire firearms from the French traders to the east. And from the Indian tribes to the west and south they acquired the horse, which had been introduced into the Southwest by the Spanish two and a half centuries earlier. These innovations made possible the political, economic,

---

1. For the early history of the Sioux see Doane Robinson, *A History of the Dakota or Sioux Indians* (2d ed. Minneapolis, 1956), chap. 1; George E. Hyde, *Red Cloud's Folk: A History of the Oglala Sioux Indians* (2d ed. Norman, 1957), chap. 1, and *Spotted Tail's Folk: A History of the Brulé Sioux* (Norman, 1961), chap. 1; and John C. Ewers, *Teton Dakota Ethnology and History* (Berkeley, 1938). For classification of the Sioux see John R. Swanton, *The Indian Tribes of North America*, Bureau of American Ethnology, Bulletin 145 (Washington, 1952), 280–84. The seven Sioux divisions were Mdewkanton, Wahpeton, Wahpekute, Sisseton, Yankton, Yanktonai (Upper and Lower), and Teton. The first four comprise the Santee or Eastern Sioux.

social, and religious life that evolved in the century preceding the conquest.

The great herds of buffalo ranging the new Teton homeland profoundly shaped this way of life. Indeed, in few other areas of the world has a single animal played so conspicuous a role in the culture of a people. Although the Tetons hunted all game animals, it was the buffalo that furnished the means of supplying nearly every material want. Buffalo meat was the staff of life and constituted the largest item of diet. Folklore credits the Indian with making use of every part of the animal, and in fact he did in times of scarcity; in times of plenty he enjoyed only the choice parts, like the tongue and hump, and discarded the rest. The hide of the buffalo provided material for clothing and moccasins, for bed covers, for "bull boats" used in stream crossings, and for every kind of container. Dressed hides sewn together and stretched over a conical framework of poles formed the familiar tepee, which provided an easily transported yet comfortable year-round shelter. Hoofs, horns, and bones found a variety of uses—ceremonial trappings, cooking utensils, awls, chisels, hide-scrapers, and other tools. Intestines and bladders were used to carry water. Sinews furnished rope, thread, and bowstrings. Hair was put to a wide range of utilitarian purposes. On the treeless prairie even the droppings were burned as fuel. Occupying so prominent a place in the material culture of the Tetons, the buffalo loomed significantly in the Tetons' conception of the universe and in their body of religious beliefs and practices. For the Plains Indians the disappearance of the buffalo was a catastrophe.

Because the buffalo were migratory, the Tetons became nomads. Living in portable skin tepees, with mobility afforded by the horse, they scattered over the plains west of the Missouri River and north of the Arkansas River. Individual bands of a tribe went their separate ways during part of the year. Each spring they gathered at a pre-arranged rendezvous and took their places in the tribal circle. As a tribe they devoted a major share of the summer to killing game and preparing the meat for winter. The organization and conduct of the hunt required elaborate rituals and for its duration consumed the energy and enthusiasm of the entire tribe. In late autumn the tribe again broke up, and the bands scattered for the winter.

Vital though the buffalo was, the Teton economy was never purely primitive. White traders supplied numerous useful items —firearms, pots, kettles, knives, awls, even beads for decoration —and in return received animal furs and skins. The Tetons regarded trade goods as indispensable, and they rarely got through a year without a journey to the trading post or a visit from an itinerant trader. Even before the close of the eighteenth century, traders had appeared on the Upper Missouri. After Lewis and Clark showed the way, the great fur companies spread up the Missouri and the Platte to play a cherished and essential role in the Teton way of life.

Ranging over a vast country, ceaselessly on the move, ever-active whether in war or in the hunt, the Teton warrior despised restraint. Self-discipline was the strongest curb on individual desires that conflicted with group welfare. But group living required group restraint, and a simple political organization evolved.

Each band had its own chief, but he was not an absolute despot ruling the destinies of his people. His duties were to carry out the will of the majority and to guard the band's customs, traditions, and religion. He could influence opinion, but he rarely acted in important matters without a mandate from the people. The rank of chief might be inherited, or attained through force of character, success in war, and acquisition of wealth. No single chief ruled the entire tribe. When the bands assembled in the summer months, such authority as existed rested in the tribal council, which governed through executive deputies and a corps of tribal soldiers. Among the Oglalas, for example, the council consisted of seven band chiefs chosen by the older men of the tribe. Their deputies, four distinguished young men, wore shirts fringed with hair as badges of office, and were called the Shirt Wearers. They governed in the name of the council and within the policy framework set by the council. They enforced their authority and that of the council through tribal soldiers, or policemen, chosen from a men's society called the *Akicita*. Given the individualistic temperament of the Sioux, these policemen commanded surprising obedience. The Oglalas explained to the anthropologist Clark Wissler that the Akicita were

> those who see that there is general order in camp when traveling from one place to another; those who attend to the duties of overseeing the buffalo hunt so that no one may chase the buffalo singly; those who see that all can charge the buffalo at once or split the party so that when one chases the buffalo one way, the other band closes in; and those who supervise the chase to get better results. They also see that no one kills another, but in case one does, they either kill him or destroy all his property, kill his horses, destroy his tipi, etc.[2]

This system of tribal government operated only during the summer months, when the bands came together as a tribe to hunt and to make war. It worked well enough, but when increasing numbers of whites moved westward in the middle nineteenth century, posing a sustained menace to the Indian way of life, it proved too weak. Paradoxically, the white officials injected more authoritarianism into the system. Ignorant of the realities of Sioux political organization, they found it convenient to deal with a tribe through a single leader and persuaded each tribe to choose a head chief.[3] Even then, the head chief had to act as the tribal council instructed. The officials' assumption that a chief ruled absolutely over his people led to many misunderstandings between the two races. Red Cloud and Spotted Tail became big chiefs by white appointment. They held less authority during the 1870s than the whites thought, but far more than would have been possible in the old days, before the whites controlled the source of food.

The highest values of the Tetons centered on war. For a young man, success in battle offered the surest and quickest path to prestige, wealth, and high rank. A collection of enemy scalps

2. Wissler, "Societies and Ceremonial Associations in the Oglala Division of the Teton-Dakota," *Anthropological Papers of the American Museum of Natural History*, *11* (1916), 9–10.

3. Hyde, *Red Cloud's Folk*, p. 67.

was his badge of success, and together with the qualities of bravery, daring, and cleverness earned him the esteem of men and the admiration of women. Early in life he developed skill in horsemanship and in the use of combat equipment—bow and arrow, lance, tomahawk, knife, shield, and, when available, rifle. He joined a war society. Each tribe had several such organizations that gave expression to the ideals of warfare. Analogous to Akicita societies in civil matters, these military societies were not in themselves fighting organizations. A member wore into battle the distinctive insignia and regalia of his society, and at its feasts and dances he boasted of his prowess and achievements, but otherwise he enlisted in war parties as an individual. Each society sought the most renowned warriors, and the warriors in turn exerted themselves to bring honor to their societies.

Organization, departure, adventures, and return of a war party aroused universal interest among the tribe. Ideally, a raiding party numbered thirty to forty men. Its objectives were to steal as many ponies and take as many scalps as possible. Any warrior might recruit and lead such an expedition. Its existence was temporary and membership entirely voluntary. When a larger number of warriors or an entire band or tribe set forth on an invasion of enemy territory, a more elaborate organization went into effect. Officers called *blotaunka* were appointed to assist the leader and regulate the march and attack. These men performed military duties similar to the civil duties of the Akicita. They served for one campaign only, but selection as a blotaunka was one of the highest military honors to which a warrior could aspire.

Women performed the vital if unheroic labor of cooking, preparing skins and robes, making clothing and lodgings, and moving camp. They also served an important function in lending inspiration to the men, for the admiration of a woman worked wonders in spurring hunter and warrior to ever loftier achievement. In sharp contrast to the boasting that trumpeted his return from war or the hunt, the Sioux man conducted his amorous pursuits with extreme shyness and circumspection. When he wanted to propose marriage, he deposited as much personal wealth as he could afford, usually in ponies, in front of the tepee of the girl's father. If the suitor was accepted, the girl moved in with him without further formality. No ceremonies or vows sanctified the contract. Divorce, while uncommon, was equally simple and accomplished without ceremony. Men of wealth often took several wives, housing them in one or more tepees. Both men and women displayed overwhelming and unconcealed affection for their children, imposing almost no discipline on them, and indulging every whim. Separation of parents from their children produced an emotional catastrophe and reunion a scene of joy.

For men and women alike, religion dominated nearly every thought and activity. It reflected their nomadic, outdoor life. Living close to nature, dependent upon its bounty for survival, the Tetons felt themselves part of nature, and nature an extension of themselves. A profusion of gods surrounded them, and one or more resided in every manifestation of nature. An early observer saw here "naught but an inextricable maze of gods, demons, spirits, beliefs and counter beliefs, earnest devotion and reckless skepticism, prayers, sacrifices, and sneers, winding and intermingling with one another, until a labyrinth of pantheism and skepticism results, and the Dakota, with all his infinity of deities appears a creature of irreligion."[4]

Yet the Sioux was not a creature of irreligion, and a distinguished ethnologist did succeed in making some sense out of his gods.[5] All gods merged to become Wakan Tanka, the Great Mysterious, who was at the same time many beings and one all-inclusive being. Each of the constituent beings possessed distinct powers and commanded a peculiar form of ritual from those who would invoke his power; and all, while individual gods in their own right, collectively constituted Wakan Tanka. All the gods that made up Wakan Tanka were benevolent gods. The Teton did not worship them as the white man worshiped his God but rather appealed to them for help and personal power.

4. Quoted in J. O. Dorsey, "A Study of Siouan Cults," *11th Annual Report of the Bureau of American Ethnology, 1888–89* (Washington, 1894), pp. 431–32.

5. J. R. Walker, "The Sun Dance and Other Ceremonies of the Oglala Division of the Teton Dakota," *Anthropological Papers of the American Museum of Natural History, 16,* Pt. II (1917).

Of the benevolent gods, Wi, the Sun, ranked as chief. He appeared in material form each day to span the heavens, then rested at night in the underworld. Patron of the four principal Sioux virtues—bravery, fortitude, generosity, and fidelity—his power might be solicited through certain offerings and ceremonies. Chief among these was the Sun Dance, in which a dancer might communicate directly with Wi. Red symbolized Wi and stood forth as the great sacred color of the Plains Indians. Blue symbolized Skan, the Sky, who resided everywhere above the ground and could sit in judgment not only upon all humans but also upon all other gods. His immense potency, captured in a fetish (object endowed with supernatural power), prevailed in all matters. Only shamans might possess such a fetish, and it could be invested with the power of Skan only through lengthy and intricate ceremony. Maka, the Earth, was the mother of all material things and patroness of all that grew from the earth, of food and drink, and of the tepee. Fetishes made of anything grown from the soil might contain Maka's potency. Her symbolic color was green. Inyan, the Rock, was ancestor of all things and all gods. He was patron of authority and vengeance, construction and destruction, implements and utensils. Anything hard as stone might become a fetish with the powers of Inyan. His symbolic color was yellow.

Other gods, lacking the enormous power of Wi, Skan, Maka, and Inyan, performed no less essential functions. The Moon, for instance, set the time for the important events of mankind, while Tate, the Wind, governed the four seasons of the year. Wohpe presided over pleasure, protected the chastity of women, and mediated between gods, between men, and between gods and men. Tatanka, the Buffalo God, watched over the hunt and decreed its success or failure.

In addition to the benevolent gods that composed Wakan Tanka, the Sioux combated or propitiated seven malevolent gods, whose sole purpose was to make trouble for Indians. The Mini Watu, for example, looked and acted like maggots and could make things rot. They were eternally trying to enter the human body. When they succeeded, they caused an infinite variety of internal tortures and tried to drive Niya, the Ghost, from the body. Less evil were the Gica, who caused annoying accidents, and the Can Oti, who forever tried to confuse man in his recognition of directions and locations. Every misfortune that befell the Indian, whether calamitous or merely irritating, might be ascribed to the activities of these malevolent gods. Various techniques, such as the smoke of sage and sweet grass, could be employed to ward off some; the powers of the medicine man were required to repel others.

The encompassing presence of the Great Mysterious and the existence of his constituent parts in every expression of nature —earth, sky, sun, animals, birds, vegetation, rocks—conditioned the daily thought and behavior of the Tetons. At Standing Rock in 1911 Chased-by-Bears described to Frances Densmore how the Sioux felt about Wakan Tanka:

> We talk to Wakantanka and are sure that he hears us, and yet it is hard to explain what we believe about this. It is the general belief of the Indians that after a man dies his spirit is somewhere on the earth or in the sky, we do not know exactly where, but we are sure that his spirit still lives. Sometimes people have agreed together that if it were found possible for spirits to speak to men, they would make themselves known to their friends after they died, but they never came to speak to us again, unless, perhaps, in our sleeping dreams. So it is with Wakantanka. We believe that he is everywhere, yet he is to us as the spirits of our dead friends, whose voices we cannot hear.[6]

In the Teton gods resided all the different kinds of power that man needed on earth. To acquire the virtues of Teton society, to achieve success in war and the hunt, to win acclaim and status in the tribe, to enjoy satisfactory family relations, and to excel in the men's societies a Teton had to possess powers that could be obtained only from these deities.

The high point in the lifelong quest for power usually came to the man in adolescence and in fact marked his initiation to manhood. He went alone to the plains, stripped to a breechcloth,

6. Densmore, *Teton Sioux Music,* Bureau of American Ethnology, Bulletin 61 (Washington, 1919), 96.

fasted, prayed, tortured himself, and humbly appealed for strength. If he experienced no vision after four days he returned home, but went again and again until the vision came. Interpreted by a shaman, it identified his guardian spirit for life. This patron being might dwell in any object, animate or inanimate, and between the youth and this object, or *totem,* sprang a spiritual relationship that lasted for the rest of his life.

If the totem happened to be a rabbit, for example, the warrior took care always to treat rabbits with reverence, never to harm them, never to eat their flesh. Caricatures of rabbits adorned many of his possessions, especially his weapons, for in war above all pursuits the power of the totem was essential. He acquired some part of the rabbit—an ear, a leg bone, a tail—to symbolize the totem, and it became the repository of his personal power, the visible link between him and all rabbits, the most sacred and valued thing he owned.

Besides the symbol of his totem, the Sioux usually collected a number of fetishes, objects that a vision or dream had suggested as possessed of supernatural power. In return for prayer, sacrifice, feasts, and protection, the fetish promoted the welfare of the owner. Unlike the memento of his totem, the fetish might lose its power and thus its sacred character.

From gods, totems, and fetishes the Tetons derived every kind of psychological power needed to make them individually and nationally strong, confident, and untroubled. Without this power they would have been an inconsequential obstacle to the westward advance of the white man.

Indispensable to the proper functioning of the religion were shamans and medicine men. Although the distinction between the two is shadowy, the shaman held higher rank, possessed greater knowledge and power, and often taught the medicine man. To these men the Tetons looked for instruction and guidance in spiritual matters, for interpretation of visions and dreams, and for mediation between man and the gods. As Capt. John G. Bourke explained to his contemporaries in 1890:

> The medicine-man of the American tribes is not the fraud and charlatan many people affect to consider him; he is,

indeed, the repository of all the lore of the savage, the pos-
sessor of knowledge, not of the present world alone, but of
the world to come as well. At any moment he can commune
with the spirits of the departed; he can turn himself into
an animal at will; all diseases are subject to his incantations;
to him the enemy must yield on the war-path; without the
potent aid of his drum and rattle and song no hunt is undertaken; from the cradle to the grave the destinies of the tribe
are subject to his whim.[7]

In addition to spiritual duties, shamans and medicine men
took charge of attacking all maladies that home remedies had
failed to cure. Malevolent gods caused sickness, and the medicine man attacked them with prayers, incantations, healing songs,
and the personal fetishes on which he had made his reputation.
He required advance payment, usually in ponies. Although his
fees were exorbitant, he frequently returned them in case of
failure. And failure often brought, in addition, physical harm
or even death at the hands of the patient's relatives. The shamans and medicine men organized dream cult societies composed of members who had experienced similar dreams. As Captain Bourke pointed out, these men exercised such enormous
influence that they virtually controlled the destinies of their
people.

Although the Sioux had many ceremonies, dances, and feasts
—some religious and others merely social—the Sun Dance was
by far the most prominent and spectacular. Indeed, its importance in the total scheme of Teton life can hardly be overesti-
mated. "The Sun Dance," Red Bird told Frances Densmore,
"was our first and only religion."[8]

The event took place each summer and lasted eight days. The
first four days were devoted to a number of ceremonies that

7. Bourke, "The Indian Messiah," *Nation* (Dec. 4, 1890), pp. 439–40.

8. Densmore, p. 86. The most authoritative treatment of the subject is Walker,
"Oglala Sun Dance," but see also Gordon MacGregor, *Warriors without Weapons:
A Study of the Society and Personality Development of the Pine Ridge Sioux* (Chicago, 1946), pp. 90–91. A graphic eyewitness account by an Army officer is Lt. Frederick Schwatka, "The Sun-Dance of the Sioux," *Century Magazine, 39* (1890),
753–59.

reinforced various ideals and customs of Sioux society. For the women, fertility and chastity found expression in rituals. For the men, there were rites to dramatize hunting, scouting, raiding, and victory over the enemy. The men's societies took in new members and staged a number of ceremonies. Feasts and give-aways alternated with the ceremonies. During the last four days men who had so vowed danced one of four grades of the Sun Dance—worshiping, supplicating, and communing with the chief god, Wi, the Sun. The fourth grade, danced on the fourth day, required the greatest self-torture. Suspended from the dance pole by rawhide thongs run beneath their chest and back muscles, often dragging buffalo skulls to increase the weight, the dancers gazed intently into the face of the sun and danced around the pole until the thongs tore through the flesh. Thus each man hoped to establish a direct relationship with Wi, and to gain Wi's power for himself and the tribe.

By accenting all the values of Teton culture, by exerting an enormous social and religious force on every individual, by strengthening the solidarity of the tribe, and by creating a sustained atmosphere charged with the most intense emotion, the Sun Dance occupied a place of incalculable importance in the life of the Teton Sioux.

This was the background that the Tetons brought with them to the reservation. This was the only life they had known and the only life they wanted to know. And this was the life that the white man, during the decade of the 1880s, set out to destroy, utterly and immediately.

3. THE NEW LIFE

WATCHED by the soldiers at Camp Robinson, Red Cloud Agency sprawled on the banks of White River near the modern town of Chadron, Nebraska. Here in 1877 Red Cloud lived with his Oglala Sioux followers. At Spotted Tail Agency, on a tributary of White River about thirty miles to the northeast, stood the tepees of the Brulé followers of the chief for whom the agency had been named. Together with other Sioux at Cheyenne River and Standing Rock Agencies, on the Missouri River to the north, these Indians had lived under the eyes of government agents while their wilder kinsmen had made the last stand of the Sioux Nation. Under such leaders as Black Moon, Sitting Bull, Crazy Horse, Gall, and Hump, these Indians had fought to assert their right to the Powder River hunting grounds. They had defied the United States Army to confine them to the reservation. On Rosebud Creek in June 1876 they stopped Brig. Gen. George Crook and forced him to turn back. On the Little Bighorn they battled Lt. Col. George A. Custer and the entire Seventh Cavalry Regiment, leaving the field strewn with the bodies of the commander and more than 200 soldiers. But these triumphs in the end brought defeat. Throughout the summer, autumn, and winter of 1876 growing hordes of soldiers hounded the Sioux so persistently that the agencies, with free rations, looked increas ingly attractive. At noon on May 6, 1877, Camp Robinson and Red Cloud Agency formed the stage for a drama full of meaning for the future of the Sioux.

Led by Oglala tribal soldiers, a mass of Indians approached the military post. Crazy Horse, Little Big Man, Little Hawk, He Dog, Old Hawk, and Big Road, astride war ponies, rode abreast. Behind each came his personal following of warriors, riding in column formation. Women, children, and old men, with all the camp equipment, brought up the rear. Between 1,100 and 1,500 people, including about 300 warriors, made up a column that spread over two miles of prairie. Singing war songs, the van marched into the military quadrangle and drew up before General Crook and his staff. The Crazy Horse hostiles laid down their arms and promised to fight no more.[1]

The surrender of Crazy Horse came as the grand climax of a series of similar scenes that had been enacted at Red Cloud and Spotted Tail Agencies throughout the spring of 1877. Pressed by soldiers in the north, one band after another had drifted in to give itself up. By summer, following the defeat of Lame Deer's Miniconjous by Col. Nelson A. Miles, nearly 4,500 hostiles had joined their tamer relatives at the two agencies. Only Sitting Bull and about 2,500 irreconcilables remained at large, and they had already sought refuge in the land of the "Great Mother," Queen Victoria's Canada. Some of Crazy Horse's people, angered by the death of their leader in a guardhouse scuffle at Camp Robinson, broke away once more and joined Sitting Bull in Canada. There, the Great Mother's redcoats turned out to be stern policemen, and the Great Father's bluecoats watched like hawks from the other side of a magic line on the prairie that the Sioux could not see. Food proved scarce and life grim. At the agencies, at least, their kinsmen ate with a degree of regularity. Finally, in July 1881, the Sitting Bull and Crazy Horse hostiles crossed the international boundary and surrendered at Fort Buford, Montana. Except for Sitting Bull, who spent the next two years confined at Fort Randall, these Indians were promptly placed on the reservation.

1. Hyde, *Red Cloud's Folk*, pp. 291–92.

The Great Sioux Reservation in 1880 was bounded on the east by the Missouri River, on the south by the Nebraska line, on the north by the Cannonball River and the present line between North and South Dakota, and on the west by the eastern fringes of the Black Hills. The seven tribes of Teton Sioux held this reservation in common, but they were individually assigned to one of six separate agencies. Both Red Cloud and Spotted Tail Agencies, which lay within the state of Nebraska, had been abandoned in the autumn of 1877 and relocated the following spring inside the reservation. Red Cloud became Pine Ridge Agency and Spotted Tail became Rosebud Agency. On the west bank of the Missouri River, from north to south, were the Standing Rock, Cheyenne River, and Lower Brulé Agencies. Across the Missouri from Lower Brulé lay the Crow Creek Agency.

Assigned to Pine Ridge were Red Cloud's Oglala Sioux, numbering about 7,300, and 500 Northern Cheyennes under Little Chief, who had successfully demanded to be returned to their northern homes from Indian Territory. At Rosebud, Spotted Tail's Upper Brulés totaled about 4,000. About 1,000 Lower Brulés lived at their agency and another 1,000 Lower Yanktonais were across the river at Crow Creek. Cheyenne River enrolled some 3,000 Miniconjou, Blackfeet, Sans Arc, and Two Kettle Sioux. About 1,700 Hunkpapa, Blackfeet, and Upper Yanktonai Sioux drew rations at Standing Rock Agency.[2]

In all, about 8,000 hostile Sioux gave themselves up between 1876 and 1881. Perhaps another 8,000 remained at the agencies during the war of 1876. Of close to 16,000 Teton Sioux on the Great Sioux Reservation in 1880, few had been much changed by contact with the white race. Just arrived from the Powder and Bighorn country, the recent hostiles retained their aboriginal customs and attitudes almost unimpaired; and agency life

2. These figures include the Sitting Bull hostiles who surrendered in 1881. They numbered about 3,000, of which 200 remained in Canada, where their descendants live today. About 1,300 of those who surrendered went to Cheyenne River Agency, 600 to Pine Ridge, a few to Rosebud, and the rest to Standing Rock. Sitting Bull and 153 followers, released from Fort Randall in 1883, went to Standing Rock. The Upper and Lower Yanktonais, though living on the Great Sioux Reservation, were not Tetons. Commissioner of Indian Affairs (hereafter CIA), *Annual Report* (1880), pp. 19, 21, 33–34, 39, 51; (1881), p. 57; (1883), p. 48.

had not seriously modified the native customs and attitudes of
Red Cloud's Oglalas and Spotted Tail's Brulés. Throughout the
1870s the agents for these two tribes exercised little real authority over the chiefs. They handed out rations but otherwise existed at the sufferance of Red Cloud and Spotted Tail. Only a
few bands, perhaps a thousand people, had lived so long near
white neighbors that, much to the disgust of their kinsmen, they
had begun to act like white men. The material culture of the
Sioux had of course been conditioned by contacts with white
traders and government officials, but, far from influencing really
basic Indian values, the white and mixed-blood traders more
often acquired Indian values themselves. The few Christian
missionaries who had labored among the Tetons since the 1840s
had made almost no headway. In 1880 the political, social, and
religious structure of the Teton Sioux remained largely intact.

The year 1880 ushered in a decade of profound stress for the
Tetons. No longer were they to have things their own way at
the agencies. They might have weak agents—although at least
three were men of strong will and determination—but always
the Indians lived with the knowledge that the white soldiers
were not far away. In the old days they could strike out for the
Powder if they did not like conditions at the agencies. Now they
knew such a course to be suicidal. No longer, as in the 1870s, was
the Great Father's chief objective to control his troublesome
wards and keep them from blocking the paths of westward expansion. Now, spurred by a growing number of Indian reform
groups in the East, the Great Father sought also to "civilize" his
Sioux children, to transform them at once into imitations of the
prosperous, God-fearing tillers of the soil who peopled the land
east of the Mississippi River. The attempt struck the Sioux with
shattering impact.[3]

3. For a discussion of Indian policy during the period see Loring B. Priest,
Uncle Sam's Stepchildren: The Reformation of the Indian Policy, 1865–1887 (New
Brunswick, 1942); Laurence F. Schmeckebier, *The Office of Indian Affairs: Its History, Activities and Organization* (Baltimore, 1927); and, as applied specifically to
the Teton Sioux, George E. Hyde, *A Sioux Chronicle* (Norman, 1956). A contemporary view is Herbert Welsh, "The Indian Question, Past and Present," *New England Magazine*, 2 (1890), 262–64.

When the hostile Sioux came to the reservation, they doubt-less understood that the life of the future would differ from that of the past. Neither they nor those who had spent the war years at the agencies, however, could have had the remotest idea of the revolutionary changes in store for them. During the following decade, the white man cut the very heart out of the only life they knew. Resentful and suspicious, the old life fresh in their mem-ories, they resisted, not altogether successfully, the substitute offered.

At once, they surrendered a large group of customs on which the old life had focused. Warfare was an activity no longer pos-sible. Planning and conducting raids, performing attendant rituals, celebrating success, and mourning failure had once con-sumed much of the time, interest, and ambition of the Tetons. Now, except when men gathered to reminisce, it consumed none. The principal means of attaining prestige, wealth, and high rank vanished the moment they arrived at the agency. War so-cieties ceased to play their vital role in Teton society and within a few years passed entirely out of existence.

The tribal economy promptly collapsed. The annual buffalo hunt was no more, not only because officials in Washington re-garded it as barbaric but also for the very practical reason that buffalo were growing increasingly scarce. That the vanishing herds symbolized their own vanishing way of life cannot have escaped the Sioux. Another important method of winning recog-nition thus disappeared, together with traditional diet, clothing, lodgings, and many objects of material culture. When buffalo drifted onto the reservation in 1882, Agents James McLaughlin and Leonard Love let the Indians of Standing Rock and Chey-enne River organize a hunt. The joy with which they greeted this opportunity—their last, as it turned out—dramatizes the psychological impact of the end of their hunting days.[4] In the first years they tried to recapture the excitement of the chase by killing issue cattle in the same manner as they had once killed buffalo. But the Sioux Commission of 1888 described this as "a disgrace to our civilization" that could only "perpetuate in a

4. James McLaughlin, *My Friend the Indian* (Boston and New York, 1910), chap. 7. Hyde, *Sioux Chronicle*, p. 68.

savage breast all the cruel and wicked propensities of his nature."
Two years later the Indian Bureau prohibited the practice.[5]

The ration and annuity system supplanted the hunt as the principal source of material needs. The Treaty of 1868, as amended by the Agreement of 1876, promised each Indian beef, bacon, flour, coffee, and clothing until such time as he could take care of himself. Although appropriations rarely provided the full amount guaranteed, and although the monotony of the fare did little to promote good health, the Sioux subsisted almost entirely on government dole throughout the 1880s.

The architects of Indian policy conceived the ration system as a bridge between savagery and civilization. At the end of the bridge the Indian would find 160 acres of land. By tilling his acres he would acquire dignity, frugality, individuality, and ultimately the benefits and responsibilities of citizenship. Once the bridge had been crossed, it could be destroyed. Zealous in their cause, reformers worked tirelessly for a law to break up the reservations and parcel out the land to individual Indians in the same manner that, at the same time, the public domain was being allotted to westward-moving homesteaders. This doctrine finally triumphed in 1887 with the passage of the General Allotment Act of Senator Henry L. Dawes.

Before the dream expressed by the Dawes Act could be made a reality, however, the Indian had to be taught to support himself. Thus the Sioux agents received instructions to break up the band camps, and to disperse the Indians over the reservation and encourage them to become farmers. The Indian Bureau furnished seeds, implements, and, finally, "practical farmers" to teach the nomadic huntsmen the arts of horticulture and husbandry.

Keeping the Sioux constantly upset, the program made little real progress. For one thing, the treaty guarantees killed incentive. The Sioux cheerfully admitted that they could not take farming seriously. "They do not wish to cultivate large fields or raise surplus crops," complained Agent McLaughlin, because "they might be dropped from the ration rolls and obliged

5. Senate Documents, 50th Cong., 2d sess., No. 17, p. 19. CIA, *Annual Report* (1890), p. clxv.

to support themselves thereafter."[6] This was, of course, precisely what the policy makers had in mind. Several times during the 1880s exasperated officials and reformers brought the Government perilously close, in the name of civilization, to repudiating the treaties.

There were other reasons, too, why the agricultural program moved slowly. Indians had never done this sort of demeaning labor before, and few could see any good reason for starting now. "An Indian's ambition does not run toward the plow and harrow," Agent V. T. McGillycuddy reminded his superiors, "but rather in the direction of prominence as a war chief or fighting man." He added that the Sioux considered themselves superior to the white man, who "is a laborer and pays tribute to the Sioux Nation by sending . . . rations and supplies of all kinds."[7] Those who allowed the agent to prod them into the fields suffered the scorn of others less willing to surrender basic Indian values. As the years passed, however, more and more were induced to scatter over the reservation, build cabins, break a patch of sod, and plant just enough seed to keep the agent from hounding them. Even then, wanderlust usually triumphed. "An Indian will build for himself a log house, plow and fence a small track of land," observed Agent J. G. Wright of Rosebud. "At the expiration of the season, if not before, he will . . . go to or with his relatives to another locality, and do all the work again for another season."[8] By the close of the decade, however, all but the most reactionary had established homesteads, whether permanent or transitory.

The land and the climate joined forces against the would-be Indian farmers. There were several good years, but in the latter part of the decade the Sioux watched the crops burn up and blow away, or disappear under clouds of grasshoppers, or turn into powder as hail beat down. The Sioux agents prefaced their annual report with generalities about what encouraging progress the Indians were making at farming, then detailed how, this year, the weather had caused the crops to fail. Years of bitter

6. CIA, *Annual Report* (1882), pp. 46–47.
7. Ibid. (1884), p. 43.
8. Ibid.

experience taught them some of the realities of dry-land farming in Dakota. White settlers learned the lesson at the same time, although later generations had to learn it all over again. Agent Charles E. McChesney of Cheyenne River flatly told the Indian Bureau in 1887: "The drawbacks to successful agriculture are so great as not to be overcome with any reasonable amount of labor," and warned that no success could be expected.[9] But so strong in the East was the image of the self-sufficient Indian farmer dwelling happily on 160 acres of land that no dissenting voice could make itself heard.

Although the emphasis remained heavily upon agriculture, two other occupations held greater promise of leading some day to self-support. As the whites themselves learned, the Sioux country was far better suited for cattle raising than for farming. And as the agents learned, the Indian was much better fitted to the life of the cowboy than to that of the farmer. The Indian Bureau in 1879 distributed nearly 3,000 head of cattle among the Sioux agencies. To the surprise of many observers, the Indians took good care of them, rarely killing either the original stock or the increase. Although the herds grew yearly, and agents unanimously suggested that here lay the true road to self-support, sufficient breeding stock was never forthcoming. Then came the terrible winter of 1886–87, which ruined most of the cattlemen of the Northwest and decreed the end of the open range. It wiped out most of the gains made by the Sioux. Even so, Agent McLaughlin reported that his Indians had worked tirelessly all winter to save their herds, and while white cattlemen suffered losses up to 75 per cent, the Standing Rock Indians lost only 30 per cent.[10] In later decades the Sioux fully justified the belief that their talents ran to stock raising, although the high beef prices of World War I lured them into selling their herds and plunging once more into poverty.

The other avocation that interested the Sioux was freighting. Rates charged by white contractors for hauling annuity goods from the Missouri River to the Rosebud and Pine Ridge Agencies proved so exorbitant that, in desperation, the Indian Bu-

9. Ibid. (1887), p. 17.
10. Ibid., p. 48.

reau paid the Indians to haul their own goods. The experiment was an unqualified success, for the Indian could satisfy his roving inclinations and earn hard cash at the same time. He knew he had a good thing and never tampered with the freight entrusted to his care. When the Fremont, Elkhorn and Missouri Valley Railroad pushed across northern Nebraska, the Indian freighters continued to haul supplies from the rail terminus to the agency. In 1884 the Pine Ridge Indians, operating 500 wagons, earned $40,000 hauling three million pounds of freight from Valentine to the agency. This same year they expanded the business by freighting 100,000 pounds of goods consigned to white merchants in the Black Hills.[11]

Stock raising and freighting were but tiny rays of light in an otherwise dark picture. The old economic order had suddenly vanished, and the Sioux found themselves hurried toward an impossible alternative that they did not wish or intend to adopt. As a result, they complied only to the extent absolutely required and subsisted almost entirely on govenment handouts. By 1890 this enervating system, as the Sioux Commission of 1889 pointed out, had drained them of the "manliness and self-respect which characterized them in their savage state."[12]

Although not so rapidly or effectively destroyed, the Teton political system experienced severe stress during the 1880s. Soon after the Sioux settled on the reservation, the Akicita societies, like the war societies, gradually quit holding meetings and finally disappeared. Their existence depended on the annual gathering of bands in tribal encampment and on the hunt. Many members discovered a compensating experience in the Indian police force, which now discharged the responsibilities of the Akicita. Other institutions whose meaning depended on the tribal circle, the Shirt Wearers, for example, likewise passed out of existence.[13]

The institutions of chief and tribal council, however, persisted. For thirty years the white man had regarded the Teton tribes as an independent nation and had insisted upon dealing with each through a head chief. An institution that may not have

11. Ibid. (1884), p. 38.
12. Senate Documents, 51st Cong., 1st sess., No. 51, p. 22.
13. Wissler, "Oglala Societies," p. 62.

existed before contact with the whites had assumed importance and authority to be reckoned with. Such chiefs as Red Cloud, Spotted Tail, and Sitting Bull clung tenaciously to the past and labored mightily to turn aside all threats to the old way of life. They were motivated not only by determination to preserve their own rank and power but also by sincere conviction that the welfare of their people demanded uncompromising devotion to time-tested values. Painfully aware that in the chiefs lay the most formidable barrier to civilization, the Government set out to strip them of their influence and break up the tribal relationship.

When officials of the Indian Bureau sent out instructions to tear down the chiefs, what they really meant was to tear down the chiefs who opposed civilization. Each tribe divided itself into factions labeled by the whites "progressive" and "nonprogressive." The progressives, for differing motives, tried to follow the path marked out by the agent. They clustered around their own leaders, some of whom were chiefs in their own right, and stood in opposition to the nonprogressive chiefs and their followers. As the progressive chiefs usually cooperated with the agent, they did not feel the pressures directed against the chieftainship. It was the rebellious ones who suffered the full weight of the Government's attack.

In the agent they encountered the first serious threat to their supremacy. Strong men like McGillycuddy and McLaughlin had many advantages in the struggle. They did not shrink from shutting off rations or employing the police to compel obedience. When confronted with an agent obviously determined to have his way or die in the attempt, the tribal councils invariably withdrew their support from a rebellious chief. They knew full well the inevitable consequence of violence—an agency swarming with bluecoats. Several times the clash of wills between Red Cloud and McGillycuddy brought Pine Ridge to the brink of revolt, but each time Red Cloud had to retreat.[14] Weak agents, however, failed to control their agencies, and the chiefs for a time enjoyed their customary authority.

14. Hyde, *Sioux Chronicle*, chap. 3, details these episodes.

The chiefs rightly viewed the Indian police force as a menace to their supremacy. As Clark Wissler points out,[15] police service called forth personal attributes cherished by Indian society and was one of the few white institutions that had enough in common with the old life to be a conspicuous success. Strong agents commanded respect and undivided loyalty from the policemen, who with few exceptions proved faithful to their trust and carried out assigned duties regardless of obstacles or opposition from their own people. For example, Red Cloud stood up to McGillycuddy and tried to prevent organization of a police force at Pine Ridge. McGillycuddy "deposed" him and recruited a highly efficient force captained by the able George Sword.[16] At Rosebud, Spotted Tail captured control of the police from the ineffectual Cicero Newell but backed down when confronted with an agent, John Cook, who insisted on commanding the force himself.[17]

In their control of the ration issue, agents discovered a powerful weapon to wield against the chiefs. The chief customarily received the entire issue of goods and distributed it among the people of his band. In 1880 McGillycuddy conceived an idea for taking this prerogative away from "these relics of barbarism." "Every man his own chief," he announced, and invited each family head who wished to draw his own rations. From eleven chiefs at Pine Ridge in 1879, he reported, this approach yielded twenty-five to thirty in 1880 and sixty-three in 1881.[18] So successful was McGillycuddy's technique that it spread rapidly to the other agencies.

Complementing the new issue system in its effect upon the position of the chiefs was the farming program. As one family

15. *Indian Cavalcade, or Life on the Old-Time Indian Reservations* (New York, 1938), pp. 132–33.

16. Doane Robinson, "The Education of Redcloud," *South Dakota Historical Collections, 12* (1924), 176–78.

17. CIA, *Annual Report* (1880), pp. 46–47.

18. Ibid., p. 41; (1882), p. 38. Consulting the Treaty of 1868, McGillycuddy thought he was acting illegally. Actually he was not, for the Agreement of 1876 expressly stated that "Rations shall, in all cases, be issued to the head of each separate family." For the first time, however, this could be tried with hope of success.

after another yielded to the agent's proddings and moved out on the reservation, the band camps dwindled. Removed from the daily guidance of the chief, no longer dependent upon his favor for their share of rations, family heads grew more independent, and the chief became correspondingly less influential.

With the weapons at its command, the Government probably could have destroyed the chieftainship by the end of the decade, although complete success might have produced worse demoralization than did partial success. The Government, however, found itself incapable of consistently following its own policy. The nonprogressive chiefs happened also to be the most powerful, and when matters arose that required Indian cooperation the first step was to convince these chiefs. At a time when Red Cloud and Spotted Tail were locked in a contest of wills with their agents, the Government provided each with a shiny black carriage and a large frame house, built within sight of the far less pretentious quarters of the agent. The chiefs were brought to Washington, lodged in a fine hotel, treated with respect by officials, lionized by the very reformers who demanded their destruction, and in all ways made to feel like foreign monarchs whose favor the United States was courting. On these occasions the voice behind the chieftainship—the tribal council—was ignored, and the chiefs were invested with greater authority than they really possessed.

Even the agents were inconsistent. Their attacks on the chieftainship were in fact personal attacks on nonprogressive chiefs. To accomplish anything they had to work either through real chiefs who happened also to be progressives or through progressives promoted to chieftainship by the agent. Thus McGillycuddy, archfoe of the chieftainship, controlled his agency through such men as Young-Man-Afraid-of-His-Horses and American Horse. He later admitted frankly that these progressives held the balance of power at Pine Ridge, and that only through them was he able to hold out for seven years against the "mob element."[19] McLaughlin, exercising firmer if less spectacular control of Standing Rock, was even more candid. "Although

19. McGillycuddy to L. W. Colby, Jan. 15, 1891, in Colby, "Sioux War," p. 179.

the Government no longer recognized the tribal authority of the chiefs," he wrote in his memoirs, "still it was easier to deal with one man of influence than to have to deal with many irresponsible ones." He dealt with Crow King, Gall, John Grass, Rain-in-the-Face, "and many others who were not chiefs originally but who were advanced as I found them influential and intelligent."[20]

On the one hand, the Government reinforced the leadership of the chief and assumed for him an authority he did not and could not possess. On the other, it undermined his leadership by deposing him or refusing to recognize his rank. The Sioux were terribly confused. One moment the Great Father acted as if they should do the bidding of the chief; the next moment he seemed to want them to throw away the chief. This unstable situation also encouraged ambitious, discontented, or resentful men to intrigue against the established chiefs and to compete for the allegiance of the people and the favor of the agent. Men who would never have dared to criticize a chief in the old days suddenly began to plot the downfall of their leaders. The murder of Spotted Tail by Crow Dog in August 1881 can be traced directly to this sort of political maneuvering. With Spotted Tail out of the way, however, no man of comparable stature emerged, and the subsequent anarchy at Rosebud amply demonstrated that the Brulés as well as the whites owed a considerable debt to the statesmanship of Spotted Tail.[21]

While the economic order crumbled and the political system buckled with the pressures of reservation life, the Government and religious denominations warred on long-established religious beliefs and social customs. In 1881 Commissioner of Indian Affairs Hiram Price voiced the guiding sentiment of the decade:

> To domesticate and civilize wild Indians is a noble work, the accomplishment of which should be a crown of glory

20. *My Friend the Indian*, pp. 90, 100.

21. Hyde, *Sioux Chronicle,* chap. 2, details this episode. See also CIA, *Annual Report* (1881), p. 54. The legal proceedings that followed this murder resulted in a Supreme Court decision that Indians could not be tried for crime under United States law and led ultimatly to extension of the law to Indian reservations. Crow Dog, however, went free.

to any nation. But to allow them to drag along year after year, and generation after generation, in their old superstitions, laziness, and filth, when we have the power to elevate them in the scale of humanity, would be a lasting disgrace to our government.[22]

The first step was to root out paganism. At the direction of Secretary of the Interior Henry M. Teller, the Commissioner of Indian Affairs on April 10, 1883, distributed a set of rules designed to stamp out "demoralizing and barbarous" customs. The directive defined a number of "Indian Offenses." It was an offense to hold feasts and dances, including the Sun Dance. It was an offense to have more than one wife. All practices of medicine men, medical and religious, were offenses. "Purchase" of wives by leaving property at the father's door was an offense. Willful destruction of property, the traditional way of showing grief over the death of a relative, was an offense.

Each agent received instructions to organize a Court of Indian Offenses charged with enforcing these rules. He was to choose three prominent Indians, preferably from the police, to serve without pay as judges. The courts were also empowered to exercise jurisdiction over misdemeanors committed by Indians, over civil suits involving Indians, and over violations of liquor regulations. Penalties at the command of the judges, subject to the agent's approval, were fines, imprisonment, hard labor, and withholding of rations. The Courts of Indian Offenses had no sanction in law, their sole justifications being inferred from the responsibility of administering Indian affairs. They finally achieved quasi-legal recognition in 1889 when Congress appropriated money for the salary of judges.[23]

Among the Sioux the court did not turn out so happily as its originators had hoped. From Rosebud, Agent Wright pointed out that the offenses, in Indian eyes, were not offenses at all and that no Indian judge would have the courage to impose punishment for their violation. Dutifully, however, he appointed three judges; but when they discovered that no salary went with the

22. CIA, *Annual Report* (1881), p. iii.
23. Ibid. (1883), xv.

job, they refused to serve, and no other Indian would accept the appointment.[24] At Pine Ridge, McGillycuddy regarded the whole idea as nonsense. In place of the court, he encouraged the progressives to organize a "permanent board of councilmen," of which Young-Man-Afraid-of-His-Horses was elected president. Although the agent reported delegating judicial responsibility to the council, there was never any doubt about who actually managed agency affairs.[25] His successor, Hugh D. Gallagher, viewed the council as a "travesty upon justice." Grumbling that "plurality of wives was an indispensable condition of membership," he abolished the organization and thereafter dispensed justice himself.[26] At Cheyenne River Agency, William A. Swan, thwarted by jealousy among the chiefs, deposed all chiefs and adopted a device patterned after McGillycuddy's council. Swan's successor, Charles E. McChesney, finally set up a court by permitting the Indians to elect the judges.[27] Only at Standing Rock did the court work well. McLaughlin's judges took their jobs quite seriously and did not even shrink from hauling the mighty Sitting Bull before the bar of justice.[28] Whether through the Court of Indian Offenses or through the Indian police, however, the agent constantly battled against the practices defined as Indian Offenses.

The practices of the medicine man were not quickly suppressed, for they could be conducted in privacy. But the new life assigned a less vital role to the medicine man, and his importance diminished. For one thing, with hunting and warfare gone, young men no longer sought personal power in a vision whose meaning depended upon the interpretation of the medicine man. One after another the medicine men died, without passing on their lore to apprentices.

The Sun Dance headed the evils regarded as antagonistic to progress. As soon as the list of Indian Offenses reached Agent Swan's desk in the spring of 1883, he made the Cheyenne River

24. Ibid., p. 42.
25. Ibid. (1884), p. 46.
26. Ibid. (1887), p. 42.
27. Ibid. (1885), p. 18; (1886), p. 53; (1887), pp. 18–19.
28. Ibid. (1884), p. 57; (1886), p. 82; (1887), p. 53.

Indians call off plans for the annual Sun Dance. They protested, but he explained that the Great Father would be highly displeased and sternly warned that anyone who tried to organize a dance would wind up in the agency jail. To give point to the admonition, at Pierre's Bottom, where the Indians staged less sacred dances for whites from across the river, he tore down the dance house and seized the drums. McGillycuddy let his Indians hold a Sun Dance in 1883, the last anywhere on the Great Sioux Reservation.[29]

With the proscription of the Sun Dance, the social and religious framework of the Sioux began to give way. No longer could they appeal directly to Wi for personal power and assistance. No longer could they experience the pervading sense of religious security that came only from the Sun Dance. No longer could the Sun Dance strengthen such values and institutions of Teton society as still existed. The Sioux had been dealt a shattering emotional blow, and their lives began to seem like a great void.

Missionaries tried to fill the void with Christianity. Since the days of Grant's Peace Policy, religious groups had intimately concerned themselves with Indian affairs. Now the Government encouraged missionaries of any denomination to go among the Indians and "assist in the great work of redeeming these benighted children of nature from the darkness of their superstition and ignorance."[30] Episcopalians, Catholics, Congregationalists, and Presbyterians spread over the Great Sioux Reservation, establishing mission churches and schools. Under Bishop W. H. Hare the Episcopalians led the field, although the Catholics were not far behind. Even though they forever criticized good old Indian ways, the missionaries were kind, and the Sioux liked most of them well enough to attend services. They could not help noting with some confusion the different ways in which missionaries of different sects urged them to worship the same god, and the ill-concealed hostility that the various sects often displayed toward one another. But this was only one of many strange inconsistencies in the white man's behavior.

On the whole, the missionaries made good progress and en-

29. Ibid. (1883), p. 22; (1884), pp. 33, 54.
30. Commissioner J. D. C. Atkins in ibid. (1885), p. xiv.

listed many adherents. There were several reasons for this. The promise of a life in paradise after death proved a strong attraction. It corresponded to the Indian's earlier vague conception of a "happy hunting ground" and held out some hope of eventual relief from the unhappy reservation life. Christian rituals, especially those of the Catholics, provided a slight compensation for the loss of the old ceremonies. Moreover, the missionaries taught that everyone was equal in the eyes of God, and the church was about the only place on the reservation where the Indian found himself actually treated as an equal by white men.

The chief explanation for the willingness of the Sioux to embrace Christianity, however, lay in the multiple character of their old pantheon. One god more or less made little difference. In earlier times, they had appealed for personal power to the many deities that made up Wakan Tanka. Now, confronted with unmistakable evidence of the power of the white man, they logically turned to the white man's God for this brand of power. But they did so without giving up the old gods. Explaining the evolution of his own religious convictions, Capt. George Sword, head of the Pine Ridge police, also explained what had happened to many of his people:

> When I believed the Oglala Wakan Tanka was right I served him with all my powers. . . . In war with the white people I found their Wakan Tanka the Superior. I then took the name of Sword and have served Wakan Tanka according to the white people's manner with all my power. I became the chief of the United States Indian police and held the office until there was no trouble between the Oglala and the white people. I joined the church and am a deacon in it and shall be until I die. I have done all I was able to do to persuade my people to live according to the teachings of the Christian ministers.
>
> I still have my Wasicun [ceremonial pouch or bundle of a shaman] and I am afraid to offend it, because the spirit of an Oglala may go to the spirit land of the Lakota.[31]

31. Quoted in Walker, "Oglala Sun Dance," p. 159. For a good discussion of the impact of Christianity see MacGregor, *Warriors without Weapons*, pp. 90–92.

The schoolteacher went hand in hand with the missionary. Education was conceived as the most important step toward racial assimilation and national citizenship. The English language and the trades and arts formed only part of the teacher's program: he must also, by example, lift "the child of savage parentage" from "the degrading atmosphere of superstition and barbarism" that surrounded him from birth. Congress signified agreement by voting ever-larger appropriations for Indian education, and the Indian Bureau organized a special Education Division. Day schools and boarding schools multiplied on the reservation, some operated by the Government, others by religious groups either from their own resources or under government contract. Indian boarding schools sprang up off the reservation at Carlisle, Pennsylvania; Hampton, Virginia; Chilocco, Indian Territory; Genoa, Nebraska; Lawrence, Kansas; and Forest Grove, Oregon. Agents were authorized to compel attendance by such methods as withholding rations, and by 1887 there were 2,020 students enrolled in 117 boarding schools, and 2,500 in 110 day schools. Such progress moved the Commissioner of Indian Affairs in 1886 to call upon all officials "who come into contact with our red brothers to impress them with the great benefits thus conferred upon them, on which their hearts should swell with grateful emotion."[32]

Capt. R. H. Pratt had just opened his famed Indian industrial school at Carlisle, Pennsylvania, when the Tetons were consolidated on the Great Sioux Reservation. Although Indian parents displayed acute anguish at any parting from their children, in the autumn of 1879 Pratt managed to talk the Rosebud and Pine Ridge Sioux out of sixty boys and twenty-four girls. On a visit to the East during this winter, Spotted Tail looked in on the school and, angered by what he saw, stormed out with nine of his children. This blow, together with the death of several children from illness, played havoc with the reputation of Carlisle among the Sioux and made recruiting almost impossible for several years. Attendance at the off-reservation schools picked up, however, in the last years of the 1880s.

32. CIA, *Annual Report* (1887), p. xvi; (1886), p. xxiv.

The off-reservation boarding school enjoyed greater qualitative success than any other educational method attempted, for it withdrew the child entirely from Indian influences and exposed him for several years entirely to white influences dosed with liberal applications of stern discipline. But even the officials of the Indian Bureau recognized a serious flaw in this apparent progress. Returned to the reservation, the graduates found themselves virtual aliens among their own people and with no occupation in which they could utilize their new-found skills and learning.[33] Many Carlisle graduates turned up later, painted and draped in blankets, as active participants in the Ghost Dance.

Designed to bring education to the Indian, boarding schools were established at each agency, and day schools were started at population centers scattered around the reservation. Parents exhibited scarcely less reluctance to send their children to schools on the reservation than off. But the agents eternally pestered them to fill the schoolhouses; finally, with the authority of the Bureau, they shut off the rations of families that refused to cooperate. Trying to fill a 100-pupil boarding school at Standing Rock, McLaughlin assigned a quota to each band and stopped issue of rations to those who failed to meet their quota. Soon he had more applicants than he could accommodate and had to turn twenty-three away. "But I afterward learned," he revealed, "that there was not an *orphan child* over five years of age left in the camps after this 'conscription.' "[34] Although Indian welfare organizations, observing the increasing attendance at schools, marveled at the progress of education on the Great Sioux Reservation, Agent L. F. Spencer of Rosebud struck a more realistic note when he declared:

> There are camps on this agency where the mere mention of a prospective school operates like a red flag on an outraged bull. Eliminate from the educational proposition sentiment and gush, and the average Indian of this agency who voluntarily sends his children to the government day-

33. Ibid. (1880), pp. 178–79; (1881), p. 53; (1884), p. 45.
34. Ibid. (1884), p. 56.

school does it either through fear of gastronomic consequences if he does not, or expects pay from the Great Father
as a premium for surrendering his children for educational
advantages.[35]

The Sioux disliked the school not only because it separated
them from their children but also because they quickly discovered that it was a place where children were subjected to a
discipline unknown at home, and to types of work that no Sioux
had ever done before. They must have dimly understood, too,
that it represented the most dangerous of all attacks on basic Indian values, the one most likely to succeed in the end because it
aimed at the children, who had known little if any of the old life.

The first day of school at Pine Ridge forcefully dramatized
this truth. A crowd of parents, curious and anxious, clustered
around the big frame schoolhouse. The children disappeared
inside, and a teacher drew the window blinds. But a breeze blew
one aside, and a father caught a glimpse of what was going on.
One matron held a boy while another sheared his long braided
hair, symbol of Sioux manhood. Instantly the mob stormed the
school and rescued the children. Only time and infinite diplomacy enabled it to reopen.[36]

By the last years of the 1880s, the Sioux had been forced to
surrender their children to the demands of education. The effect was to heighten the resentment of the adults and to confront the children, exposed to both Indian and white environ-
ment, with seriously conflicting values.

The Government and the religious groups had evolved a program of breath-taking scope for making over the Indian and, in
their optimism, looked forward to reaching the goal in an im-
possibly short time. Had they aimed for success in 100 years
instead of 10, they would still have needed a corps of agency
officials of the most exceptional caliber. Simply to manage a
large agency and do nothing but maintain tranquillity demanded abilities that few men possessed, for as Bishop Hare

35. Ibid. (1887), p. 43.
36. Hyde, *Sioux Chronicle*, pp. 100–01.

remarked, "Indian life is a tangle of intrigue and diverse parties and clashing plans and interests through which the benevolent, no matter how clever, may find it hard to make his way."[37] To also transform several thousand primitives into copies of the typical white citizen clearly demanded agency officials with an enormous range of skills.

The spoils system of appointment did well to produce an agent who could uphold his authority. With each change of administration, virtually every Indian official from Secretary of the Interior and Commissioner of Indian Affairs to the lowest agency employee gave way to a replacement appointed mainly for political reasons. When Grover Cleveland led the Democrats to power in 1885, after twenty-four lean years on the outside, more than fifty of the fifty-eight Indian agents surrendered their jobs to Democrats. Although the Indian Service contained some dedicated and capable people, they were the exception. Carl Schurz observed as late as 1894: "A thoroughly competent, honest, and devoted Indian agent is, according to my experience, so rare a jewel that, were I at the head of the Interior Department [he once was], nothing could induce me to part with him."[38] Herbert Welsh, Secretary of the Indian Rights Association, told of a state governor who laughingly admitted that for party workers fit for nothing else, he usually found jobs in the Indian Service.[39] An Indian inspector reported finding an "abandoned woman" running an Indian school, a lunatic in charge of another.[40]

The Indian reform organizations performed notable service by publicizing the often disastrous, always damaging consequences of the spoils system. Toward the end of the decade they made some progress. The Indian Rights Association took credit for influencing President Benjamin Harrison to appoint Thomas

37. Quoted in M. A. DeWolf Howe, *The Life and Labors of Bishop Hare* (New York, 1911), p. 204.

38. Schurz to Herbert Welsh, April 6, 1894, Schurz Papers, Library of Congress, quoted in Mary A. Johnson, *Federal Relations with the Great Sioux Indians of South Dakota, 1887–1933* (Washington, 1948), p. 16, note 56.

39. Welsh, "The Meaning of the Dakota Outbreak," *Scribner's Magazine*, 9 (1891), 449.

40. Board of Indian Commissioners, *Annual Report* (1889), p. 139.

J. Morgan as Indian Commissioner in 1889.[41] An ex-Baptist preacher of the staunchest rectitude, Morgan justified the faith of the reformers not only by translating their ideas as fully as possible into policy but also by working assiduously to extend the merit system over large blocks of jobs. Throughout the 1880s, however, corruption, incompetence, and short tenure burdened the conduct of Indian affairs.

The spoils system dealt less severely with the Sioux in the 1880s than with many tribes. James McLaughlin brought intelligence, fairness, judgment, and authority to Standing Rock, and he enjoyed a smooth channel of communication to his people through his Indian wife. He won the respect of reformers, Army officers, Indian officials, and most of the tribal leaders of his agency. The powerful political support of the Roman Catholic Church ensured a long tenure. For all his blustering theatrics, McGillycuddy made a good agent, and there were many who said that the troubles of 1890 would never have got out of hand if he had not been removed in 1886 to make way for a deserving Democrat. James G. Wright at Rosebud and Charles E. McChesney at Cheyenne River also proved superior to the usual appointees. But there were enough agents like the weak Cicero Newell and the corrupt L. F. Spencer to cancel out the McLaughlins and add the weight of mismanagement to the immense burdens already borne by the Sioux.

By the end of the decade these burdens had plunged the Sioux to depths of despair unprecedented in their history. Virtually every meaningful custom had been attacked or proscribed, every institution damaged or destroyed. That they could not avoid adopting some of the alien customs and institutions thrust upon them only intensified their grief over the loss of the old. A pervasive feeling of bitterness, helplessness, and futility gripped the Sioux.

41. Indian Rights Association (hereafter IRA), *Seventh Annual Report* (1889), p. 10.

4. THE LAND AGREEMENT

THE TETONS had signed many treaties with the United States, and each surrendered more land. The first was in 1851. The great covered-wagon migrations of the 1840s, followed by the acquisition of Oregon and California by the United States, suggested the desirability of clearing the Indian tribes from the Platte Valley route to the Pacific. After a lavish distribution of presents near Fort Laramie in 1851, the Tetons and other tribes of the northern Plains set their marks to the treaty. After 1851 these tribes continued to roam from the Upper Missouri to the Arkansas, for the treaty granted this right. But for the first time, they had a homeland assigned to them. The territory of the Tetons was enclosed by the Heart, Missouri, White, and North Platte Rivers, and the Black Hills.

A block of treaties with the tame bands along the Missouri River in 1865 foreshadowed the second fundamental document defining Teton-white relations. On its face, the Treaty of 1868 appeared an abject white surrender to Red Cloud's demand, reinforced by two years of successful warfare, to abandon the Bozeman Trail, which ran through the Powder River country to the Montana gold fields. But the goal of civilizing the Indians had begun to form in the minds of Eastern humanitarians, and the Treaty of 1868 laid the groundwork for the effort. True, the Government gave up the Bozeman Trail forts and guaranteed the Powder River country as unceded hunting grounds. But the treaty also drew new boundaries around the Sioux homeland, and in subsequent years these took on far more meaning than the empty guarantee of the Powder River country. The present borders of South Dakota west of the Missouri River enclosed the Great Sioux Reservation, and, although few of the chiefs understood it, they had agreed to settle within the reservation. Many, including Red Cloud himself, set the pattern. Lured by free rations and annuities, they established themselves at the newly built agencies. Settling the Indians in one place was the first step toward launching the civilization program.

The third important document was called an "agreement" because the House of Representatives, angry at the Senate's exclusive prerogative of ratifying treaties, had brought about the destruction of the Indian treaty system in 1871. In 1875 the Government ordered the Sioux to vacate the Powder River hunting grounds and withdraw to the Great Sioux Reservation, and it fought the war of 1876 to enforce the order. At the same time, gold having been discovered in the Black Hills, government commissioners set forth to reduce the Great Sioux Reservation by purchasing the rich Hills. Impelled by more promises of rations and annuities together with some thinly veiled intimidation, the chiefs who were not fighting bluecoats on the Powder signed the Agreement of 1876 and thus gave up the triangle of land formed by the forks of the Cheyenne River.

In none of the treaty councils were the chiefs fully informed of the contents of the documents they were asked to sign. Treaty commissioners made much of the rations and other gifts that were promised but said little if anything about the land and freedom the Indians would be expected to surrender. This they were left to discover later. Repeatedly victimized, it is not surprising that the Sioux brought to all subsequent councils a profound distrust of the white man, together with an imperfect knowledge of the actual provisions of the treaties and agreements that regulated their relations with the Government.

By 1880 eastern Dakota had filled with settlers. Railroads had reached the Missouri River and stopped. The Great Sioux Reservation denied more than 43,000 square miles to settlement and economic exploitation and cut off the Black Hills from the rest of the territory. Settlers demanded that the Indian move aside. In Congress, Delegate Richard F. Pettigrew sponsored a bill to provide for a commission to go to Dakota to learn if the Sioux cared to cede about half the Great Sioux Reservation to the United States and accept in return clear title to five separate reservations. The bill slipped through as a rider to the sundry civil appropriations bill in August 1882.

Secretary of the Interior Henry M. Teller, a westerner thoroughly in sympathy with Pettigrew's aims, named Newton Edmunds to head the commission. A former governor of Dakota Territory and a master at negotiating with Indians, Edmunds went beyond the intent of the law—instead of merely sounding out the Sioux on the proposal, he set forth to secure their assent. He brought intense pressure to bear, made much of the many advantages to the Indians, and barely mentioned that he was asking them to part with half their remaining land. They grew dizzy under the avalanche of words. At each agency the chiefs held out as long as they could, but someone always started a stampede and they lined up to sign. Edmunds returned to Washington early in 1883 and announced that the Sioux had accepted the agreement.

The Indians protested that they had been victimized, and they had. The document bore only the signatures of 384 chiefs and headmen—not the three-fourths of all adult males required by the Treaty of 1868. The Indian rights organizations went into action, and Congress sent the agreement back to the reservation for the necessary signatures. The Indians would not sign, and it failed to gain Congressional approval. Again the Sioux had seen confirmed the conviction that the whites could not be trusted. No matter how purely motivated, any future attempt to reduce the Great Sioux Reservation would at once encounter the legacy of the Edmunds Commission.

In the General Allotment Act of 1887, sponsored and championed in the Senate by Senator Henry L. Dawes, the advocates of opening the Sioux Reservation had at last a legal framework

REDUCTION OF THE GREAT SIOUX RESERVATION
1868 to 1890

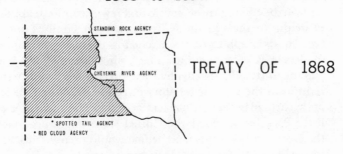

TREATY OF 1868

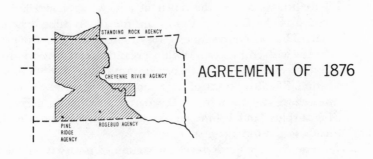

AGREEMENT OF 1876

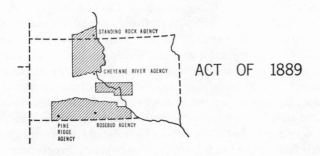

ACT OF 1889

for achieving their purpose. Allotment in severalty had been incorporated into a number of treaties and had been tried among a few tribes. The Dawes Act, with a few exceptions, applied the principle to the remaining Indians. Each family head would receive upon application a patent for 160 acres of land, others for less in varying amounts. The United States would hold the patents in trust for twenty-five years. With the patent went citizenship in the state or territory of residence. When all Indians on a particular reservation had accepted allotments, or sooner if the President decided, the United States might negotiate with the tribe for its surplus land, which would then be thrown open to settlement under the Homestead Laws.[1]

Reformers hailed the dawn of a new era and confidently looked to the Dawes Act as a cure for all ills afflicting the Indian. The Dakota promoters, for different reasons, also greeted the law with enthusiasm. Within a year they had hurried through Congress a bill applying its provisions to the Great Sioux Reservation. The Sioux Act of 1888, however, reversed the order of procedure laid down by the Dawes Act. It called for negotiations for surplus land before surveys had been run and allotments made to the Indians.

The Great Sioux Reservation contained nearly twice the land needed for allotments. The plan was to set aside six separate reservations—Pine Ridge, Rosebud, Cheyenne River, Standing Rock, Crow Creek, and Lower Brulé—on which the allotment program could be carried out at a leisurely pace. The surplus land, about nine million acres, would be purchased from the Sioux at fifty cents an acre, restored to the public domain, and immediately thrown open to settlement under the Homestead Laws. In return for surrendering their right to "joint undivided occupancy" of the Great Sioux Reservation, the Indians would receive a number of benefits. They would have clear title to their land instead of mere right of occupancy. Proceeds from the sale of the surplus land to settlers, after reimbursing the Government for expenses incurred by the Act, would go into a perman-

---

1. CIA, *Annual Report* (1887), pp. iv–x and 274, reproduces the law and discusses its proposed application in terms of contemporary official thinking. See also Schmeckebier, *Office of Indian Affairs,* pp. 78–81.

ent Sioux fund whose interest, at five per cent, would be spent on educational programs. Also, the Government promised to continue for another twenty years the educational benefits of the Treaty of 1868, to furnish the Sioux with up to 25,000 cows and 1,000 bulls, and to give to each family head and single adult who took land in severalty two milk cows, a pair of oxen, farming tools, a two-year supply of seeds for five acres, and twenty dollars in cash. In keeping with the Treaty of 1868, the Act could not take effect until three-fourths of all adult males had agreed to its provisions.[2]

The commission appointed to obtain these signatures consisted of Capt. Richard H. Pratt, Reverend William J. Cleveland, and Judge John V. Wright of Tennessee. Pratt seemed an admirable choice for chairman. As head of the Carlisle Indian School, he had worked closely with Indians for a decade. It did not follow, however, that he was trusted and revered by the Indians. On the contrary, insofar as the Sioux remembered him at all, he was the stern officer with the big nose who had taken their children to a far-off place from which some never returned. They had no great love for the man who was expected to convince them that the land agreement was a good thing.

As Pratt was to find out, the Sioux had already made up their minds. Delegations from each agency had gathered at Rosebud to agree upon a united stand. Ignorant of the forces that shaped their destiny, the Sioux failed to see that the combination of reformer and land boomer inevitably meant the end of the Great Sioux Reservation. All they knew was that another commission was coming to talk them out of their land. Judging from past experience, the commissioners would talk long and convincingly. They would make many appealing promises that would later, if they materialized at all, somehow get twisted into considerably less attractive shape. Their big mistake in dealing with the Edmunds Commission, the delegates decided, lay in arguing at all. This time they would put forward leaders to say no, then turn a deaf ear to all further talk.[3]

2. See CIA, *Annual Report* (1888), pp. 294–301, for the text of the act.

3. The report of the commisson was published as Senate Documents, 50th Cong., 2d sess., No. 17.

The commission started at Standing Rock Agency in July 1888. Agent McLaughlin regarded the terms of the act as unfair. Although he had to cooperate with the commissioners, the Indians knew where his sympathies lay.[4] They stood firm. Pratt began by having his assistants pass out copies of the act, but the Hunkpapas and Yanktonais suspiciously refused to touch the paper. Pratt next launched his presentation. He explained that "no character of threat, menace or force was to be used to induce them to assent; that it was a matter which was to be left to their own free will." He then hinted darkly that failure to sign the agreement would make "further action which may be taken in regard to the reservation problematical and uncertain". (Commission Report, p. 5) Thereafter, explicitly or implicitly, threat and menace formed the basis of his argument.

Day after day for nearly a month, the Standing Rock people listened with polite dignity as Pratt explained the act, section by section, over and over. Forgetting their compact of silence, they put forward John Grass and three others to speak. The chiefs declared that the Government could not be expected to honor these promises any more that it had past promises. Besides, the Sioux did not have more land than they and their children would need. Even if they did sell, half the land was unfit for farming and could not be sold to settlers. It seemed all wrong, moreover, that the Government would offer the Indians fifty cents an acre, then sell it for $1.25 an acre. For each argument Pratt had a convincing reply, but the Sioux refused to be convinced.

Finally, Pratt asked the Standing Rock Indians to step forward and sign. The law required each Indian to signify acceptance or rejection by signing one of two papers. This was something new and aroused deep suspicion. Although twenty-two Indians placed their marks on the agreement, the rest bluntly declined to sign either paper and marched out of the council hall to return to their homes.

Soundly defeated at Standing Rock, the commissioners boarded a steamer on August 21 and sailed down the Missouri

4. McLaughlin, *My Friend the Indian*, pp. 275–76.

to Crow Creek and Lower Brulé. At both agencies a sizable group of progessives stood ready to sign, but the proposal excited much heated opposition, too. At Lower Brulé, where 244 made their marks on the agreement, old Iron Nation led his following out of the council. At Crow Creek 120 signed, but 282 refused to sign either acceptance or rejection.

Even if Pine Ridge, Rosebud, and Cheyenne River voted overwhelmingly for the agreement, Pratt still lacked the necessary three-fourths majority. And all the news from these agencies indicated even more stubborn opposition than that encountered at Standing Rock. He hastened to a council of war with Secretary of the Interior William F. Vilas, who was vacationing at Madison, Wisconsin. Back at Lower Brulé, Pratt summoned the Sioux agents and the leading men of each tribe to convene there for a council on September 22.

The delegates, 150 in all, stood united in opposition to all of Pratt's persuasion and threats. But there were also signs of weakening. The chiefs made much of the absurdly low price offered for their land, thus implying that a higher price might be acceptable. They also thought they saw an opportunity for a trip to Washington—the Sioux chiefs immensely enjoyed such excursions—and suggested that maybe a talk with the Honorable Secretary of the Interior or the Great Father himself would produce a compromise. Pratt ridiculed the idea that Congress would even think of raising the price and categorically declared that a trip to Washington was out of the question.

Their mission a total failure, the commissioners went home to write a scathing denunciation of the Sioux and their obstinate refusal to recognize something so clearly in their best interest. The report ended by suggesting that the Government put the agreement into effect without their consent.

The Government was not ready for such drastic action. In October the chiefs got their trip to Washington. Sixty-one heard the Secretary of the Interior offer to recommend to Congress some liberal changes in the agreement, including one dollar an acre for their land. A majority of the delegation, forty-seven in number, turned in a report holding out for $1.25 and even more generous concessions. They had had their vacation in Washington and now were beginning to think that maybe a compromise was not possible after all. In truth, the Interior Department had been cleverly maneuvered into paying sixty-one railway fares and a large hotel bill without receiving much in return.

Supporters of the program drew up another bill, far more generous than its predecessor, and closed ranks for another try. In the national elections of 1888, the Republicans, led by Benjamin Harrison, turned out the Democrats; but if anything they were even more committed to breaking up the Great Sioux Reservation, for Dakota stood overwhelmingly in the Republican camp. Added impetus came in February 1889 with passage of the Omnibus Bill, which provided for admission to statehood in November 1889 of North and South Dakota together with Washington and Montana. Congress enacted two measures for opening the Sioux land. One, part of the Indian Appropriation Act signed on March 2, 1889, empowered the President to appoint another commission to negotiate the best agreement possible and submit it to Congress for ratification or rejection. The other, the Sioux Act of March 2, 1889, spelled out new terms of an agreement that the Indians must either accept or reject as a whole. Although the commission was appointed under the first act, it was instructed to present the second act to the Sioux. Only if they turned down this new proposal was the commission to negotiate.

The Sioux Act of 1889 embodied a number of concessions which its supporters hoped would break down some of the opposition. Most important, it raised the price to be paid the Indians for the ceded land. On the assumption that settlers would claim the best land first, the Sioux were to be paid $1.25 an acre for all land homesteaded by whites during the first three years, seventy-five cents an acre for land sold in the next two years, and fifty cents an acre for all remaining land. Rather than deduct the expense of administering the program from the proceeds of land sales, as contemplated by the Act of 1888, the United States now offered to bear the entire cost. The prospect of having to take their land in severalty had greatly upset the Indians. The Act of 1889 specified that the allotment program could not be started on a reservation until favored by a majority of adult males, and then family heads would receive 320 instead of 160 acres plus the benefits promised by the Act of 1888, except that fifty dollars instead of twenty dollars would be spent for physical improvements on the property of each allottee. Finally, to meet an unrelated complaint, the act appropriated $28,500 to compensate the followers of Red Cloud and Red Leaf for ponies seized by the Army during the war of 1876.[5]

As chairman of the Sioux Commission, President Harrison appointed Charles Foster, former governor of Ohio. William Warner of Missouri, another prominent Republican and national commander of the Grand Army of the Republic, also received an appointment. Both were able men but had no experience with Indians. The third member of the commission was the one who was expected to sell the proposition to the Indians: Maj. Gen. George Crook knew Indians as well as any white man in the country. The Sioux knew him, too, for they had fought his soldiers and surrendered to him back in the 1870s. How far they shared the prevailing white belief that Crook was the best friend they ever had is less apparent. They probably accorded him more trust than they did most whites. But the undeniable fact remained that, in uniform or out, General Crook revived unpleasant memories.

Again the Sioux agreed among themselves to resist all blandishments and, come what may, to withhold their marks from the agreement. At each agency the people chose several chiefs to do all the talking and to say that they had decided to reject the agreement. But this year they were not dealing with a Captain Pratt. Crook knew how to handle Indians. The commissioners acted as if they had all the time in the world. Great feasts were staged to put the Sioux in a contented frame of mind, and dancing, banned since 1883 as an Indian Offense, once more enlivened the agencies. In council, the commissioners displayed infinite patience and good will. They professed complete indifference to whether the Sioux accepted the act or not. Their mission was simply to explain it and record the vote.

Nevertheless, the "threat and menace" that characterized the

5. See CIA, *Annual Report* (1889), pp. 449–58, for the text of the act.

proceedings of 1888 dominated the councils of 1889, although more subtly. Crook, Foster, and Warner clearly saw what would happen if this agreement failed. They and the agents knew that the Sioux would have to give up their land, and probably with considerably less compensation than provided by the agreement. The welfare of the Sioux demanded acceptance, and the commissioners recognized the urgency of securing a favorable vote. As Bishop Hare remarked, the commission, "convinced that the bill was essential, carried persuasion to the verge of intimidation. I do not blame them if they sometimes did. The wit and patience of an angel would fail often in such a task."[6]

Crook did not mince words. There can be little doubt of his sincerity when he laid the unpleasant facts squarely before the Sioux:

> Last year when you refused to accept the bill Congress came very near opening this reservation anyhow. It is certain that you will never get any better terms than are offered in this bill, and the chances are that you will not get so good. And it strikes me that instead of your complaining of the past, you had better provide for the future. . . . It strikes me that you are in the position of a person who had his effects in the bed of a dry stream when there was a flood coming down, and instead of finding fault with the Creator for sending it down, you should try and save what you can. And that when you can't get what you like best you had better take what is the best for you. [Commission Report, p. 172.]

He also heaped scorn upon them, as when he told the Rosebud Indians:

> When I left you before I expected much good of you, and here after eleven years I come back and find that you have done but very little towards civilization. You have been

6. Bishop Hare to Secretary of the Interior John W. Noble, Jan. 7, 1891, reproduced in Mooney, *Ghost-Dance*, p. 841. The report of the Sioux Commission of 1889 is in Senate Documents, 51st Cong., 1st sess., No. 51.

contented to sit down and eat rations, thinking the Government is always going to keep you. . . . This indolent life you have been living has made squaws of you, and if you don't work and help yourselves you will get such a bad record that the Government will have to send out dolls and rattles to amuse you. [p. 50.]

The Sioux had many anxieties—some well grounded, others illogical. The 181 pages of fine print that make up the transcript of council proceedings are heavily laden with childish complaints of real or imagined grievances. The record also yields significant clues to the temper of the Sioux and the motives for their opposition. It reveals, first, a deeply rooted suspicion of any proposal from the Government. The Indians searched for deception in every clause of the agreement and every utterance of the commissioners. At Rosebud, after ex-Governor Foster had finished reading the agreement, Swift Bear insisted that he have for his own use the copy that had been read, and no other. At Standing Rock, John Grass requested that the Indians be permitted to have their own stenographer to record what was said.

Beyond the suspicion, the record reveals a paralyzing fear. The Sioux feared the incomprehensible. Acres, principal and interest, and invisible boundary lines had little real meaning to them. And they feared the unknown. Their present situation, bad as it was, seemed preferable to one that, even though endlessly explained by the commission, remained beyond their ability to comprehend.

In the councils at each agency, the greatest confusion and anxiety sprang from the conviction that the agreement would kill the Treaty of 1868, whose benefits had been extended by the Agreement of 1876. Over and over the commissioners emphasized that one would not affect the other, that the two would run side by side until the Treaty of 1868 died. The Sioux could not grasp such a relationship. At Pine Ridge, Old-Man-Afraid-of-His-Horses waved a copy of the treaty and declared, "When this paper was given to me at the treaty of 1868, the commissioners at that time told me that I would have to wait for the time called for, and then I would have a right to make another treaty. . . . It

seems you are in a great hurry," he concluded. "The time when
we will sign again will be twenty-one years" (p. 79).

The complicated system of pricing the surplus land badly
disturbed the Indians. No one could predict how many settlers
would establish homesteads during the first three or even five
years. What prevented the white man from waiting five years and
then taking all the land at fifty cents an acre? The commissioners
could not say how much would be paid in total for the ceded
territory. Here, surely, was evidence that the Great Council in
Washington had set a clever trap. "Now, my friend," one chief
addressed General Crook at Cheyenne River, "there is nothing
on a foundation at all. Everything is just wobbling. Even you
yourselves don't know the price we are going to get for anything.
So even you don't know, and I don't know, and I am afraid of
that." And, added another chief, "Suppose we go to work and
sign this bill now. They would take that bill there and keep it
there until it comes to 50¢ an acre, and that is what don't suit
us" (p. 169).

The matter of compensating the Red Cloud and Red Leaf
people for their confiscated ponies sparked considerable discussion among all but the beneficiaries. Those of the Standing Rock
and Cheyenne River Indians who had remained at peace in 1876
pointed out that they, too, had lost ponies. The only difference
was that they had voluntarily surrendered theirs as an earnest
of good faith, while those of Red Cloud and Red Leaf had been
seized to prevent a threatened flight to the hostile country. Crook
knew that this was so, but all he could do was to promise to tell
the Great Father about the injustice.

And what about their rations, the Sioux asked. It was no secret
to them that the Government wanted to make them self-supporting and do away with rations altogether. Again and again the
commissioners explained that the Agreement of 1876 guaranteed
rations until the Sioux could support themselves, and the land
agreement had nothing to do with that. But many Indians could
not shake the haunting fear that once they had given up their
land the food supply would be shut off.

At first glance it seems incredible that the Sioux, as the transcript clearly shows, could be so united in opposition to the

agreement, yet approve it by an overwhelming majority of 4,463 out of 5,678 eligible to vote. The answer lies in the expert way in which General Crook guided the commission to its goal. The technique was to bury the Indians under mountains of words while working behind the scenes to lure individuals away from the influence of the chiefs. If a considerable stampede could be started, even the most determined opponent, afraid of being excluded from the benefits, would rush to sign. With the help of the agents and the half-breed squaw men, who could read the newspapers and recognized the truth of Crook's warning, this is precisely what happened.[7] In its report to the Secretary of the Interior, the commission candidly described the method:

> It was soon discovered that it was impossible to deal with the Indians as a body in general councils. The matter had been already decided as the result of their tribal councils, and that when all were present each one sustained the other in the opposition to which each had pledged himself. It was therefore determined to endeavor to convince individuals that substantial advantages to the Indians as a whole would result from an acceptance of the bill. For a time the task seemed almost hopeless, but persistence prevailed and interest was awakened. As soon as the question became debatable the situation changed and success was assured. [p. 21]

Even so, there were some exciting moments. At Cheyenne River on July 18, Chasing Crow led the first contingent of defectors forward to sign. Pandemonium broke loose and two painted warriors rushed to the table brandishing war clubs. Indian policemen seized them. Amid shouts and "great commotion," the signing continued. Similar disturbances, engineered by the reactionary Hump, chief of police, hampered subsequent signings. Crook spoke gruffly and summoned Maj. George M.

---

7. The brief excerpts from Crook's diary reproduced in Martin F. Schmitt, ed., *General George Crook, His Autobiography* (Norman, 1946), pp. 283–89, show how the general went about this. See also McLaughlin, pp. 284–85. McLaughlin, who believed the agreement as favorable as the Sioux would ever get, spent an entire night working on John Grass. When Grass changed front next day, the Standing Rock Indians followed suit.

54   CHAPTER FOUR

Randall from nearby Fort Bennett to sit in on the proceedings.
The blue uniform spoke more eloquently than words, and the
troublemakers took the hint. Later, even Hump signed. Less
serious trouble erupted at Rosebud and Pine Ridge. At Standing Rock, Sitting Bull tried to break up the signing but failed.

With more than the necessary signatures, the commissioners
boarded a train for Chicago. They left behind at each agency a
divided people. Progressive and nonprogressive emerged more
sharply defined than ever, and each faction harbored the bitter-
est resentment toward the other. Those who had refused to sign
blamed not only the Sioux Commission but also their tribesmen
who had weakened and voted for the agreement. The contention
spread even to the reservation day schools, where fist fights and
worse among the children revealed the depth of the cleavage
among the parents.[8]

Intense argument exploded over the matter of rations. Fear
that the Government would cut rations once it obtained the
Sioux land had cropped up repeatedly in councils with the commissioners. They had promised over and over that acceptance of
the agreement could in no way influence the amount of food
issued, and they emphasized this in their report: "Without our
assurances . . . it would have been impossible to have secured
[the Sioux] consent" (p. 23). Nevertheless, the ever-suspicious
nonprogessives predicted a reduction in rations now that the
Government had their land. Certain that even the white man
could not be that stupid, the progressives just as assuredly ridiculed the idea.

The nonprogressives pointed out that they were already being
counted. A census agent, A. T. Lea, had started work on the
Rosebud Reservation before the Crook Commission arrived.
Since the days of the old Red Cloud Agency, nothing excited such
fury as a census. Many Sioux suspected that Lea's presence had
something to do with rations. It did. Congress had insisted that
the Indian Bureau find out if rations were being issued to non-
existent Indians. As a matter of fact, the Sioux for years had
used various clever devices to inflate their numbers. If any ever

8. See, for example, Frank B. Fiske, *Life and Death of Sitting Bull* (Fort Yates,
N.D., 1933), pp. 27–28.

worried over the ethics of the practice, they could console themselves that shrinkage of beef on the hoof between delivery and
slaughter often ran as high as thirty per cent, surely more than
compensating for the overcount. It would take Lea two years to
finish the census, and therefore no immediate ration cut could
be expected as a result of his labors. Still, his very presence
heightened the agitation over food that the land sale had started.

The progressives and nonprogressives did not have long to
argue. The commissioners had been gone hardly two weeks when
the order came: reduce the beef issue at Rosebud by two million
pounds, at Pine Ridge by one million, and at the other agencies
by proportional amounts. By the same Indian Appropriation Act
under which the Sioux Commission was appointed, Congress in
an economy move had cut the appropriation for subsistence and
civilization of the Sioux for the fiscal year 1890 to $900,000—
$100,000 less than for the two previous years. The new Com-
missioner of Indian Affairs, Thomas J. Morgan, had no choice
but to cut rations.[9]

The Sioux Commission had not lied. The land agreement had
nothing to do with the quantity of rations. But this was a subtlty
that the Sioux could hardly be expected to appreciate. They
understood only one thing: the Government had tricked them
again. "When it became generally known that the reduction was
really going to be made," reported Agent Hugh Gallagher from
Pine Ridge, "it caused intense feeling against the Sioux Commission among those who had signed the bill. They were made
the targets for derision by the non-signers, who called them fools
and dupes and told them they were now getting their pay in the
same coin that had been received before whenever they were so
foolish as to make contracts with the whites."[10]

Greatly upset by the beef reduction (Foster dashed off a sharp
note of protest to Commissioner Morgan on August 29), the
Sioux Commission won approval to bring a delegation of chiefs

9. CIA, *Annual Report* (1891), pp. 32–35, 192. Inspector F. C. Armstrong to
Secretary of the Interior John W. Noble, April 7, 1890, printed in *Cong. Rec.*, 51st
Cong., 2d sess., 22, Pt. II (Jan. 27, 1891), 1882. Report of the Sioux Commission
of 1889, pp. 23–24.

10. CIA, *Annual Report* (1890), p. 49.

to Washington. There, perhaps the Indians could be shown why their rations had been slashed, and at the same time high officials could be impressed with the gravity of the action. Moreover, the commissioners had said they would try to win for the Sioux certain concessions not covered by the agreement. Although they had stressed that these were not promises, the Sioux had regarded them as such. It therefore seemed wise to make certain not only that everyone concerned agreed on what these benefits were but also that the high officials appreciated the degree to which the honor of the Government had been committed. The Indian delegates, happy at vacationing in Washington once again, showed up at the Interior Department on December 18, 1889. They talked Secretary John W. Noble to the verge of exasperation, then repaired to the White House for a short session with the President himself.[11]

The chiefs returned to their homes somewhat happier because the report of the commissioners, submitted to the Secretary of the Interior the day before Christmas, clearly stated that the Sioux had signed only because they trusted the commission to secure for them a long list of additional benefits. Many of these—employment of Indians at agencies where possible, equality of mixed bloods with full bloods, construction of gristmills, removal of the ban on "innocent dances"—lay within the administrative province of the Secretary of the Interior, who agreed to most of them. But the really important ones required Congressional action. Among them were increased educational appropriations, prompt availability of interest on the three million dollar permanent fund, legislation for apportioning the permanent fund and its interest among the new reservations according to population, an appropriation to compensate the Cheyenne River and Standing Rock Indians for ponies seized in 1876, and, above all, an appropriation of $100,000 to restore the cut in the beef allowance.[12]

Although the hope born of the council with the Great Father gladdened the Sioux a bit, it was still a bad winter on the reserva-

11. See Report of the Sioux Commission of 1889, pp. 218–33, for transcript of the councils.

12. Ibid., pp. 23–32.

tion. There was hunger and perhaps even some starvation. With reduced rations and the failure of their own crops, the Sioux found it hard indeed to keep the family kettle full enough.[13] There was sickness. Epidemics of measles, influenza, and whooping cough swept the camps with fatal effect. At Pine Ridge alone the death rate rose to 45 a month in a population of 5,550.[14]

Then came the cruelest blow of all. On February 10, 1890, President Harrison announced acceptance of the land agreement by the required three-fourths majority of adult males and threw open the ceded territory to settlement.[15] The promises had not been carried out. No surveys had been made to determine the precise boundaries of the new reservations. No provision had been made for Indians living in the ceded land to take allotments there. Here was the ultimate in bad faith.

A group of townsite boomers tried to stake claims on the Lower Brulé land but were prevented by troops hastened from Fort Randall.[16] Otherwise, the expected rush failed to materialize: the bad years had dramatized the hazards of farming in the Dakotas. For the Sioux this was a blessing and a curse. On the one hand, it undoubtedly saved them from swarms of land-

13. Morgan to Secretary of the Interior John W. Noble, Jan. 5, 1891, in CIA, *Annual Report* (1891), pp. 191–95, sets forth complete statistical data on the Sioux ration situation during this period. Commissioner Morgan had no reason to falsify the figures, for the blame demonstrably lay with the House of Representatives, and he said so. He claimed that each Sioux received 1.9 pounds of beef per day plus flour, bacon, coffee, sugar, corn, and beans, and he allowed about fifteen per cent for shrinkage of beef on the hoof. Capt. F. A. Whitney, who personally investigated the question at Rosebud, allowed thirty-five per cent shrinkage and arrived at a per capita allowance of ten ounces a day, which is still above the starvation level. See Whitney to Adjt. Rosebud Agency, Nov. 27, 1890, encl. to Brig. Gen. John R. Brooke to Asst. Adjt. Gen. Div. of the Mo., Pine Ridge, Nov. 30, 1890. (Hereafter, all correspondence not otherwise identified is from the National Archives.) There is also abundant testimony that the Sioux were in truth starving. So conflicting is the evidence, and so replete with variables is the problem, that the safest conclusion is that the Sioux were very hungry, and perhaps individuals were actually starving.

14. "Rev. William J. Cleveland's Investigation of the Causes of the Sioux Trouble," IRA, *Ninth Annual Report* (1891), pp. 39, 57.

15. James D. Richardson, ed., *A Compilation of Messages and Papers of the Presidents, 1789–1897* (Washington, 1898), *8*, 94–97.

16. Morgan to Sec. Int., Feb. 4 and 8, 1890; Actg. CIA R. V. Belt to Agt. Anderson, Feb. 12, 1890; Sec. War, *Annual Report* (1890), *1*, 191–92.

hungry whites who would have shown scant regard for Indian rights. On the other, it reinforced their apprehension that they might receive only fifty cents or seventy-five cents an acre for the ceded land. The price of $1.25 held for only three years.

In issuing the proclamation before fulfilling the promises of the Sioux Commission, President Harrison had acted on the recommendation of Secretary of the Interior Noble. Transmitting the commission's report on January 30, Noble had declared:

> In my own judgment, the act should now be proclaimed, the surveys made as soon as possible, and the Secretary of the Interior required, so far as he may, without further legislation, to carry into effect the recommendations of the Commission; and the further recommendations of the Commission be transmitted to Congress for action by it in accordance with the spirit and fair understanding of the negotiations exhibited to have taken place between the Commission and the Sioux.
>
> It may be relied upon, I think, that the legislative branch of the Government will execute what it believes to have been this understanding with the Indians, in good faith. The burdens assumed are light in comparison with the benefits obtained [nine million acres of land], and there will be no substantial reason for refusing to supplement the act assented to by such further provisions as are recommended to make it fair and acceptable.[17]

The President sent the report to Congress on February 10, together with the draft of a bill incorporating all the recommendations of the commission, and urged that the legislation be enacted at once.[18]

As February, then March, then April slipped by, the awful realization dawned upon the Sioux that the Great Council in Washington, having got their land, had no intention of making good the promises of the Crook Commission. The general had died in March 1890, a bad omen. Said Red Cloud to Father F.

17. Report of the Sioux Commission of 1889, p. 9.
18. Ibid., pp. 1–11.

M. Craft, missionary at Pine Ridge, "Then General Crook came; he, at least, had never lied to us. His words gave our people hope. He died. Then hope died again. Despair came again."[19]

The Senate, traditionally liberal and humanitarian in dealing with the Indian problem, passed the bill on April 26. But the House of Representatives held the purse strings and declined to untie them. Not only this but the House also delayed passage of the regular Indian Appropriation Act for fiscal year 1891 until August 19, 1890, too late for clothing and other annuity goods to reach the agencies until winter was well advanced. And the act carried only $950,000 for subsistence and civilization of the Sioux, still $50,000 short of the amount required for the full ration allowance.[20]

On the Sioux Reservation an old Indian, with singular appropriateness, remarked to Reverend William J. Cleveland: "They made us many promises, more than I can remember, but they never kept but one; they promised to take our land and they took it."[21]

19. Quoted in John G. Bourke, *On the Border with Crook* (New York, 1891), p. 486.
20. CIA, *Annual Report* (1891), pp. 182–91.
21. IRA, *Ninth Annual Report* (1891), p. 29.

5. THE INDIAN MESSIAH

THE LAND AGREEMENT shook the Teton tribes with more violence that anything in their history, and it threw into sharp focus all the resentments and frustrations built up in a decade of reservation life. The winter of 1889–90—with unrelieved hunger, disastrous epidemics, the opening of the ceded lands, and the continued inaction of Congress on the recommendations of the Crook Commission—emptied the Tetons of hope.

Then, in March 1890, eleven Indians returned to Pine Ridge, Rosebud, and Cheyenne River from a long journey to the west. They told a wonderful tale. A Messiah had appeared on earth. He preached a new religion. It was a religion that offered hope for the Indian race—hope not dependent upon promises of the white men. He held forth a vision of paradise in which not only the Sioux but all Indians would at last be free of the white burden and reside for eternity in a blissful land. By simply believing in the Messiah, practicing the tenets of his faith, and dancing a prescribed "Ghost Dance," they could bring forth a new world where everything was even better than it used to be.

The first vague rumors of the Messiah had begun to circulate among the Sioux eight months earlier. On July 23, 1889, a young schoolteacher named Elaine Goodale, accompanying a party of

Oglalas on an antelope hunt in hope of gaining insight into the Sioux mind, wrote in her diary:

> So tired I fall asleep before supper. Later in the night a cry is raised: "A traveler comes!" Chasing Crane, on his way home from Rosebud, is welcomed with supper and a smoke. God, he says, has appeared to the Crows! In the midst of a council he came from nowhere and announced himself as the Savior who came upon earth once and was killed by the white men. He had been grieved by the crying of parents for their dead children, and would let the sky down upon the earth and destroy the disobedient. He was beautiful to look upon, and bore paint as a sign of power. Men and women listen to this curious tale with apparent credence. A vapor bath is arranged, and I fall asleep again to the monotonous rise and fall of the accompanying songs.[1]

The tale reached the Sioux Reservation while the Crook Commission was making the rounds of the agencies and just before the ration cut. With the white man causing them so much grief, the Tetons were much interested in the vague reports of a God who had come to earth to rescue the Indians from adversity. In the autumn of 1889 the Oglalas of Pine Ridge convened a council to talk over the rumors. Red Cloud and Little Wound (non-progressives) and American Horse and Young-Man-Afraid-of-His-Horses (progressives) presided. They chose representatives to journey westward in search of the truth. Similar councils at Rosebud and Cheyenne River also selected emissaries. In all, there were eleven and they traveled together. From Pine Ridge went Good Thunder, Yellow Breast, Flat Iron, Broken Arm, Cloud Horse, Yellow Knife, Elk Horn, and Kicks Back. Short Bull and Mash-the-Kettle represented Rosebud, and Kicking Bear represented Cheyenne River.[2] Of these men, Short Bull

1. Elaine Goodale Eastman, "The Ghost Dance War and Wounded Knee Massacre of 1890–91," *Nebraska History, 26* (1945), 28.

2. Porcupine, George Sword, and William T. Selwyn—the first two, Indians, and the last, a mixed blood—are the main authorities for the gathering of the delegates. See, respectively, Brig. Gen. T. H. Ruger to Adjt. Gen. U.S.A., June 25, 1890; Selwyn to Agt. E. W. Foster, Nov. 25, 1890; and George Sword, "The Story

and Kicking Bear were to become the most ardent disciples of the new religion among the Tetons.

Kicking Bear was about forty-one years old, a mystic with a modest reputation as a medicine man. In the old days he had been a mighty warrior and an intimate of Crazy Horse. He had taken many ponies in raids on the Crows and other enemy tribes and had distinguished himself in 1876 at the Rosebud, Little Bighorn, and Slim Buttes. By birth an Oglala, he became a Miniconjou band chief through marriage to Woodpecker Woman, niece of the Miniconjou chief, Big Foot. Uncompromising hatred of the white man and all his ways, refusal to adjust to the new life, mystical leanings, and rank and reputation made Kicking Bear a natural leader in the quest for the old life.[3]

Short Bull, Kicking Bear's brother-in-law, was a medicine man in Lip's Wazhaza band on Pass Creek. Three or four years older than Kicking Bear, Short Bull had also been a notable warrior and, after the surrender, had become a leading nonprogressive. A sharp-faced man of small stature, he was kind, generous, and well liked—traits that Agent James G. Wright mistook for lack of force and influence. Short Bull's career as a Ghost Dance leader amply demonstrated his qualities of leadership.[4]

The Teton delegation journeyed first to Wind River Reservation, Wyoming. Here they found that other tribes had dispatched emissaries to search for the prophet. Five Shoshonis, three Northern Cheyennes, and an Arapaho from Oklahoma joined the Sioux. At Fort Hall Agency, Idaho, five Bannocks and Western Shoshonis joined the party. Southward to Salt Lake City the pilgrims made their way, then traveled by train to western Nevada. Some Paiutes furnished them with wagons, in which

---

of the Ghost Dance," trans. Emma Sickels, *Folk-Lorist, 1* (1892–93), 28–31. See also George Bird Grinnell, "Account of the Northern Cheyenne Concerning the Messiah Superstition," *Journal of American Folk-Lore, 4* (1891), 65–66; and Lt. N. P. Phister, "The Indian Messiah," *American Anthropologist,* o.s. *4* (1891), 105–08.

3. David H. Miller, *Ghost Dance* (New York, 1959), pp. 3–14, 286–91, based on interviews with Cheyenne River Indians.

4. Ibid., pp. 40, 42. J. R. Walker Interview, Ricker Collection (Walker was agency physician at Pine Ridge in the early years of the twentieth century and knew Short Bull). James G. Wright (the elder) to CIA, Jan. 22, 1891.

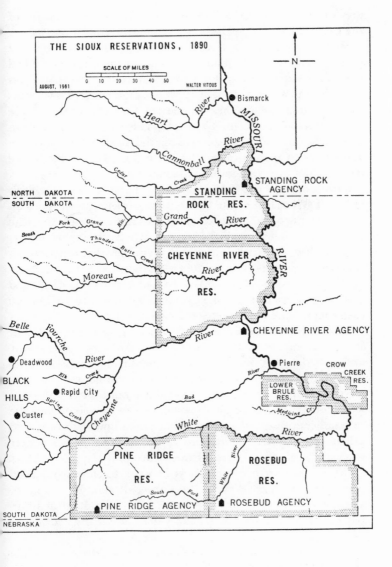

THE SIOUX RESERVATIONS, 1890

SCALE OF MILES
0   10   20   30   40   50

AUGUST, 1961   WALTER VITOUS

— N —

Bismarck

Heart   River

Cannonball   River

MISSOURI

Cedar   Creek

STANDING ROCK AGENCY

NORTH   DAKOTA

SOUTH   DAKOTA

STANDING
ROCK   RES.

South   Fork   Grand   Riv.   Grand   River

Thunder   Butte   Creek

CHEYENNE RIVER

River

RIVER

Moreau

RES.

Belle   Fourche

Deadwood

River

Elk   Creek

River

CHEYENNE RIVER AGENCY

BLACK

Rapid City

Pierre

CROW
CREEK
RES.

HILLS

Spring   Creek

Bad

River

LOWER
BRULE
RES.

Custer

Cheyenne

Medicine   Cr.

White   River

PINE   RIDGE

White   River

RES.

ROSEBUD

South   Fork

RES.

PINE RIDGE AGENCY

ROSEBUD AGENCY

SOUTH   DAKOTA

NEBRASKA

they drove to the Paiute Reservation at Walker Lake, south of the Central Pacific Railroad. Here dwelt the Indian Messiah.

He was a Paiute sheepherder named Wovoka, and his rise had been spectacular. On January 1, 1889, only a year earlier, he had been an obscure shaman. On this day an eclipse of the sun was visible in the western states, and Wovoka experienced a wonderful vision. He "went to heaven and saw God and all the people who died a long time ago."[5] When he came back to Nevada from heaven, he came as the Messiah of the Indian race. He came with a new religion and with a mandate from God to rescue his people from the darkness that awaited them.

Such a miracle was nothing new to Mason Valley. Wovoka's father, Tavibo, had created similar excitement among the Paiutes about 1870 and had even attracted some interest among the neighboring Bannock and Shoshoni tribes. From his father, Wovoka had acquired a degree of mysticism that contributed, nearly twenty years later, to the vision that led to his own notoriety. From his father, also, Wovoka had learned sleight-of-hand and other tricks of the magician's art that made up part of the stock in trade of every successful medicine man.

After the death of Tavibo, Wovoka went to live with David Wilson, a white rancher in Mason Valley. Adopted by the family and named Jack Wilson, Wovoka came under Christian influences. The Wilsons read aloud the family Bible, and Wovoka learned about the white man's God and about his son, Jesus. He learned that Jesus was a great medicine man who could heal the sick and control the elements, and he noted how the whites had killed Jesus by nailing him to a cross. These stories deeply marked the youthful mind of the future prophet.

In addition to conventional Christian teachings absorbed from the Wilsons, Wovoka encountered another brand of Christianity. By 1890 Mormon families had spread out in all directions from the Great Salt Lake Valley, and many had settled

---

5. Mooney, *Ghost-Dance*, p. 764. Unless otherwise cited, this account of Wovoka's background is drawn from Mooney and from Paul Bailey, *Wovoka, the Indian Messiah* (Los Angeles, 1957). Mooney's book is the most comprehensive source of authoritative information about the Ghost Dance. Bailey's work is a competent biography of Wovoka.

in Nevada. In the theology of the Church of Jesus Christ of Latter-Day Saints, Indians occupied a place of special significance, and Mormons took special interest in them. Wovoka was exposed to Mormon teachings but rejected them. Nevertheless, they were almost certainly among the factors that shaped his mind.[6]

Another influence went into the making of this prophet. For two years he worked in the hop fields of California, Oregon, and Washington. On Puget Sound he learned of the Shaker religion, which since about 1880 had swept the tribes of the region. This religion reflected the influences to which its founder, a Squaxon Indian named John Slocum, had been subjected. It was a strange combination of Catholic pageantry, Presbyterian austerity, and pagan witchcraft. Significantly, trances formed an important part of its ceremonies. Despite the efforts of the agents to suppress it, the Shaker religion held powerful sway over the tribes of the Pacific Northwest. Wovoka learned the doctrine, participated in some of its rituals, and observed its regenerating effect upon converts.

Back in Mason Valley, Wovoka, now about thirty-five and an intelligent, handsome Indian, became in the late 1880s a successful shaman, moderately wealthy and respected by his people. He longed for more. Gambling his reputation on a spectacular stratagem, he publicly vowed to cause ice to float down Walker River in midsummer. With numerous witnesses, he did. From that day forward, the Paiutes revered him as one of the great shamans of all time. What they never knew was that the Wilson boys, to help their adopted brother advance in his chosen profession, had filled a wagon with blocks of ice from the Wilson ice house and

6. The link between the Mormons and the Messiah Craze is shadowy and probably never will be sharply defined. Many whites, some in high places, accused them of fomenting the Indian troubles of 1890—an accusation that doubtless originated in the widespread hostility to Mormons and ignorance of their theology. Existing evidence will not sustain the charge but does suggest that the Mormons contributed indirectly to the form the religion assumed, as indeed did all Christian teachings. Some accounts speak of whites participating in Ghost Dances at Walker Lake. It is entirely possible that they were Mormons, for Joseph Smith, founder of Mormonism, had prophesied in 1843 that the Messiah would come to earth in mortal form during the year 1890.

surreptitiously dumped them in the river above the place appointed by Wovoka as the scene of his miracle.

Wovoka prayed for still greater things. His motivation was more than personal ambition. Like most other Indians in 1889, he was bewildered and tormented. The customs, beliefs, and values of the white people had crushed the old Indian life. Traditional views of the universe seemed no longer valid. Yet the white man's views of the universe were not satisfactory either. In groping for basic explanations, in longing to roll back the years, Wovoka differed from few of his race. But he had the determination coupled with the ability to do something about the conflict.

"When the sun died" on January 1, 1889, the Paiutes were filled with fear. They shouted, wailed, and fired guns into the air trying to drive off the evil monster that threatened to devour the sun, most powerful of Indian deities. Wovoka lay ill with fever on a pallet in his tule wickiup. A vision came to him. He died and went to heaven, where he spoke with God. God was very much like the God described in David Wilson's Bible, and heaven was a heaven such as the white man conceived. Yet at the same time it was a heaven inhabited by Indians—all the Indians who had once lived on earth. They enjoyed peace, happiness, and prosperity. No one grew old, and everyone remained free of sickness and want. Here in short was the old life made infinitely better.

God told Wovoka to take a message back to earth. If the Indian people followed His commandments, as preached by Wovoka, they might join their ancestors in heaven and enjoy the Utopia Wovoka had seen. To bring about this millennium, they must be industrious, honest, virtuous, peaceful. In fact, although not stated, they must follow a code of conduct almost identical to the white man's Ten Commandments. The admonition against fighting was stressed. This was indeed a revolutionary doctrine to a people whose highest values were based on success in war. In addition to adopting these moral precepts, Indians must perform at stated intervals a dance that God taught Wovoka. It was this "Ghost Dance" that became the most spectacular and widely known feature of the religion.

Finally, as evidence of his divine mission, God gave Wovoka command of the elements. By exercising this power, he could make the sun shine or make the heavens drop rain or snow. With a mandate to assume command in the West, while leaving the East to "Governor Harrison," Wovoka returned to earth and began to preach to his people.

The following summer he staged an impressive demonstration of his supernatural power. The captain of the Indian police, Josephus, came to Wovoka and told him that the crops were dying and that unless it rained soon there would be much suffering in Mason Valley. Wovoka said: "You can go home and on the morning of the third day you and all the people will have water." Josephus spread word among both Indians and whites that the drought would soon end. Rain began to fall at once, and by the third day the Walker River had overflowed its banks. Like most medicine men, Wovoka was doubtless an extraordinarily skilled weather forecaster, but from then on few Paiutes doubted his story of the journey to heaven.[7]

The Paiutes became devoted adherents of the Ghost Dance religion, and Wovoka organized dances in Mason Valley and at Pyramid Lake, to the north. Word of the new Messiah soon reached nearly every reservation in the West; paradoxically, innovations of white civilization spread the news faster and farther than could have been possible in the old days. Indians now communicated by mail with members of distant tribes simply by getting a friend who had been to school to write a letter in the English language. Railroads now blanketed the West, and the trainmen made little effort to prevent Indians from riding the cars. Traveling by railroad to other reservations had become a favorite pastime, and the teachings of the prophet were spread orally from one reservation to another. Thus the Sioux had learned of the religion by word of mouth from the Shoshonis and by letter from tribes all over the West.

7. A. I. Chapman to Brig. Gen. John Gibbon, Dec. 6, 1890, in Sec. War, *Annual Report* (1891), *1*, 191–94. Gibbon had sent Chapman, an Army scout, to learn the origins of the Messiah Craze then sweeping the western tribes. Josephus, corroborated by two white employees of the agency, related the story to Chapman. The whites of Mason Valley confirmed that the rain came as Wovoka had predicted.

The Sioux emissaries and their companions reached Mason Valley early in 1890. They were not the only Indians who had come. Representatives of many of the important tribes of the Plains and mountains had converged on Walker Lake at the same time early in the year. Agent C. C. Warner counted thirty-four delegates, and there were doubtless more. They were the vanguard of the procession that in the next several years would travel to Mason Valley.

Agent Warner, who administered the two Paiute agencies from headquarters at Pyramid Lake, attached little importance to this unusual gathering of Indians. He did not report the arrival of emissaries from other tribes until nearly a year later, and then only because the Indian Bureau, confronted with open warfare among the Sioux, was frantically trying to find out what had started the whole thing. As late as October 1891 he wrote that he could furnish little information on the Ghost Dance religion because he was "pursuing the course with [Wovoka] of nonattention or a silent ignoring."[8]

The delegation that included the Sioux probably stayed in Mason Valley about a week. They reverently paid homage to the great medicine man, listened to his sermons, and learned the movements of the Ghost Dance. The message they heard was truly revolutionary. Deeply rooted in Christianity, it demanded attitudes and practices leading inevitably to progress in civilization, and as a stimulus to such progress it was worth a thousand reform policies devised in New England drawing rooms. This truth, however, escaped the architects of Indian policy, who regarded the Ghost Dance religion as a monster of paganism that would stamp out the progress of a decade. There was reason for their misunderstanding, for the doctrine underwent many changes as it spread out from the source. Each tribe shaped the religion to the framework of its own mythology, and each individual adherent added further embellishments of his own. The white friends of the Indian had, after all, to base their judgments on distorted fragments of the doctrine that came from many different sources.

8. Warner to James Mooney, Oct. 12, 1891, in Mooney, *Ghost-Dance*, p. 767.

Yet the few perceptive whites who took the trouble to investigate learned the truth of the matter. One such, Capt. Hugh L.
Scott, wrote his superiors that Wovoka "has given these people
a better religion than they ever had before, taught them precepts which, if faithfully carried out, will bring them into better
accord with their white neighbors, and has prepared the way for
their final Christianization."[9] Another was the Smithsonian Institution's able ethnologist James Mooney. In 1891, while the
religion still gripped the tribes, he went west and, by means of
specialized training and a sympathetic approach, learned all any
white man possibly could about it. He won an interview with
Wovoka himself and thus obtained the true version of the doctrine. Later he verified Wovoka's statements by interviewing
Ghost Dancers throughout the West.

According to Mooney's findings, Wovoka promised his followers to regenerate the earth. He declared that a new world
was being prepared for the Indian race. It was already advancing
from the west and was expected to arrive in the spring of 1891.
The ground would tremble as a signal for Indians everywhere
to fix in their hair sacred feathers by which to soar aloft while
the new land covered the old. The new land would push the
white people before it, back across the ocean to where they came
from in the first place. When the cataclysm subsided, the Indians
would lower themselves from the sky. Here they would find all
Indians who had once lived on earth—friends, relatives, and
ancestors. Together they would enjoy eternal life, unmarred by
pain, sickness, discomfort, want, or death. On every side, deer,
antelope, and elk would roam in abundance, and herds of buffalo
such as only the old people could recall would once more blacken
the prairie.

By praying, dancing the Ghost Dance, and singing the Ghost
Dance songs, Indians could "die" and journey to this paradise
for brief visits before it actually appeared. Wovoka taught the
delegates the mechanics of the dance and the words of some songs.
By dancing, singing, and praying, they worked themselves into
emotional frenzies. They went into trances that enabled each

9. Report of Feb. 10, 1891, quoted in ibid., p. 783.

to "die" for a short time and to see what the future held in store for the Indian race.

But there was a price for this. The religion imposed a rigid moral code, grounded in Christian ethics and departing radically from ancient attitudes and habits. "Do no harm to anyone. You must not fight," Wovoka enjoined the disciples. A people who had fought for centuries, who loved to fight, whose greatest aspirations centered on war and whose greatest rewards sprang from war, were told to put away all weapons and trophies of war, to think gentle thoughts, and to harm no person, red or white. "Do not tell lies." "When your friends die, you must not cry." Since all dead Indians were to return, there was no need to cry, to mutilate and torture their bodies, to cut off their hair, and to destroy property. And finally, a blanket injunction to cover all else, "Do right always."[10]

Yet, as powerfully as Christianity influenced the Ghost Dance religion, there were features, such as the dance itself, that evoked the old pagan religion; and the object of the whole movement, of course, was the restoration of the old savage life and its dominant values. Christianity and paganism had united to form the common denominator of a doctrine that offered grounds for belief to all Indians, progressive and nonprogressive alike. Such a combination appealed strongly to the heart and mind of the American Indians of 1890.

Throughout the history of the world, such a combination has appealed to other peoples similarly afflicted. The Ghost Dance religion was by no means unique; on the contrary, it bore striking resemblances to earlier primitive religious movements. Wovoka was but one of a long line of aboriginal mystics who sought to rid their people of an alien oppressor and lead them into the promised land. By such teachings the Tewa medicine man Popé united the Pueblos of the Rio Grande to expel the Spaniards in 1680. The Ottawa chief Pontiac used a like doctrine to forge the confederation that in 1763 nearly drove the English from the Appalachian frontier. Early in the nineteenth century Tecumseh and his religious ally, the Prophet, built a similar confederation that wrought destruction in the Old Northwest until shat-

10. Ibid., p. 782.

tered at the battle of Tippecanoe. In 1881 the Apache medicine man Nakaidoklini stirred up the White Mountain Apaches with such teachings, and as late as 1887 the prophet Sword Bearer excited the Crows with promises of an approaching millennium.

Nor were the antecedents of the Ghost Dance confined to American aborigines. Condorcanqui, who united the Peruvian natives against the Spanish in 1781, and the Mahdi of Allah, who inflamed the tribes of the Sudan against the British and seized Khartoum in 1885, are but two of many native leaders elsewhere on the globe who preached tenets that would have been familiar to Wovoka.

Mooney himself saw the Ghost Dance in its larger context— and not just a phenomenon of primitive peoples. Any race that has been crushed as were the American Indians, he observed, is likely to turn to a self-appointed redeemer. "Hope becomes a faith and the faith becomes the creed of priests and prophets, until the hero is a god and the dream a religion, looking to some great miracle of nature for its culmination and accomplishment. The doctrines of the Hindu avatar, the Hebrew Messiah, the Christian millennium, and the Hesunanin of the Indian Ghost dance are essentially the same, and have their origin in a hope and longing common to all humanity."[11]

Broken Arm, Elk Horn, and Kicks Back left their comrades at Walker Lake and visited some tribes in the Pacific Northwest. The rest of the apostles turned homeward, the Sioux reaching their agencies in March 1890. At Pine Ridge, Rosebud, and Cheyenne River they told the wonderful story. The Messiah had indeed come to earth to save his Indian children. He had scars on his hands and feet, evidence of treatment many centuries ago by the white men.[12] There was other proof of divinity: Once as

11. Ibid., p. 657.
12. Mooney concluded that Wovoka did not claim to be the Son of God. But as the delegates of 1889–90 universally conceived him as the Messiah, and as they all told of the scars on his hands and feet, I have chosen to use the term Messiah freely. It is possible that by 1891, when Mooney went west, Wovoka had modified his story from that of 1890. The important point, however, is that whether Wovoka actually represented himself as the Messiah or merely as a prophet, the delegates believed he was the Messiah.

they watched he made two birds talk to each other; another time he caused two horses to do the same. During the journey home they had come upon a herd of buffalo, by 1890 a rarity on the plains. The Sioux remembered the Messiah's words: "On the way home, if you kill any buffalo, cut [off] the head, the tail, and four feet, and leave them, and that buffalo will come to live again." They killed one of the animals and, after devouring the carcass, left the useless parts enumerated by Wovoka on the prairie. Before their eyes the buffalo came to life and ambled away. Also on the return trip, still a long way from home, they grew weary. Calling upon the Messiah for help, they went to sleep one night and next morning awoke to find themselves much closer to their destination.[13]

The delegates related how the prophet had given them a graphic preview of the world to be gained by embracing his religion. "We looked and we saw a land created across the ocean, on which all the nations of Indians were coming home." (This phrase, "nations of Indians coming home," found its way into the lyrics of numerous Ghost Dance songs.) In this land they visited friends long dead. Chasing Hawk, recently deceased, and his wife, killed in war many moons before, lived in a large tepee of buffalo skin. (The Sioux now lived in dark log cabins; on ration day at the agency they camped in cheap canvas tepees.) Good Thunder saw his son, who also had died in battle long before, and talked with him in his tepee. But the delegates were permitted only a brief glimpse of this land, the Messiah explaining that "it was not time for that to take place."[14]

The apostles added to Wovoka's message a touch of their own —a tragic one as it turned out. The doctrine as taught by the Paiute prophet was entirely pacifistic. Indians need only follow his moral precepts and dance the Ghost Dance to bring about the new order. Above all, he stressed the importance of avoiding violence, even in thought. Every other tribe absorbed this commandment, but not the Sioux. The bitterness engendered by the land agreement and the ration cut left them with too much hatred toward the white man. As described by the Sioux emis-

13. Sword, "Story of the Ghost Dance," pp. 29–30.
14. Ibid.

saries, the doctrine of peace became a doctrine, if not of war, at least of vicious antagonism to the whites.

The contrast between the story told to his people by Porcupine, the Northern Cheyenne delegate from Tongue River, and that told by the Sioux is instructive.[15] Porcupine's recollection of Wovoka's description of his crucifixion and return displays no particular hostility toward the white man. The Messiah said that "after God made the earth the people were afraid of me and treated me badly. This is what they done to me." He exhibited the scars on his hands and feet. "I did not try to defend myself; I found my people were bad, and so went back to heaven and left them." Now God had sent him back to "renew everything as it used to be and make it better." The Sioux version of the same story took on decidedly militant overtones. "The white people are not good," said the Messiah. "They killed me, and you can see the marks of my wounds." But now he came as a savior of the Indians, and the whites could not harm him. If soldiers tried to arrest him, he would, merely by raising his arms, "knock them into nothingness." Or he would cause the earth to "open and swallow them in."

Porcupine enjoined the Cheyennes: Wovoka "told us not to quarrel or fight or strike each other, nor shoot one another; that the whites and the Indians were to be all one people." The Sioux proclaimed that the Messiah, as punishment for three centuries of oppressing the red race, would wipe the white race from the earth. The whites "have treated the Indians very bad all the way through," ran the Sioux story, and the Messiah is "going to exterminate the whites by some phenomenon in the spring of 1891." Thus the whites were not to be gently pushed aside, but violently and vengefully destroyed. And a time, the spring of 1891, had been set. From this idea, it was for some only a short mental leap to the belief that force would help prepare for the day of deliverance. William T. Selwyn, mixed-blood postmaster at Pine Ridge, asked a Ghost Dancer "if their father advises them to cause trouble on the whites by next spring." "That was the

15. The Sioux version that follows is from ibid., the Cheyenne version from Porcupine's narrative in Ruger to Adjt. Gen., June 25, 1890.

orders they had from their father," was the reply, "but [the orders] will be kept secret."[16]

The story of the apostles sped to the remotest corner of each of the newly created reservations. Everyone talked of the new religion, but not everyone believed. The progressives, mostly the young who had known little of the old life, found the tale hard to swallow. Yet they were too much Indian to dismiss it lightly, and only a few of the more courageous spoke up in ridicule. The nonprogressives, largely those of middle and advanced age who had suffered most from the conflict between new and old values, had few doubts. The glowing promises gave them new hope, and they looked eagerly to the apostles for instruction in the Ghost Dance.

At Rosebud, Short Bull and Mash-the-Kettle began holding councils as soon as they returned in March 1890. Agent J. George Wright immediately saw that something was amiss. Although newly appointed, he was not without experience. His father had been agent at Rosebud from 1882 to 1886, and he himself had served L. F. Spencer as clerk from 1886 to 1889. Wright owed his appointment to the Crook Commission. General Crook suggested to the Secretary of the Interior that Spencer's love of graft and strong drink impaired his usefulness as agent, and he recommended Wright as successor. The new administration had just begun to purge the Indian Service of political undesirables, and Crook's advice opportunely provided an excuse to get rid of Democrat Spencer. Although mild mannered, Wright in his quiet way made a good agent. When he learned of Short Bull's councils, he sent policemen to sit in on a few and report what was agitating the Brulés and disrupting the farming program. Then he called Short Bull into his office and lectured him with unaccustomed sternness. Meekly, the medicine man promised to stop holding councils, and there is no evidence that he failed to keep his promise.[17]

Pine Ridge required more firmness. Here a Democrat, Hugh D. Gallagher, still clung to his post, although the Republican

16. Selwyn to Foster, Nov. 25, 1890.
17. IRA, *Tenth Annual Report* (1892), p. 45. CIA, *Annual Report* (1891), p. 411.

ax was soon to fall. An elderly politician from Indiana, he had served satisfactorily and enjoyed a quiet tenure. In April, Postmaster Selwyn told Gallagher about the religious excitement that was sweeping the reservation and reported that Good Thunder and his colleagues had called a council to inaugurate the Ghost Dance. Gallagher summoned Good Thunder and two others and quizzed them about the matter. They refused to talk, so he locked them in jail. After two days, although they still declined to answer the agent's questions, they promised to hold no more councils and were released. Here, as at Rosebud, the apostles either quit preaching or else continued in secret.[18]

At Cheyenne River, Charles E. McChesney, soon to give up his post to a Republican, considered the new religion so unimportant that he did not interfere with Kicking Bear's agitation. He knew something of the doctrine but expected nothing to come of it. Kicking Bear and his followers wrote letters to the other agencies summoning all Sioux to a grand council at Cheyenne River to receive instruction in the Ghost Dance. But after Gallagher and Wright intervened, the Rosebud and Pine Ridge Sioux gave up the idea of attending, and the excitement subsided at Cheyenne River too. Kicking Bear went off to visit the Arapahoes in Wyoming.[19]

The Indians of Standing Rock, Crow Creek, and Lower Brulé undoubtedly heard of the coming millennium, but the news created no great enthusiasm. None of the tribes at these agencies had sent representatives to Nevada, and none of the delegates from the other agencies had as yet attempted to introduce the dance among them.

The Sioux agents had failed to take the Ghost Dance religion seriously, and none had received any hint of its militant trappings. They did not report the talk of a Messiah until queried by their superiors. Garbled rumors reached Washington early in June 1890. A Sioux youth attending the Presbyterian college at Pierre, South Dakota, received a letter from relatives at Pine Ridge advising him that there might be an uprising soon. He

18. Selwyn to Foster, Nov. 25, 1890. Sword, "Story of the Ghost Dance," p. 30.
19. Ibid. McChesney to CIA, June 16, 1890. Wright to CIA, same date.

told a white friend, a resident of Pierre named Charles L. Hyde, who on May 29 wrote to the Secretary of the Interior that "the Sioux or a portion of them are secretly planning and arranging for an outbreak in the near future." The Acting Commissioner of Indian Affairs, Robert V. Belt, promptly called for a report from each of the Sioux agents.[20]

Gallagher and McChesney acknowledged that a religious excitement was current among the Sioux but minimized its importance. It would die out, they believed, when the Messiah failed to appear at the appointed time. Wright set the unrest down to dissatisfied nonprogressives. At Standing Rock, James McLaughlin, of all agents the best informed about doings on his reservation, had heard nothing of the Messiah and detected nothing unusual among his people.[21]

The replies of all the agents leave little doubt that the Sioux had no thought of going to war. Clearly, the doctrine preached by the apostles had not in June 1890 won the implicit faith of large numbers of Sioux, and nowhere had the Ghost Dance itself been formally inaugurated.[22] It is entirely possible, indeed probable, that had Congress at this time restored the ration cut and carried out the promises of the Crook Commission, the Ghost Dance religion would have quietly run its course as it did among the other tribes affected by Wovoka's teachings. But Congress had other matters to debate more weighty than Indian

20. Hyde to Sec. Int., May 29, 1890. Belt to Sioux agents, June 7. Belt to Sec. Int., same date.

21. Gallagher to CIA, June 14, 1890. McChesney to CIA, June 16. Wright to CIA, same date. McLaughlin to CIA, June 18.

22. I can find only one source, the report of Dr. Daniel Dorchester, Superintendent of Indian Schools, in CIA, *Annual Report* (1891), p. 529, that explicitly states that a Ghost Dance was organized before August 1890. The weight of evidence, admittedly largely negative and indirect, leads me to discount Dorchester's statement. Mooney, pp. 846–47, citing Dorchester, says that a Ghost Dance was held at No Water's camp near Pine Ridge about the middle of June and that Ghost Shirts were here worn for the first time. A glance at Dorchester's report shows that Mooney misread it. After writing "As early as about the 20th of June the ghost dance commenced among the Sioux," Dorchester goes on to quote an eyewitness account of a Ghost Dance at No Water's camp that Mooney takes to be a description of the June 20 affair. The account, however, begins, "We drove to this spot about 10:30 o'clock on a delightful October day."

appropriations. And the summer of 1890 only multiplied the miseries that beset the Sioux.

Hunger continued to stalk the reservations. Bishop Hare estimated that rations, even when carefully husbanded, lasted only two-thirds of the period for which they were issued. An officer stationed at Fort Niobrara, thirty-eight miles southeast of Rosebud Agency, recalled that throughout the summer Brulé families trooped down from the agency to beg at the fort. Regulations authorized the post commissary officer to issue food to visiting Indians. They took advantage of this, then went to beg for the garbage of the company kitchens and the refuse of the slaughter pens. Citizens of nearby Valentine told similar stories.[23]

But there was also reason for hope. The farming season began auspiciously. A heartening number of Indians planted seeds, and heavy spring rains got them off to a good start. (This may partly explain why the agents had been able to suppress the Ghost Dance religion so easily.) Then in mid-July scorching winds whipped across the prairie. Day after day they pounded the crops relentlessly. Elaine Goodale, journeying from the Black Hills to the Missouri and north to the Cannonball inspecting Indian schools, recalled the scene: "The pitiful little gardens curled up and died in the persistent hot winds. Even young men displayed gaunt limbs and lack-luster faces. Old folks lost their hold on life, and heart-broken mothers mourned the last of a series of dead babies."[24] In many areas oats, wheat, vegetables, and even the range grass were totally destroyed. Elsewhere a third to a half of the crops managed to survive. In neighboring Nebraska and eastern South Dakota, settlers abandoned their homesteads by the score. The Sioux had no place to go. The disaster this year exceeded that of previous years, for now they desperately needed the food. That they had permitted themselves hope in June only magnified the impact of the disaster in August.

---

23. Lt. W. P. Richardson, "Some Observations upon the Sioux Campaign of 1890–91," *Journal of the Military Service Institution of the United States, 18* (1896), 520.

24. Elaine Goodale Eastman, "Ghost Dance War," p. 29.

Other grievances piled on top of hunger. The new boundary between Pine Ridge and Rosebud Reservations, running due south from the mouth of Black Pipe Creek, upset Chief Lip's Wazhazhas, who lived along this creek and Pass Creek, to the east. Technically Brulés, these people had joined the Oglalas in 1854 and lived with them until 1876, when they rejoined Spotted Tail's Brulés to avoid the trouble with the Army that Red Cloud's leadership gave promise of provoking. Although they had drawn their rations at Rosebud Agency, their ties with the Oglalas were still strong, and, when the new boundary threw them into Pine Ridge Reservation, they insisted upon being counted on the Pine Ridge rolls.

To the Wazhazhas the solution was simple and logical. To Commissioner of Indian Affairs Morgan it was equally simple and logical: "The Indians whose case is now under consideration, belonging to and receiving rations and annuities at the Rosebud Agency, as they do and did at the date of the Sioux Act, have as I conceive, no interest in the lands of the Pine Ridge Reservation, although residing on a portion thereof." This being clearly evident, he saw no course but to move the families across the line. But one of Secretary Noble's inspectors thought otherwise, and Morgan was directed to find out how the Rosebud and Pine Ridge people as a whole felt about it. As might have been predicted, they could not agree. Noble was all set to end the controversy by sending the families to Rosebud when Agent Wright pointed out that the line had never been surveyed and that they might already be living on the Rosebud side. As no surveyors could be spared, Wright and Gallagher were told to run the boundary. But the Wazhazhas took matters into their own hands and stampeded toward Pine Ridge Agency. They went into camp on Wounded Knee Creek, about fifteen miles east of the agency, and vowed to stay there until they had their way.

At this juncture, to compound the confusion, about half the Lower Brulés suddenly decided that they wanted to move from their agency on the Missouri down to Rosebud and live with the Upper Brulés. Morgan patiently explained the legal reasons why they could not, but the Lower Brulés were not impressed. By the end of the summer, no decision had been reached on either question, and everyone involved was confused and angry.[25]

The census begun the previous summer also irritated the Sioux. On top of a long-standing aversion to being counted, they were sure that it would produce another ration cut. All over the Rosebud Reservation, Census Agent A. T. Lea encountered trickery, evasion, and opposition. Old White Horse, a notable nonprogressive, went a step further and bluntly refused to submit his band to enumeration. Inspector W. W. Junkin happened to be visiting the agency, and Lea called for help. The Secretary's "Big Cats" usually inspired the Sioux with more respect than the "Little Cats," who, as resident agents, took orders from the Commissioner of Indian Affairs; but Junkin made no headway. Finally, he had Wright suspend beef issues to White Horse's band and had the police throw White Horse, High Hawk, and Lance in the agency jail. This brought the rebels to terms. Lea finished at Rosebud in late May and moved on to Pine Ridge. Here he ran into the same obstacles and could not have finished the job without constant help from the police. Although the final count showed little change since 1880 in the total number of Teton Sioux, the Rosebud figure dropped by nearly 2,000— principally, explained Wright, because of fatal epidemics. (The Brulés had been overcounting themselves, too.) Reduction in population, of course, brought further reduction in rations.[26]

Always uneasy in the presence of bluecoats, the Sioux this summer lived under more than ordinary military scrutiny. The 500 Cheyennes under Little Chief enrolled at Pine Ridge had been agitating for seven years to transfer to the Tongue River Reservation in Montana, where their kinsmen lived. In the spring of 1890 they had begun to act very much as if they in-

25. Belt to Sec. Int., June 12, 1890. Morgan to Wright, July 31. Morgan to Gallagher, same date. Morgan to Wright, Aug. 30. Belt to Senator H. L. Dawes, Sept. 5. Belt to Senator R. F. Pettigrew, Oct. 2. Belt to Agt. A. P. Dixon, Lower Brulé, same date. Capt. F. E. Pierce to CIA, Feb. 12, 1891. Philip Wells Interview, Ricker Collection.

26. "Proceedings (Condensed) of a Council Held with the Rosebud Agency Indians, April 24, 1890, by Inspector Junkin." Junkin to Sec. Int.: "Report on Census Troubles," April 27, 1890. A. T. Lea to CIA, April 28. CIA, *Annual Report* (1890), p. 45.

tended to go without permission. Upon an inspector's recommendation, Secretary Noble asked for soldiers to move in and
by their presence suggest to the Cheyennes the folly of such a
course. Two troops of cavalry from Fort Meade set up camp at
Oelrichs, west of Pine Ridge on the trail to Tongue River. Here
they remained during the summer, keeping the reservation under observation.[27]

Other soldiers marched down Cheyenne River uncomfortably
close to Cheyenne River Reservation. About 130 nonprogressives from this reservation, incensed over the land agreement,
had moved eighty miles up the river in order to live as far as
possible from the agency. McChesney feared they would molest
the whites expected to occupy the land that had been opened
to settlement south of the river. He asked for soldiers. Three
troops of cavalry and two companies of infantry from Fort
Meade, Capt. A. G. Henissee commanding, established a "camp
of observation" near the forks of Cheyenne River. All summer
they kept watch.[28]

The anguish of the summer of 1890, so patently attributable
to the white man, dramatized to the dullest Sioux the depths to
which the tribes had been depressed. Sensing perhaps the final
chance to restore their waning power, the nonprogressive chiefs
on each reservation stiffened their opposition to official policies
and made a desperate bid to enlist adherents from the progressive and uncommitted ranks. They recited the impressive list of
grievances amassed in a decade of reservation life, dwelt at length
on the land agreement and its sequel of broken promises, and recalled the days when the Sioux lived unrestrained by reservation
boundaries and senseless regulations. Always a source of trouble
to the agents, these chiefs now became causes for alarm.

At Standing Rock, Sitting Bull bore the standard of reaction.
Unlike other hostile leaders, notably Gall, Sitting Bull refused
to be reconstructed. Surrounded by most of the nonprogressive
element of Standing Rock, he lived with his family in a small

27. Belt to Sec. Int., April 14, 1890. Morgan to Sec. Int., April 23. Sec. War, *Annual Report* (1890), *1*, 188, 192.

28. McChesney to CIA, March 8, 1890. Brig. Gen. T. H. Ruger to Asst. Adjt. Gen.
Div. of the Mo., April 19.

log cabin on Grand River, forty miles southwest of the agency. Except for a tour as a feature attraction of Buffalo Bill's Wild West show, he had carried on a constant feud with McLaughlin from the first. Backed by the power of the Government, the agent usually won the battles. But Sitting Bull refused to concede him victory in the war. "Crafty, avaricious, mendacious, and ambitious," McLaughlin characterized his adversary in later years. "I never knew him to display a single trait that might command admiration or respect."[29] Even so, he was still the greatest chief and medicine man of the Sioux Nation, an elder statesman whose political, military, and religious triumphs of old had left him with a reputation and a demeanor of authority that few Hunkpapas or Yanktonais, even progressives, could resist when it came to a showdown.

So troublesome had Sitting Bull and his lieutenants become by 1890 that McLaughlin seized the flimsiest pretext to try to rid himself of them. When the Indian Bureau in June passed on Charles Hyde's warning of an impending uprising and called for reports from the agents, McLaughlin, while denying that his people harbored hostile intentions, suggested the removal from Standing Rock of "the leaders of disaffection"—Sitting Bull, Circling Bear, Black Bird, and Circling Hawk. Such a move, he believed, "would end all trouble and uneasiness in the future."[30] He was doubtless correct, but the Indian Bureau quite rightly took no action, for none of these men had committed any overt act to justify their removal.

McLaughlin's troubles were minor compared with those at Cheyenne River, Pine Ridge, and Rosebud. His nonprogressives formed a smaller share of the total population than on any other reservation, and he enjoyed the support of such influential leaders as John Grass, Gall, and Crow King. At Cheyenne River the most influential men were Hump and Big Foot, both vocal spokesmen for the old life. Hump had played an important role in the Custer Battle, but his later service as scout for General

29. *My Friend the Indian*, pp. 180–81. For a laudatory biography of Sitting Bull see Stanley Vestal, *Sitting Bull: Champion of the Sioux* (2d ed. Norman, 1957).

30. McLaughlin to CIA, June 18, 1890.

Miles had earned him the confidence of Army officers and had led to his appointment, paradoxically, as chief of police at Cheyenne River. His band, numbering nearly 600, lived on Cherry Creek, about sixty miles west of the agency. All attempts to break up this nest of reaction had failed. Wearing his badge and uniform, Hump had led the opposition to the Crook Commission, although in the unpredictable shifting of Indian politics he had later signed the land agreement. Big Foot had not, and he had angrily led his band up Cheyenne River. Eighty miles west of the agency they built cabins and, under the vigilant eyes of Captain Henissee's soldiers, sullenly watched settlers trickle into the ceded land across the river.

Red Cloud still ranked as the top nonprogressive at Pine Ridge. The stature he had won in the war of 1866–68 over the Bozeman Trail, coupled with two decades of readiness to sound the trumpet of freedom, left him the undisputed patriarch of the Oglalas. But he was old and his eyes were failing. Although he held the respect of his people, his grip had loosened, and such mildly reactionary chiefs as Little Wound and Big Road were gaining influence. American Horse and Young-Man-Afraid-of-His-Horses championed the progressive cause, but their role in selling the land agreement had weakened their authority. Agent Gallagher, moreover, had alienated these chiefs. The reactionaries thus regained some of the power that McGillycuddy had labored to destroy, and the police lost much of the effectiveness they had achieved under McGillycuddy. Gallagher's replacement would suffer the consequences of this shift in power relationships.[31]

At Rosebud, the bulwark of reaction, no single chief enjoyed the eminence of Red Cloud. After Crow Dog murdered Spotted Tail in 1881, a squad of Brulés maneuvered to seize his mantle, but none possessed the requisite qualities. The principal contenders in 1890 were Two Strike, Crow Dog, High Hawk, Turning Bear, Lance, and Eagle Pipe. Of these men, only Two Strike was actually a chief. He and Spotted Tail had been youthful companions in the long-ago wars against the Pawnees, and it

31. See especially McGillycuddy to Colby, Jan. 15, 1891, in Colby, "Sioux Indian War," pp. 178–80.

was in a battle with the Pawnees that Two Strike had gained his name. Now, although a prominent chief, Two Strike was seventy years old and was growing infirm and senile.[32]

That the chiefs sensed a favorable climate for a comeback and that their efforts enjoyed a measure of success were symptoms of the deep distress felt by the Sioux. The underlying causes had operated for ten years. The immediate causes were the broken promises of the Crook Commission and the crop failure that, together with reduced rations, forecast hunger and possibly starvation in the months ahead. Only a catalyst was needed to turn sullen resentment into violent protest. In midsummer Kicking Bear returned from his visit to the Arapahoes and told of the regeneration Wovoka's religion had worked upon this tribe. Again he preached to the Sioux his own twisted version of the Paiute prophet's doctrine. The hot winds that withered the cornstalks nourished the seed of the Ghost Dance religion. This time it took root and sprang into full bloom before the agents could act.

32. James G. Wright (the elder) to CIA, Jan. 22, 1891. J. George Wright (the younger), notes on Rosebud chiefs, encl. to Lt. Col. J. S. Poland to Asst. Adjt. Gen. Div. of the Mo., Jan. 13, 1891. Hyde, *Sioux Chronicle*, pp. 207, 266. Hyde, *Spotted Tail's Folk*, p. 31.

6. CRISIS FOR THE SIOUX AGENTS

IN WYOMING, Kicking Bear had watched the Arapahoes dance the Ghost Dance and go into trances that enabled them to see friends long dead and wonders of the world to come. Returning home, he stopped early in August for a visit with the Oglalas at Pine Ridge. His story of the miraculous happenings among the Arapahoes caught the Sioux at the climax of the terrible summer. They were ripe for just such miracles themselves. Kicking Bear fired the Oglalas with the faith and taught them the mechanics of the dance.[1]

Red Cloud shrewdly avoided committing himself. If the story were true, he said, "it would spread all over the world." If it were false, he stated for the agent's benefit, "it would melt like the snow under the hot sun."[2] Other chiefs were not so cautious. At

1. I deduce Kicking Bear's role in the Ghost Dance revival from the following known facts. He went to visit the Arapahoes shortly after the religion was first suppressed in late spring. Dances were organized shortly after his return. They appeared first at Pine Ridge in August, then at Rosebud and Cheyenne River in September, and finally at Standing Rock in October.

2. Capt. Marion P. Maus, "The New Indian Messiah," *Harper's Weekly, 34* (1890), 944.

his camp on Medicine Root Creek, Little Wound called together his people and advised: "My friends, if this is a good thing we should have it; if it is not it will fall to the earth itself. So you better learn this dance, so if the Messiah does come he will not pass us by, but will help us to get back our hunting grounds and buffalo."[3] Some 300 people were soon staging regular Ghost Dances there. On Wounded Knee Creek, Big Road, Shell Boy, and Good Thunder (one of the delegates of 1889 to Mason Valley) organized another dance, which attracted 250 people. Torn Belly, His Fight, Bear Bone, and Jack Red Cloud, the old chief's son, enlisted 600 dancers at a camp on White Clay Creek north of the agency. A fourth dance group, with 150 members, sprang up on Porcupine Creek under the guidance of Knife Chief, Iron Bird, and Whetstone.[4]

From their cheerless cabins the dancers gathered. Just as in the old days, they pitched tepees on the valley floor near the cottonwood groves that fringed the creek. Surrounded on all sides by lodges, the circular dance ground was the focus of activity. The dancers cut a sapling and mounted it in the center. From the top of this prayer tree fluttered a small American flag or strips of brightly colored cloth. From its base the leader of the Ghost Dance presided over the ceremonies.[5]

They began at dawn with the cleansing and purifying rite of the sweat bath. The sweat lodge was a diminutive structure shaped of willow wands and covered with skins. The entrance

---

3. "Dr. V. T. McGillycuddy on the Ghost Dance," in Stanley Vestal, ed., *New Sources of Indian History, 1850–1891* (Norman, 1934), pp. 88–89.

4. D. F. Royer to CIA, Nov. 18, 1890.

5. This description of a typical Ghost Dance is constructed from the following eyewitness accounts of separate dances: Mooney, *Ghost-Dance*, pp. 788–89, 822–23, 915, 924–25; Mooney, "The Indian Ghost Dance," *Collections of the Nebraska State Historical Society, 16* (1911), 168–86; Sword, "Story of the Ghost Dance," pp. 28–31; "An Officer," "The Sioux of South Dakota," *Frank Leslie's Illustrated Newspaper, 71* (Dec. 20, 1890), 372; E. B. Reynolds to CIA, Sept. 25, 1890; Mrs. James A. Finley, "The Messiah Superstition," *Journal of American Folk-Lore, 4* (1891), 67–68; Mrs. Z. A. Parker, "Ghost Dance at Pine Ridge," ibid., pp. 160–62; Warren K. Moorehead, "The Indian Messiah and the Ghost Dance," *The American Antiquarian and Oriental Journal, 12* (1891), 161–67; and Gen. L. W. Colby, "Wanagi Olowan Kin (The Ghost Songs of the Dakotas)," *Proceedings and Collections of the Nebraska State Historical Society, 2d ser. 1* (1895), 131–50.

opened to the east, greeting the morning sun. Facing it from a mound of earth, a buffalo skull peered inside. Like inverted bowls, sweat lodges dotted the valley around the village. Clad only in breechcloths, several dancers entered the lodge and squatted on a carpet of freshly cut wild sage. The medicine man heated stones on a fire nearby and with forked sticks passed them through the entrance. The disciples rolled them into a hole dug in the center of the lodge and poured cold water on them. Outside, the medicine man prayed, while inside his followers sweated in billowing clouds of steam trapped by the tightly fastened lodge cover. Purged of moral impurity, the men emerged at length and plunged into the nearby stream.

Next the leader and his assistants prepared the people for the dance. The face of each was painted. Forehead, cheeks, and chin bore circles, crescents, and crosses that symbolized sun, moon, and morning star. Colors varied, but red, the color of Wi, the Sun, became also the color of the Ghost Dance among all the western tribes. Wovoka had so decreed, and he gave small cakes of red ochre to the apostles who came to Mason Valley. These cakes from the Messiah himself were much sought after. A few grains mixed with the locally made paint of the Sioux helped a dancer to experience the vision he sought in the Ghost Dance and also had value as a weapon against the malevolent gods who caused illness.

No other part of the body was painted, for Ghost Dancers were fully clothed. The central feature of the costume, worn above buckskin leggings, was the Ghost Shirt. It was a sacklike garment of cotton cloth or muslin ornamented, like the face, with painted circles, crescents, and crosses, and with designs symbolizing the eagle, magpie, crow, sage hen, and other birds and animals having special significance in Sioux mythology. Many were fringed and adorned with feathers. The medicine man preached that the Ghost Shirt made its wearer invulnerable to rifle bullets. If soldiers fired at an Indian so protected, the bullets would fall harmlessly to the ground. The idea behind the Ghost Shirt was not new: warriors had long carried ceremonial devices and had even worn "medicine shirts" designed to turn away the bullets and arrows of the enemy. Other Ghost Dancing tribes adopted the Ghost Shirt, but only the Sioux invested it with bulletproof qualities.

The dancers believed, and they drew courage from the conviction that no longer were the bluecoats to be dreaded. The Sioux apostles had perverted Wovoka's doctrine into a militant crusade against the white man. Now they removed any reason the faithful might have to fear open conflict with the white man. The mixture was indeed explosive.

As in the world to come there would be no white men or material reminders of white men, so in the Ghost Dance Wovoka had ordained that nothing of white manufacture could be worn or carried. This injunction applied to all metal objects, including knives, guns, and the silver jewelry and belts of which the Sioux were so fond. In the earlier dances the Sioux usually heeded this rule, but as time went on and the dance turned increasingly down belligerent paths, an occasional rifle or carbine made its appearance in the dance circle.

Eagle feathers fixed in the hair completed the attire. These, Wovoka had explained, would enable the people to mount into the sky when the millennium came. But they possibly took on another purpose as the dance grew more turbulent. George Sword's vague explanation, which doubtless suffered in translation, suggests that the Sioux regarded the eagle feathers as another magic weapon against the whites. "The ghost dancers all have to wear eagle feather on head," he declared. "With this feather any man would be made crazy if fan with this feather."[6]

The dance began about noon. Dancers of all ages and both sexes sat in a large circle facing the center of the dance ring. Often, when several hundred participated, they ranged themselves in concentric circles. The dance leader, flanked by his assistants, took station at the foot of the prayer tree and gave detailed instructions to his followers. Then, raising his arms to heaven, he prayed: "Great Wakan Tanka: We are ready to begin the dance as you have commanded us. Our hearts are now good. We would do all that you ask, and in return for our efforts we beg that you give us back our old hunting grounds, and our

6. "Story of the Ghost Dance," p. 31.

game. Oh, transport such of the dancers as are really in earnest to the Spirit Land far away and let them there see their dead relatives. Show them what good things you have prepared for us and return the visitors safely to earth again. Hear us, we implore."

The people stood and clasped hands. Someone started a ghost song. It was rhythmic but without rhyme, and evoked misty images of the past. The singer began softly:

> Someone cometh to tell news, to tell news;
> There shall be a buffalo chase,
> There shall be a buffalo chase;
> Make arrows; make arrows.

The song rose slightly in intensity and took on emotion. The dancers bent their knees to produce a rise and fall of their bodies, and with a shuffling side step started the dance rings moving slowly and hypnotically to the left. The people joined the singing, softly at first but with rising volume and quickening tempo.

> Raise the tepee, hurry, raise the tepee, hurry,
> I wish to cook soon, I wish to cook soon;
> Drive the pins around the tepee,
> Drive the pins around the tepee;
> Saith thy mother, saith thy mother.

After half an hour the dancing stopped. "Weep for your sins," cried the dance leader. A great moan punctuated by piercing wails of the women rose from the dance rings. Dancers rolled on the ground crying for forgiveness. Others crowded around the prayer tree to thrust gifts among the limbs. A few cut their bodies in the ancient fashion of showing grief and smeared blood on the tree. The leader signaled, and the dancers, re-forming the circles, sat down. He preached a short sermon. The dance resumed, the people moving faster now, showing exaltation, singing of the world of the future.

> The people are coming home,
> The people are coming home,
> Saith my father, saith my father,
>   Saith my father.

> The time cometh, I shall see him,
> The time cometh, I shall see him,
> Saith thy mother, saith thy mother.

Faster went the circle, bending and weaving with the contortions of the dancers. Their arms and legs twitched, and their bodies shook as if possessed of demons. They leaped erratically forward, backward, and into the air. Songs gave way to wails and shouts. The holy men dashed around the circle, waving eagle feathers and exhorting dancers to yet higher pitches of delirium. They pulled the most excited from the ring and gently pushed them to the ground. Hovering over a prostrate dancer, the medicine man muttered incantations and gazed deeply into the subject's eyes. "He stared into my eyes like a snake," recalled one, "and then I knew no more." Rigid bodies littered the dance circle, their spirits gone for a visit to the other world. People who had not achieved the ultimate raced to and fro, butted trees, and threw themselves violently to the ground, all in a supreme effort to gain admission to the Spirit Land. A white observer described how "several in their frenzy rushed against our horses and were thrown headlong to the ground." In utter chaos the dance went on and on "until all became so exhausted as to be able only to writhe on the ground, screaming and moaning all the time."

Those rewarded with a journey to the Spirit Land told wondrous tales of their adventures, inspiring others to struggle yet harder to bring on a vision. Little Horse described how

> two holy eagles transported me to the Happy Hunting Grounds. They showed me the Great Messiah there, and as I looked upon his fair countenance I wept, for there were nail-prints in his hands and feet where the cruel whites had once fastened him to a large cross. There was a small wound in his side also, but as he kept himself covered with a beautiful mantle of feathers this wound only could be seen when he shifted his blanket. He insisted that we continue the dance, and promised me that no whites should enter his city nor partake of the good things he had prepared for the Indians. The earth, he said, was now worn out and it should be repeopled.

He had a long beard and long hair and was the most handsome man I ever looked upon.

Little Wound had even more remarkable experiences:

When I fell in the trance a great and grand eagle came and carried me over a great hill, where there was a village such as we used to have before the whites came into the country. The tepees were all of buffalo hides, and we made use of the bow and arrow, there being nothing of white man's manufacture in the beautiful land. Nor were any whites permitted to live there. The broad and fertile lands stretched in every direction, and were most pleasing to my eyes.

I was taken into the presence of the great Messiah, and he spoke to me in these words:

"My child, I am glad to see you. Do you want to see your children and relations who are dead?"

I replied: "Yes, I would like to see my relations who have been dead a long time." The God then called my friends to come up to where I was. They appeared, riding the finest horses I ever saw, dressed in superb and most brilliant garments, and seeming very happy. As they approached, I recognized the playmates of my childhood, and I ran forward to embrace them while the tears of joy ran down my cheeks.

We all went together to another village, where there were very large lodges of buffalo hide, and there held a long talk with the great Wakantanka. Then he had some squaws prepare us a meal of many herbs, meats, and wild fruits and "wasna" [pounded beef and choke-cherries]. After we had eaten, the Great Spirit prayed for our people upon the earth, and then we all took a smoke out of a fine pipe ornamented with the most beautiful feathers and porcupine quills. Then we left the city and looked into a great valley where there were thousands of buffalo, deer, and elk feeding.

After seeing the valley, we returned to the city, the Great Spirit speaking meanwhile. He told me that the earth was now *bad* and *worn out;* that we needed a new dwelling place where the rascally whites could not disturb us. He further instructed me to return to my people, the Sioux, and say to them that if they would be constant in the dance and pay no attention to the whites he would shortly come to their aid. If the high priests would make for the dancers medicine shirts and pray over them, no harm could come to the wearer; that the bullets of any whites that desired to stop the Messiah Dance would fall to the ground without doing any one harm, and the person firing such shots would drop dead. He said that he had prepared a hole in the ground filled with hot water and fire for the reception of all white men and non-believers. With these parting words I was commanded to return to earth.[7]

Seeking such experiences, the people danced, with periodic intermissions ordained less by the dance leader than by the limits of physical endurance, until time for the evening meal. After dinner they kindled bonfires and danced until nearly midnight. Then they dispersed to their tepees. At first the dances were staged only on Sunday, "the great medicine day of the white man." Later, as the faithful increasingly pinned all their hopes on the promises of the apostles, they abandoned their cabins and fields to live continuously at the dance camps. The dances grew more frequent, and day after day the dance grounds displayed alternating scenes of solemnity and pandemonium.

The dance began on the Pine Ridge Reservation early in August and within the next two weeks excited increasing numbers of Oglalas to a feverish pitch of enthusiasm. Agent Hugh Gallagher became alarmed. His district farmers urged him to make decisive use of the Indian police to suppress the dance by force. He, too, favored firm measures and, against the advice of Interpreter Philip Wells, began to concentrate the police at the agency. On August 22 he sent a squad to Torn Belly's camp on White Clay Creek, eighteen miles north of the agency, with instructions to break up the dance and send the people home. The

7. Both quotations are from James P. Boyd, *Recent Indian Wars* (Philadelphia, 1891), pp. 189–91, 194–95.

police returned the following morning to report that they had been ignored and that the Indians were preparing to dance the next day, Sunday, August 24.

Gallagher decided to look over the situation himself. On Sunday morning, at the head of twenty policemen, he rode to the dance grounds. With him went Philip Wells and Special Agent E. B. Reynolds, who happened to be visiting Pine Ridge.[8] Reaching the destination, they found some 150 tepees littering the valley around the cabins of Torn Belly's band. A dance ground lay in the center of camp, dominated by a prayer tree from which flew an American flag. About 600 people had assembled, but none was to be seen. They had learned of the agent's approach, called off the dance, and taken cover in a grove of trees along the bank of White Clay Creek.

Gallagher led his men into the deserted dance circle and halted. At this moment an Indian with a rifle raced from one of the cabins to the bank of the stream. Another emerged from a thicket and joined the first. They dopped to their knees and confronted the intruders with the muzzles of Winchester rifles. This made Gallagher angry, and he snapped an order for the police to arrest the challengers. Wells translated the order, then, sensing that the agent was asking for more trouble than he could handle, promptly countermanded it on his own responsibility.

When the police failed to advance, Gallagher himself rode toward the two Indians, Wells crowding in front of him. Suddenly the heads of several more Indians appeared above the crest of the creek bank. The agent stopped. "What do you mean when I come as your agent to talk to you and you draw guns on me?" he demanded. Wells translated, adding, in a more conciliatory tone, "Father [one of the men was the father of a good friend of Wells], I want you to obey me; put that gun down and come here." The Indian placed the rifle on the ground and answered, "Yes, my son, I will obey you." Then, to Gallagher, he said, "If

8. The account of this episode is drawn from Gallagher's annual report, Aug. 26, 1890, in CIA, *Annual Report* (1890), p. 49; Wells to McLaughlin, Oct. 19, 1890, in Vestal, *New Sources of Indian History*, pp. 5–6; Reynolds to CIA, Sept. 25, 1890; and Philip Wells Interview, Ricker Collection.

you have come to talk to me as my father, why bring so many guns?"

While the agent tried to explain this away, another Indian rose from behind the creek bank and hurled a challenge at the police lieutenant: "Where is Thunder Bear? Why don't he stand in sight?" Thunder Bear accepted the challenge. "Here I am in sight. If you cannot see me I will come closer to you." He moved toward the bank. Now more Indians came into view, brandishing their rifles and making it abundantly clear, as Special Agent Reynolds later recalled, that they "were ready to seal their religious convictions at the mouth of smoking rifles and in defense of what they deemed a religious rite." The police drew their revolvers, and for one tense moment the antagonists tottered on the brink of battle.

At this critical juncture, Young-Man-Afraid-of-His-Horses rode into the dance circle. His very presence subdued the passions of both sides. Wells made haste to explain that the agent had come with no intention of interfering with the ceremony, but simply to see what it was all about. Mollified, the warriors lowered their rifles.

Torn Belly came out of the timber and joined the group. Wells asked if he would announce to his people that the agent would like to hold a council at the agency the following week in order to discuss the new religion. Torn Belly thought a little, then declared that it did not seem quite proper to make such an announcement. After all, it was Sunday and the people were in the midst of religious services. But if the other headmen had no objection, he would do as asked. Torn Belly went into the trees and shortly returned, shook hands with the whites, and said he would be happy to make the announcement. He also invited the visitors to stay and watch the Ghost Dance so they could see for themselves that it was not harmful. The Indians emerged from the trees and, as the whites watched, resumed the dance.

Gallagher and Reynolds were probably the first officials to witness a Ghost Dance. It alarmed both. Reynolds reported to Washington his conviction that "steps should be taken to stop it" and ominously predicted that "this can only be done by the military unless the cold weather accomplishes it." Gallagher warned his superiors that the new religion might have unhappy consequences "should there be no restriction placed upon it."

He for one had no intention of trying to restrict it. Very soon it would become a Republican problem. Early in August he had received the long-expected word from Washington that his services were no longer required. A Republican agent had been appointed. While Gallagher sat anxiously in his office awaiting the arrival of his successor, the Ghost Dance swept through the Oglalas and, in the wake of Kicking Bear's triumphal journey homeward, jumped the reservation boundary and ignited the Brulés of Rosebud.

The craze seized the Rosebud people in September, taking hold first at the camp of White Horse (who had been jailed the previous spring for obstructing the census) and from there spreading swiftly to the other nonprogressive camps. People abandoned their farms and stock, withdrew their children from school, and flocked to the dance centers. As one of the original delegates to Mason Valley, Short Bull again rose to prominence as the ranking apostle of the Ghost Dance among the Brulés.

About the middle of September the Brulés trooped into the agency for the biweekly ration day. The Ghost Dance adherents talked of nothing but the new religion and exchanged stories of their adventures in the Spirit Land. Suddenly a rumor flashed through the camps that soldiers were on the reservation, come to stamp out the Ghost Dance and punish the dancers. Instantly the men stampeded to their tepees. They stripped to breechcloths, donned war paint, and snatched their weapons. Before Agent Wright could find out what had happened, they were galloping southward from the agency. Riding out in pursuit, Wright discovered them drawn up across the road to Fort Niobrara waiting for the troops. With difficulty he convinced them that the report was false, and they returned to the agency.

Angry over the episode, Wright decided that the time had come for a showdown. Next day he assembled the Brulés and announced that the Ghost Dance must stop. Until he was satisfied that it had stopped, there would be no rations. The people went home to reflect with empty stomachs on the true depths of their devotion to the religion. All but a small corps of fanatics placed their stomachs first, and the agent lifted the suspension of ration issues.[9]

Then one of the Secretary of the Interior's inspectors, J. H. Cisney, arrived at Rosebud to investigate the unusual reduction in population recorded by Census Agent Lea. The census counted only 5,250 Indians, yet Wright had regularly received rations and annuities for 7,500. The inspector quickly concluded that Wright had pocketed the value of a year's supplies for more than 2,000 Indians and summarily suspended him. Although Wright managed to prove his innocence and was back on the job by early December, the inspector's action forced him to leave his post at a critical time.

Late in September, Special Agent E. B. Reynolds came from Pine Ridge to act temporarily in Wright's place. The Brulés took advantage of his ignorance of conditions and personalities at Rosebud to resume the Ghost Dance. Harangued by Short Bull, they were soon beyond control. Every cent went for arms and ammunition. In order to get money, the Indians traded ponies and sold possessions for a pittance. At the trading posts they cashed receipts for firewood delivered to the agency for one-third their face value. They openly slaughtered breeding stock for food and defied anyone to stop them. Reynolds sent policemen to arrest two particularly bad offenders. Seventy-five armed warriors intervened, and the police returned empty-handed. The captain reported that his men were powerless to enforce the rules and regulations of the Indian Bureau. When Reynolds remonstrated with the dancers, they replied that they would rather die fighting than from starvation. Besides, there was no reason to fear death, for when the millennium came next spring all dead Indians would be resurrected. Finally, early in November, Reynolds reported to Washington that "there appears to be but one remedy . . . and that is a sufficient force of troops, to prevent an outbreak, which is imminent and which any one of a dozen unforseen causes may precipitate."[10]

9. Wright's annual report, Aug. 27, 1891, in CIA, *Annual Report* (1891), pp. 411–12.

10. Reynolds to CIA, Nov. 2, 1890.

Having kindled the fires of defiance at Pine Ridge and Rose-bud, Kicking Bear reached home about the middle of September. Long noted for the recalcitrance of its nonprogressives, Cheyenne River promptly took to the Ghost Dance with enthusiasm. Indeed, as Kicking Bear's headquarters, it became the fountain-head of all wisdom and lore of the doctrine, and Indians from other Sioux reservations came by the score to seek inspiration from the most incendiary of all the Sioux apostles. At his Cherry Creek camp, Hump threw off his police uniform and, donning the Ghost Shirt, presided over a succession of wild dances that soon attracted about 400 Miniconjous. Equally fanatical dances consumed the energy of Big Foot's band on Cheyenne River, beyond the western edge of the reservation. The band of 128 that had moved there in the spring swelled to 300. An officer stationed at Captain Henissee's "camp of observation," two miles west of Big Foot's village, wrote that the dances "are held by day and night; in fact, as long as they are able to move and keep awake, the Indians continue their efforts to please the Great Spirit."[11]

The capable Charles McChesney no longer administered Cheyenne River. A Republican agent had taken over on September 1. Under "Home Rule," a new twist to the spoils system that put agency appointments entirely in the hands of senators and representatives, Cheyenne River became the patronage preserve of South Dakota's Congressman J. A. Pickler. He had named one Perain P. Palmer to replace McChesney. Palmer may have been, as Pickler assured Secretary of the Interior Noble, "a cool man and a man of good judgment," although some observers formed different evaluations; but he was thrust without experience into a difficult job at a difficult time. He proved no match for such determined zealots as Kicking Bear, Hump, and Big Foot.

Palmer started out by informing the dancers that the Interior Department was displeased with their behavior. They replied, he somewhat plaintively reported to the Indian Commissioner, "that the Indians is displeased with the Department *and will dance.*" Next he turned to Straight Head, new captain of police,

---

11. *Frank Leslie's Illustrated Newspaper*, 71 (Dec. 20, 1890), 372.

and had him send some men up the river to stop the proceedings at the camps of Hump and Big Foot. The dancers met the intruders with Winchesters, which the police revolvers could not match even had the lawmen been disposed to use them. Several times in September and October, Palmer tried to break up the dance in this way, but on each occasion the police returned to report failure. Suffering repeated setbacks and sinking prestige, the force began to fall apart as, one after another, the policemen turned in their badges. Finally, on November 10, Palmer reported that "there is no doubt now that the Hostile Indians at all the dancing camps are preparing to defy the authority of the Department."[12]

At Standing Rock, Sitting Bull had listened anxiously to the reports that came from the southern agencies. He importuned Agent McLaughlin for a pass to visit Cheyenne River but was repeatedly turned down. Unable to escape the watchful eyes of the agent's spies at Grand River, he finally sent an invitation to Kicking Bear to bring the word to the Standing Rock Sioux. The apostle arrived at Grand River on October 9 and revealed the mysteries to Sitting Bull. In a public oration, Kicking Bear glowingly described his meeting with Wovoka and enumerated the miracles vouchsafed by the Nevada prophet. Then he taught the Grand River people the dance.[13]

McLaughlin immediately sent Captain Crazy Walking and Lieutenant Chatka with eleven policemen to eject Kicking Bear from the reservation. But a badge was no guarantee against the mysterious powers of the Ghost Dance apostle, and the captain, awed by the spectacle of the dance and the force of Kicking Bear's personality, could not find the courage to carry out his instructions. He told Sitting Bull that Kicking Bear must leave, then he hastily led his men back to the agency. McLaughlin next assigned the mission to Lieutenant Chatka, who set out with only two men. Of sterner mold than his captain, Chatka marched

12. My sources for Cheyenne River are P. P. Palmer to CIA, Oct. 11 and 25, Nov. 10 and 28, 1890.

13. McLaughlin, pp. 184–90, reproduces Kicking Bear's speech verbatim. It was repeated to him word for word, "with that accuracy of memory that marks the unlettered," by One Bull, an Indian policeman who was also Sitting Bull's nephew.

through a ring of dancers on the morning of October 15 and commanded Kicking Bear and his six companions to obey the agent's order forthwith, then escorted them to the reservation boundary.[14]

But the damage had been done. Sitting Bull set up a prayer tree and erected a large tent from which to superintend the dances and daily deliver himself of revelations. He may truly have believed the Messiah's message; more likely, he saw in it a new weapon to raise against McLaughlin and restore his own power among the Hunkpapas. His biographer, Stanley Vestal, contends that he wanted to believe and tried very hard to induce a vision, but in the end failed because he was too much Indian to embrace a faith founded on the teachings of Christianity.[15] To an extent, also, he became a prisoner of his own zealous followers, who demanded that he lead them into the promised land so eloquently portrayed by Kicking Bear. Whatever his personal convictions and motives, Sitting Bull did in fact act the part of apostle of the Ghost Dance at Standing Rock.

The Yanktonais and, to a lesser degree, the Blackfeet Sioux held aloof. They had advanced much farther on the white man's road than the Hunkpapas. McLaughlin estimated that the religion infected about 450 people, almost entirely among the followers of Sitting Bull.[16] The Grand River schoolteacher, John M. Carignan, observed in his classroom an index of the intensity of their devotion. The sixty pupils who showed up on September 1 dwindled to three in October. The children, the parents explained, could not come to school because they had to go to "church" every day.[17]

Congregational missionary Mary Collins tried to stop the dancing. For several years she had run a small mission at Little Eagle, ten miles down Grand River, and had carried on a friend-

14. Ibid., pp. 189–93. McLaughlin to CIA, Oct. 17 and Nov. 19, 1890, CIA, *Annual Report* (1891), pp. 328–31.

15. Vestal, *Sitting Bull*, chaps. 34 and 35.

16. *My Friend the Indian*, p. 192.

17. Carignan narrative in Fiske, *Life and Death of Sitting Bull*, p. 32. This and another Carignan narrative in Vestal, *New Sources of Indian History*, pp. 1–4, are the best sources on events at Grand River.

ly rivalry with Sitting Bull for the spiritual allegiance of the people who lived along the river. She and her assistant, Mr. Grindstone, "a little old man but possessed [of] a great deal of character," would charge into the dance circles and challenge the Great Mysterious to make good his promise, relayed by Sitting Bull, to cause the earth to swallow the unbeliever. She for one believed that these demonstrations shook the faith of many Hunkpapa dancers.[18]

Another who grappled with the craze was Mrs. Catherine Weldon, a neurotic Boston widow who first came to Standing Rock in the summer of 1889 to fight the Crook Commission on behalf of the National Indian Defense Association. Fascinated by the aboriginal splendor and charming manners of Sitting Bull, she returned in the spring of 1890 and filed on a homestead north of the Standing Rock boundary. She lavished money and expensive gifts on Sitting Bull and was always welcome in the Grand River camp. To McLaughlin's vast annoyance, she appointed herself adviser to the Hunkpapas in all their dealings with the Government. Dakota newspapers labeled her "Sitting Bull's White Squaw." In fact the old chief, taking at face value her insistence upon performing his domestic chores, did propose to make her his third wife—an overture she indignantly rejected. Mrs. Weldon threw all her energy into the fight against Kicking Bear's teachings, then gave up in despair and went home. "If I had known what obstinate minds I had to contend with," she later wrote, "I would not have undertaken this mission to enlighten and instruct them. It was money, health and heart thrown away."[19]

As the Grand River dances grew stormier, settlers along the east bank of the Missouri River and at Bismarck and Mandan grew increasingly apprehensive. Newspapers reflected their

18. Mary C. Collins, "A Short Autobiography," in Vestal, *New Sources of Indian History*, pp. 66–67.

19. Fragments of Mrs. Weldon's letters to Red Cloud, Sitting Bull, and McLaughlin were found in Sitting Bull's cabin after his death. They are printed in Vestal, *New Sources of Indian History*, pp. 92–115. In a letter to the CIA, Oct. 17, 1890, McLaughlin vented his annoyance at Mrs. Weldon. Before printing it in the CIA *Annual Report* of 1891, pp. 328–29, the Indian Office softened his harsh remarks and deleted Mrs. Weldon's name altogether.

alarm. McLaughlin saw a chance to reopen a question that had been dormant since June. On October 17 he wrote a long letter to the Commissioner of Indian Affairs describing the progress of the dance at Standing Rock. While expressing confidence that he could control any trouble that might spring from the religion, he spelled out the one move that in his judgment would assure return to normalcy: "I would respectfully recommend the removal from the reservation and confinement in some military prison . . . of Sitting Bull and the parties named in my letter of June 18 last . . . some time during the coming winter and before next spring opens."

Acting Commissioner Belt (Commissioner Morgan was in Oklahoma inspecting Indian schools) recognized the need for some move to repress the excitement and thought McLaughlin's recommendation likely to achieve results. But the arrest of Sitting Bull and his associates had to be carefully engineered. The criticism that it would inevitably generate in some quarters must fall elsewhere than on the Interior Department. His recommendation to Secretary Noble was therefore that the Secretary of War be asked to have the Army arrest Sitting Bull and the other chiefs and imprison them "until such time as their presence on the reservation may not be deemed dangerous to the peace of the Indians."[20]

But Noble was not yet ready to open such a Pandora's box. Belt's response to McLaughlin's proposal, dated October 29, expressed the Secretary's reluctance to act so boldly. The agent must tell Sitting Bull and other troublemakers that the Secretary was "greatly displeased with their conduct" and would hold Sitting Bull to "a strict personal responsibility for the misconduct, acts of violence, or any threats, actions, or movements" to which any of the Sioux might be influenced by the Hunkpapa leader. Such behavior would be severely punished. To show his good faith, Sitting Bull must submit to government authority immediately and cause his people "to turn their backs upon the medicine men who are seeking to divert the Indians from the ways of civilization."[21] More conversant with Indians than his

20. Belt to Noble, Oct. 24, 1890.
21. Belt to McLaughlin, Oct. 29, 1890, in CIA, *Annual Report* (1891), p. 330.

superiors, McLaughlin did not hasten to make himself look silly by conveying the message to Sitting Bull.

He did, however, go to Grand River to view the situation in person. On November 16 he and his interpreter, Louis Primeau, walked in on a Ghost Dance in full swing. Nearly 100 people— men, women, and children—were gyrating rhythmically around the prayer tree while another 200 watched. From his headquarters tepee, Sitting Bull and his assistant, Bull Ghost, directed the proceedings. A young girl went into a trance and "died." Carried to the tent, she lay on the ground while Sitting Bull interpreted her conversation with long-dead relatives in the Spirit Land. Wisely deciding not to interrupt the ceremonies, McLaughlin and Primeau went to the cabin of Henry Bull Head, police lieutenant who lived up the river, and spent the night.

Early next morning, McLaughlin confronted Sitting Bull as he emerged from a sweat bath. For seven years these two had struggled for mastery of the Standing Rock Sioux. Each was an unyielding partisan of his own way of life, and each was incapable of appreciating or even understanding the other's point of view. Now, as a curious throng gathered, the antagonists once more—for the last time—faced each other. McLaughlin persuaded, threatened, and cajoled, to no avail. Sitting Bull offered to settle the whole affair. He and the agent would journey together from tribe to tribe, following the stories to their source at the foot of the Rocky Mountains. If the Messiah in the end was shown not to exist in all the splendor that had been told, Sitting Bull would return to Standing Rock and kill the religion. If the stories proved true, however, McLaughlin must quit interfering. Such a journey, replied McLaughlin, would be like chasing last year's wind. Instead, Sitting Bull should come to the agency where, in one evening, he would convince him of the falseness of the doctrine. Sitting Bull promised to think over the proposal, and on this indecisive note the conference ended. Mc-Laughlin and Primeau returned to the agency.[22]

As it turned out, Sitting Bull found it inadvisable to leave Grand River long enough for a visit to the agency. Perhaps he

22. McLaughlin to CIA, Nov. 17, 1890, in CIA, *Annual Report* (1891), pp. 330–31. McLaughlin, *My Friend the Indian*, pp. 201–07.

recalled the soldiers at nearby Fort Yates, who on ration day ostentatiously paraded back and forth and fired their wagon guns at targets. He was not ignorant of McLaughlin's wish to see him behind bars, and for some weeks he had been sending others to draw his rations.

As a matter of fact, McLaughlin wanted no help from the soldiers. Proud of his long service, his apparent immunity from the spoils system, and the record that had earned him the applause of Army officers and reformers alike, he again assured the Indian Bureau of his ability to contain the religious mania. He looked to the deep snows and howling northers of winter as powerful allies in the effort. But Sitting Bull, turning a practiced eye on nature's weather indicators, announced to his followers: "Yes, my people, you can dance all winter this year, the sun will shine warmly and the weather will be fair." The winter of 1890–91 was one of the mildest on record.[23]

McLaughlin's request for Sitting Bull's arrest having met a chilly reception in Washington, he advanced another idea. He proposed, if the Bureau concurred, to inform the Grand River Indians that those who wished to go on record as opposed to the Ghost Dance must come into the agency, camp a few weeks, and be enrolled. Rations would be withheld from all who declined the invitation. McLaughlin was sure that most of Sitting Bull's people would desert their leader when their stomachs were put in jeopardy. Judging from the lessons of a decade, he was right. The letter outlining this plan went to Washington on November 19. It promptly got swallowed by the rush of events.

McLaughlin had controlled his own reservation. Cheyenne River and Rosebud, although exciting places in October and November, were also still under control. Crow Creek and Lower Brulé had yet to be infected. But at Pine Ridge matters had grown progressively worse, and by the third week of November they reached a climax.

Trouble had started with a vengeance on October 9, when the new Republican agent relieved Hugh Gallagher. Under Home Rule, Senator Richard F. Pettigrew claimed the patronage of Pine Ridge. He chose Daniel F. Royer, physician, druggist, newspaperman, and banker of Alpena, South Dakota. Two terms in the territorial legislature constituted Royer's sole qualification for the job. He knew nothing about Indians. In fact, they made him uneasy—a truth the Oglalas were not slow to perceive. They dubbed him "Young-Man-Afraid-of-Indians." His whole attitude toward his charges, recalled schoolteacher Emma Sickels, was "Oh please be good and don't make any trouble."[24] In all the history of Pine Ridge, no worse time could have been found to pin the destinies of the Oglalas to such a temperament.

It was a mean trick the spoils system had worked on Royer. The political plum turned out to be fiery red pepper, and now that he had swallowed it there was no way to get rid of it. "I think he has got an elephant on his hands," Interpreter Philip Wells wrote McLaughlin, "as the craze had taken such a hold on the Indians before he took charge."[25] Worse yet, Royer found on his desk when he arrived a message from Acting Commissioner Belt instructing him to "warn the Indians that said 'ghost dance' will not be allowed on any occasion."[26] Lacking McLaughlin's realism, Royer dutifully relayed the warning. The dancers ignored it, and, not knowing what to do next, he kept on warning them. Already he was thinking how comforting the sight of blue uniforms would be at the agency, and on October 12, after four days on the job, he alerted Belt to the possibility that troops might have to be summoned.[27]

Royer was probably not aware how discordant his words would sound in the Indian Office. For years, Army officers had vigorously denounced the civilians for the way they handled Indian affairs. Time and again, mismanagement had led to hostilities, a call to arms, and some dead soldiers as the price of corruption or incompetence. The officers considered themselves much better equipped to run an agency than the party faithfuls,

24. Sickels to L. W. Colby, Jan. 15, 1891, in Colby, "Sioux Indian War," p. 184.
25. Wells to McLaughlin, Oct. 19, 1890, in Vestal, *New Sources of Indian History,* p. 5.
26. Belt to Royer, Oct. 3, 1890.
27. Royer to Belt, Oct. 12, 1890.

and several times since the Civil War Congress had come within
a few votes of registering agreement by transferring the Indian
Bureau to the War Department.

The Bureau had no more vociferous critic in the military
ranks than Maj. Gen. Nelson A. Miles, new commanding general
of the Division of the Missouri, which embraced much of the
plains and mountain West. Miles had one of the most impressive
Indian-fighting records in the Army. He was also pompous, vain,
outspoken, and dogmatic; and it was whispered that he had
presidential ambitions. The last thing Belt wanted was Miles'
troops on the Sioux reservations. Once the Army had a foot in
the door, anything might happen, even full military control of
Indian affairs. Understandably, therefore, Belt fired a letter back
to Royer on October 18: "I approve of your course in using persuasion with the chiefs and think you had better continue in that
direction."[28]

Persuasion failed. The dancers grew more and more fanatical.
They withdrew their children from school, slaughtered breeding stock, and contemptuously defied the police and the agent.
The progressives—Young-Man-Afraid-of-His-Horses, American
Horse, Blue Horse, Standing Soldier, Spotted Horse—threw
their influence behind the agent's efforts, but they lacked the
power they had once wielded. Red Cloud still perched on the
fence. He avoided openly condoning the dances, but the dancers
suspected that his sympathies were with them.

As chairman of a commission investigating certain complaints
of the Northern Cheyennes, General Miles visited Pine Ridge
on October 27 to listen to Little Chief's reasons why his people
should live with their kinsmen in Montana. Royer unburdened
himself to the great authority on Indians. Miles said that the
craze would die out by itself. Next day he held a council with
the Oglala chiefs and gave them a fatherly lecture. Little Wound
rose to speak. He wanted his people to quit trying to act like
whites, he declared. They were Indians and should live like
Indians. By dancing the Ghost Dance, they could achieve this
purpose. They therefore intended to dance as long as they

28. Belt to Royer, Oct. 18, 1890.

pleased. And furthermore, would the general please write this down and show it to the Great Father? Miles must have been more than a little surprised. For an Indian to talk this way to a bluecoat who wore two stars on his shoulders was indeed a rarity. It reveals the extent to which the dancers had drawn courage from the personal immunity promised by the prophets. The following day, after the commissioners had departed, Royer called in the chiefs and tried more persuasion. "They simply laughed and said that they would keep it up as long as they pleased."[29]

Reporting developments at Pine Ridge to Belt on October 30, Royer violently exposed in one breathless sentence his agitation, helplessness, and resentment over what he deemed lack of understanding and sympathy from his superiors:

> Your Department has been informed of the damage resulting from these dances and of the danger attending them of the crazy Indians doing serious damage to others and the different Agencies I suppose report about the same but I have carefully studied the matter for nearly six weeks [sic] and have brought all the persuasion to bear on the leaders that was possible but without effect and the only remedy for this matter is the use of military and until this is done you need not expect any progress from these people on the the other hand you will be made to realize that they are tearing down more in a day than the Government can build in a month.[30]

The day after Royer mailed this letter, there were ominous happenings at Red Leaf's camp, near the Rosebud boundary. Short Bull, the Brulé apostle, delivered a dramatic sermon to an assembled multitude. Alluding to the promised land, he shouted: "I have told you that this would come to pass in two seasons, but since the whites are interfering so much, I will advance the time from what my Father above told me." At the end of one moon, he promised, the earth would shake and the wind blow and "we will go among our dead relations." To prepare

29. Royer to Belt, Oct. 30 and Nov. 18, 1890.
30. Royer to Belt, Oct. 30, 1890.

for the great day, he enjoined, the faithful must immediately gather at the mouth of Pass Creek and for a full moon (the month of November) zealously dance the Ghost Dance.

The white man must not be permitted to interfere with this last burst of dancing before the millennium:

> There may be soldiers surround you, but pay no attention to them, continue the dance. If the soldiers surround you four deep, three of you on whom I have put holy shirts will sing a song, which I have taught you, around them, when some of them will drop dead, then the rest will start to run, but their horses will sink into the earth; the riders will jump from their horses, but they will sink into the earth also; then you can do as you desire with them. Now you must know this, that all the soldiers and that race will be dead; there will be only five thousand [Indians?] left living on the earth. My friends and relations, this is straight and true.[31]

With the road to paradise thus dramatically shortened, many Brulés and some Oglalas flocked to Short Bull's standard. For the next three weeks families and small bands made their way to the mouth of Pass Creek. Kicking Bear showed up to lend the weight of his authority to the proceedings. Swift runners kept Sitting Bull informed of developments at Pass Creek and importuned him to join the assemblage.

Short Bull's doctrine, though militant, was defensive. The awesome supernatural weapons he had described were to be used only if the whites tried to break up the dance. But to many of his followers, animated by religious excitement and driven by hatred of the whites, the distinction between offense and defense was fine indeed. Increasingly, they talked of a holy war against the white man. With an inconsistency not uncommon in fanatical religious movements, the time of the uprising was set to coincide with emergence of the spring grasses, long after the time just set by Short Bull for the millennium. Army reports from the Upper Missouri stated that emissaries from Sitting

31. The speech, as reported by Capt. C. A. Earnest from Rosebud, is printed in Sec. War, *Annual Report* (1891), *1*, 142–43, and in Mooney, *Ghost-Dance*, pp. 788–89.

Bull had urged tribes as far north as Canada to unite in the spring at Bear Butte, near the Black Hills, to drive the whites from the country. Whether Short Bull, Kicking Bear, and Sitting Bull encouraged such talk is not apparent, nor is it apparent how much the talk represented actual intentions.

Illustrating the temper of the Ghost Dancers was an incident that happened to James "Scotty" Philip, a rancher who lived at the mouth of Grindstone Butte Creek, in the ceded tract. On November 18 a small band of Brulés under Yellow Thigh, destined for Pass Creek, camped at the Philip Ranch. The twelve men were surly, and they carried their Winchesters ostentatiously. One of them boasted of the day when he had smashed open the heads of white children and drunk the blood of white women. The time was coming, he vowed, when he would do it again. That the buffalo had vanished did not mean the Indians could no longer make war. Right now, he gloated, Philip and other cattlemen were raising horses for the Sioux to ride and cattle for them to eat during the approaching hostilities. (General Miles was even then pointing out this truth to his superiors.) Philip had already had twenty cattle killed, and his neighbors had lost both cattle and horses to passing Indians.[32] As Agent Reynolds had pointed out, with the dancers in this frame of mind, any one of a dozen unforeseen causes might touch off an explosion.

At Pine Ridge the last vestige of Royer's authority vanished. On November 11 this was made publicly and unmistakably clear.

It was ration day. Canvas-covered wagons crowded with Indians in their best finery converged on the agency. At noon everyone gathered at the corral. White herders turned loose the steers one by one, and the men, in the old way of hunting buffalo, shot them down with Winchesters. (The Indian Bureau had already issued orders to stop this "barbarous" custom.) Then they skinned and dressed the meat and divided it among the

32. Telegram, Miles to Adjt. Gen., Nov. 26, 1890, repeating telegram from Gov. A. C. Mellette of South Dakota, same date. For a biographical sketch of Philip see George Philip, "James (Scotty) Philip," *South Dakota Historical Collections, 20* (1940), 358–406.

families. With the ration cut, it did not go far. Women lined up at the commissary, sacks in hand, to draw their meager allotment of flour, bacon, coffee, and sugar. The three trading posts were crowded, and beyond the agency buildings there was horse racing and dancing.

An Indian named Little, wanted by the police for killing cattle, flaunted his immunity around the agency. Royer sent Lieutenant Thunder Bear and a squad of policemen to take him into custody. They found Little outside the combination dispensary and police assembly room. Inside the assembly room, the Oglala headmen were in council. Next door, Dr. Eastman examined patients. A full-blooded Santee Sioux, he had just been appointed agency physician. Already he had begun to court Elaine Goodale, one of the schoolmistresses.

Thunder Bear accosted Little and informed him that he was under arrest. Little drew a butcher knife. Instantly a mob of 200 Ghost Dancers surrounded the police, shouting and brandishing knives, tomahawks, and rifles. The council broke up and the headmen rushed outside. Dr. Eastman came to the door to watch. The dancers seized the police. There were menacing shouts to kill the lawmen, burn the agency, and take control.

The commanding voice of American Horse rose above the din:

> Stop! Think! What are you going to do? Kill these men of our own race? Then what? Kill all these helpless white men, women and children? And what then? What will these brave words, brave deeds lead to in the end? How long can you hold out? Your country is surrounded with a network of railroads; thousands of white soldiers will be here within three days. What ammunition have you? What provisions? What will become of your families? Think, think, my brothers! This is a child's madness.

"This man's voice had almost magic power," recalled Dr. Eastman, and dead silence fell upon the mob. Then Jack Red Cloud rushed up to American Horse, shoved the snout of a cocked pistol in his face, and yelled, "It is you and your kind who have brought us to this pass!" With supreme dignity and disdain, American Horse turned his back, slowly mounted the steps to the council room, and closed the door behind him. While the police watched helplessly, the warriors drifted from the scene, taking Little with them. The following day, Royer received a message from Little. It demanded the dismissal of all the policemen who had attempted to arrest him, on penalty of serious trouble the next ration day. Threats were also made against American Horse, and with his wife he moved in for a time with Dr. Eastman. The dancers had openly defied the agent and his police and had got away with it.[33]

The agents in the field and the Indian Bureau in Washington of course had not been operating in a vacuum during these trying weeks. Commanders at the military posts ringing the Sioux country kept their superiors at department and division headquarters fully informed of developments on the reservations. In Washington, copies of the agent's reports were referred to President Harrison and to Secretary of War Redfield Proctor and Maj. Gen. John M. Schofield, commanding the Army. The authorities in Washington grew increasingly concerned as the reports from the Sioux country piled up on their desks. Even more disturbing were the pressures coming from the citizens of Nebraska and North and South Dakota.

Beginning as early as September, all sorts of wild rumors swept these states. The agents had lost control. The Sioux were preparing to descend on ranches and settlements with torches and tomahawks. They had broken loose. They were just over the next hill. At Rushville, Valentine, Pierre, Bismarck, and a score of villages rimming the reservations, settlers met to draft resolutions calling for help. They asked for soldiers to come to their protection, for mobilization of the state militia, for arms and ammunition with which to defend themselves. Telegrams, petitions, and resolutions deluged the governors of each state, senators and congressmen in Washington, and the executive officials responsible for Indian affairs. Newspapers took up the cry, spreading wild stories with incendiary prose and demanding military action against the Sioux. Panic-stricken people aban-

33. Eastman, *Deep Woods to Civilization*, pp. 93–96.

doned their homesteads and took refuge in the settlements.
Many, ruined by the drought anyway, went back East to begin
new lives. It would be an unfair exaggeration to accuse all these
westerners of booming an Indian war. But these were hard times,
and it could not be denied that large-scale military operations
would restore a measure of prosperity.

The cries of anguish rang in the White House and had to be
heeded. Besieged on all sides and unable to get a clear picture of
the situation, the President on October 31 directed the Secretary of War to order an investigation into conditions in the
Sioux country. General Miles had not returned from his travels
with the Cheyenne Commission, but Brig. Gen. Thomas H.
Ruger, commanding the Department of Dakota, went to Standing Rock and Cheyenne River to investigate.

At Standing Rock, Ruger conferred with McLaughlin and
the commander of adjacent Fort Yates, Lt. Col. William F. Drum.
The general saw that McLaughlin had his people under control
and believed that the agent and Colonel Drum could handle
any trouble that arose. All three officials agreed that Sitting Bull
must be removed from the reservation, and all three agreed that
the task could best be accomplished after winter had set in, by
the Indian police supported as necessary by Drum's soldiers.

Ruger next went down to Cheyenne River. Here the situation
was less reassuring but still not dangerous. Like Standing Rock,
Cheyenne River had a military post, Fort Bennett, within easy
supporting distance. Ruger ordered a company of infantry up
from Fort Sully to reinforce the company already at Bennett.[34]

Meanwhile, at Pine Ridge, a thoroughly shaken Royer began
to bombard the Indian Office with telegrams begging permission
to come to Washington and explain matters in person. "The
police force are overpowered and disheartened," he warned on
the day after the Little affair, "we have no protection, are at the
mercy of these crazy dancers."[35] Denying the request to visit
Washington, Belt dryly pointed out that if conditions were as
chaotic as represented, it hardly seemed an appropriate time for

34. Ruger to Asst. Adjt. Gen. Div. of the Mo., Nov. 16 and 26, 1890, in Sec. War,
Annual Report (1891), *1*, 189–91.
35. Royer to Belt, Nov. 12, 1890.

the agent to leave his post. At the same time he could no longer afford to withhold troops from Pine Ridge. On November 13 Belt recommended to Secretary Noble that the War Department be advised of the emergency at Pine Ridge and asked to help. Noble went to the President, who on the same day directed the Secretary of War "to assume responsibility for the suppression of any threatened outbreak, and to take such steps as may be necessary to that end."[36]

In Chicago, General Miles alerted his subordinate headquarters at Omaha and St. Paul to have units ready for dispatch to the Sioux reservations. But it took another frantic appeal from Royer to set them in motion. On November 15 he telegraphed:

> Indians are dancing in the snow and are wild and crazy. I have fully informed you that the employees and government property at this agency have no protection and are at the mercy of the Ghost Dancers. Why delay by further investigation? *We need protection and we need it now.* I have submitted to you the result of 6 weeks calm conservative investigation and nothing short of 1000 soldiers will settle this dancing. The leaders should be arrested and confined in some military post until the matter is quieted and this should be done at once. Royer, Agt.[37]

Two days later, November 17, Miles instructed Brig. Gen. John R. Brooke, commanding the Department of the Platte, to send troops to Pine Ridge and Rosebud and to deploy the bulk of his command along the railroad and telegraph lines west and south of the reservations.[38]

Were troops necessary? It is a significant question, for the arrival of soldiers on the reservations united the dancers in armed defense of religious freedom and was therefore the immediate cause of the hostilities that later broke out. The answer,

36. Belt to Royer, Nov. 12, 1890. Belt to Noble, Nov. 13. President Harrison to Sec. Int., same date.

37. Royer to Belt, Nov. 15, 1890.

38. Williams by command of Miles to Brooke, Nov. 17, 1890. Miles to Adjt. Gen., same date.

it seems evident, is yes. The dancers at Pine Ridge composed about forty per cent of the population, at Rosebud thirty per cent (compared to fifteen per cent at Cheyenne River and ten per cent at Standing Rock).[39] These people were belligerent, suspicious, and excited to the point of irrationality. They expected the white men to interfere with the dance and were prone to consider the most innocuous administrative action as interference. With this state of mind, it was only a question of time until another incident such as the attempted arrest of Little ended in bloodshed. By the middle of November the lives of government employees at Pine Ridge, if not at Rosebud, were clearly in danger.

But the conditions that made troops necessary in November could almost certainly have been avoided if Congress had fulfilled its obligations to the Sioux earlier in the year, and if the spoils system had not placed inexperienced agents at Rosebud, Cheyenne River, and Pine Ridge at a critical time. The old agents—Wright, McChesney, and McGillycuddy, or even Gallagher—could probably have kept the situation in hand until spring failed to bring the expected millennium. Commissioner Morgan correctly assessed the matter when he informed the Secretary of the Interior: "Without denying that there was some real cause for alarm in the beginning of the troubles there [Pine Ridge], I am constrained to the belief that if the emergency had been met by decision and firmness, the excitement might have been allayed and quiet restored without resort to military aid."[40]

39. The figures are those of Rev. William J. Cleveland and are generally supported by reports of the agents. IRA, *Ninth Annual Report* (1891), p. 30.

40. Morgan to Noble, Dec. 12, 1890.

7. THE ARMY MOVES IN

AT DAWN ON NOVEMBER 20, 1890, Dr. Eastman was asleep
in his quarters at Pine Ridge Agency. Suddenly his assistant
rushed into the bedroom and exclaimed, "Come quick, the
soldiers are here." The Indian doctor threw off the covers and
went to the window. The sun had just burst over the knifelike
ridges dotted with stunted pine from which the agency took
its name. The shafts of sunlight illuminated a cloud of dust
rising from the road to Rushville. The agency sprang to life.
Government employees gathered in front of the frame buildings,
and the nearby camps of Red Cloud and Red Shirt bustled with
the aimless commotion that always marked an Indian village
taken by surprise.

The column entered the agency compound. In the van rode
Brig. Gen. John R. Brooke with Agent Royer and Special Agent
James A. Cooper, whom Belt had sent to fortify the frightened
Royer. Next, in column of fours, came three troops of the Ninth
Cavalry Regiment, guidons snapping overhead. They were Ne-
gro soldiers, each huddled in a buffalo overcoat topped by a
muskrat cap.[1] Instantly the Indians dubbed them "buffalo sol-

1. The 9th and 10th Cavalry and the 24th and 25th Infantry were Negro regiments with white officers.

diers." Behind the horsemen marched solid ranks of infantry, four companies of the Second Regiment and one of the Eighth Regiment. Completing the martial display, a Hotchkiss cannon and a Gatling gun rattled along in the rear of the caravan. The 170 cavalrymen and 200 infantrymen paraded through the agency and, on its west edge, pitched neat rows of tents on a plateau commanding the valley.

At this same dawn hour of November 20 the people at Rosebud Agency awoke to a similar spectacle—the whites with relief, the Indians with alarm. Lt. Col. A. T. Smith with three companies of the Eighth Infantry, two troops of the Ninth Cavalry, and a Hotchkiss gun had reached the bluffs above the agency at 4:00 A.M. At first light the weary column, composed of 120 infantrymen and 110 cavalrymen, swung down the slope and into the agency.

For the first time since the war of 1876, the soldiers confronted the Sioux.

Much careful planning lay behind the simultaneous arrival of troops at Pine Ridge and Rosebud. In Chicago's Pullman Building, where a suite of offices overlooking Lake Michigan housed the headquarters of the Army's Division of the Missouri, General Miles had pondered the delicate situation. The Indians were not at war, and war was to be avoided if at all possible. Yet war was entirely likely, for no one knew what the Ghost Dancers intended or how they would react to the appearance of troops.

If war came, what were the odds? On the one side, there were about 16,000 Tetons with perhaps 4,000 fighting men. How many would join the hostiles could not be estimated. During the decade of peace most of the Indians had bought the latest version of their favorite firearm, the Winchester repeating rifle or carbine, from traders and the merchants of Valentine and Rushville. Many whites thought that, with the disappearance of the buffalo, the Indian had lost his ability to make war. But Miles knew that domestic cattle and horses now covered the Sioux homeland, affording the Indians a reliable supply of food and transportation. The Sioux, he later wrote, were "far better prepared to wage a war than at any previous time in their history."[2]

But the Army, too, had assets. True, it was as usual unprepared. Garrisons of the scattered forts had stagnated during the years of peace. Training and equipment had suffered neglect. Single-shot Springfield rifles and carbines introduced in 1873 still served as the standard arm. Ammunition, quartermaster supplies, and, above all, wagons and mules had dwindled in quantity to a level inadequate to support emergency field operations. The Division of the Missouri had been reduced in the latest Army reorganization, leaving Miles with only two departments and slightly more than 4,000 combat troops, plus staff.

These deficiencies could be remedied in time. They were far overshadowed by one enormous advantage that Miles had not enjoyed as a regimental commander in 1876 and 1877. A cordon of military posts connected by railroad and telegraph lines now surrounded the Indian homeland. Commanders could communicate almost instantly with subordinates and rush troops in a matter of hours to any point on the perimeter of the Sioux country.

While weighing these considerations, Miles faced the immediate task of restoring order at Pine Ridge and Rosebud. Although the Sioux reservations lay in General Ruger's Department of Dakota, the troops in General Brooke's Department of the Platte were better placed to move swiftly to the trouble spots.[3] On November 17, back from a hurried consultation with Secretary of War Proctor in St. Louis, Miles began wiring instructions to Brooke at Omaha. Commands were to concentrate on the railroad at Valentine and Rushville and, in a night march, hurry simultaneously to the agencies. Brooke himself was to go to Pine Ridge. His mission there was to afford protection to government employees and property and separate the loyal from

2. Sec. War, *Annual Report* (1891), *1*, 143–45; see also Miles to Adjt. Gen., Nov. 28, 1890.

3. The Department of Dakota, with headquarters in St. Paul, consisted of the states of Minnesota, North and South Dakota, and Montana. The Department of the Platte, headquarters in Omaha, consisted of the states of Iowa, Nebraska, Colorado, and Wyoming, the Territory of Utah, and part of Idaho.

the "turbulent" Indians. If this sparked war, he was to deploy the infantry to protect settlements and guard supply trains and to hold the cavalry in mobile columns to pursue and destroy the hostiles.[4]

Brooke planned to have columns at Rosebud and Pine Ridge on the morning of November 20. On the evening of the 18th, two special trains left Omaha bearing wagons and Companies A, B, C, and D of the Second Infantry under Maj. Edmund Butler from Fort Omaha. At midnight General Brooke and his aide boarded a third train and settled themselves in the private coach of the manager of the Fremont, Elkhorn and Missouri Valley Railroad for the trip to Rushville.[5] Pausing at Valentine next morning, Brooke conferred with Lt. Col. A. T. Smith, who commanded Fort Niobrara. As the train pulled out of the station, Smith pointed his column north for the thirty-mile hike to Rosebud.

By early afternoon of the 19th Brooke had reached Rushville, where Royer and Special Agent Cooper met the train. At Brooke's request, Royer had ridden down from Pine Ridge to discuss the situation at the agency with the general. The newspapers charged that he had taken fright and abandoned his post, but both Brooke and Cooper later endorsed Royer's explanation.[6] Company C, Eighth Infantry, and Troops F, I, and K, Ninth Cavalry, had hastened up from Fort Robinson to join the infantry from Omaha. On the evening of the 19th, the column set forth on the road to Pine Ridge.

The bluecoated specter that had haunted the Sioux for a decade, that in times of stress had always restrained them from carrying defiance beyond the agent's limit of tolerance, had at

4. Williams (Asst. Adjt. Gen. Div. of the Mo.) to Brooke, Nov. 17, 1890 (three telegrams); Nov. 18 (two telegrams); Williams to Ruger, Nov. 18.

5. Omaha *Daily Bee*, Nov. 20, 1890.

6. Royer to Belt, Nov. 21, 1890; Cooper to Belt, same date. Some writers have described with relish how Royer galloped down the main street of Rushville shouting that the Indians had broken and were descending on the settlements. Given Royer's excitable temperament, the story is easy to believe and may well be true. That he abandoned his post, however, is not a necessary corollary and is discredited by the testimony of Cooper and Brooke.

last materialized in their midst. Rumors of the mobilization of troops had reached the Oglalas and Brulés on November 19 and were confirmed on the 20th. The progressives, joined by a number of dancers alarmed at what their activities had wrought, took fright and promptly heeded General Brooke's order, relayed by swift-riding Indian policemen, to abandon their homes and gather at the agency. By November 23 hundreds of families who wished to be counted as "friendlies" had come in. Missionaries, schoolteachers, farmers, and other whites who worked in the outlying reservation districts also assembled under the guns of the soldiers. Tepees littered the bottom lands surrounding Pine Ridge Agency, a picture of disorder contrasting sharply with the ranks of A-tents that marked the military camp. Sentries patrolled the agency streets and stood guard at the key buildings. General Brooke placed a twenty-four-hour guard on the Oglala boarding school, keeping 100 youngsters locked inside—partly, thought Elaine Goodale, as security for the good behavior of the parents.

The arrival of troops electrified the die-hard Ghost Dancers. On Medicine Root, Wounded Knee, and White Clay Creeks, the followers of Little Wound, Big Road, and No Water at first milled about in confusion, not knowing quite what to do. Then Little Wound took charge, and the dances resumed with a fury born of the crisis. On the nights of November 20 and 21, under Little Wound's orders, painted warriors decked in war costume dashed through the countryside, alerting all who wished to be numbered with the faithful to assemble on White River at the mouth of White Clay Creek. On the 22nd Census Agent Lea came to the agency and reported the dancers already massing at the appointed rendezvous. They disclaimed any intention of taking the offensive but vowed to defend themselves if attacked. "If the soldiers come here," said one, "we will treat them the way we did the agent and his policemen." The rebels declared that they would dance all winter, then in the spring go on a "big hunt"—the warpath, thought Lea. Meanwhile, they would ignore the agent and the troops. "Nor will they pay attention to the regulations of the Department," Lea relayed; "what little they get from it they can well do without." These Oglalas were well armed and supplied with plenty of ammunition, and they maintained an efficient system of picket outposts and roving scouts.[7]

At Rosebud the arrival of troops triggered a virtual stampede of Brulés, about 1,100 people instantly heading west. Part, under Two Strike, made directly for Pine Ridge. The old chief, whose mental stability had been increasingly questioned of late, vowed to stab General Brooke as the first act of war. But he stopped on Wounded Knee Creek, fifteen miles east of Pine Ridge Agency, and joined the 700 discontented Wazhazhas who had fled Pass Creek during the boundary controversy in July. The rest of the defecting Brulés, led by Eagle Pipe, Turning Bear, High Hawk, Lance, No Flesh, Pine Bird, Crow Dog, and White Horse, congregated in the northwest corner of the Rosebud Reservation and soon turned up at the mouth of Pass Creek to swell the ranks of Short Bull's followers. On November 25 Short Bull broke camp and moved up White River to unite his people with the Oglala dancers at the mouth of White Clay Creek.[8]

Meanwhile, General Miles continued the military build-up. His appeal for restoration of the former division boundaries had been heeded, and he could now call on troops in Kansas, Oklahoma, New Mexico, and Arizona. Within the week following November 20, General Brooke was heavily reinforced at Pine Ridge. Col. Frank Wheaton marched in with the remaining four companies of the Second Infantry. Another troop of the Ninth Cavalry came from Fort McKinney, Wyoming, under Maj. Guy V. Henry, who took command of the squadron of the Ninth. (At the battle of the Rosebud, in 1876, the Sioux had shot away half his face.) On November 26, after a tedious train ride from Fort Riley, Kansas, the entire Seventh Cavalry, Col. James W. Forsyth commanding, arrived at Pine Ridge. (At the Little Big-

7. Cooper to Belt, Nov. 22, 1890, encl. letter from Lea, same date. See also Miles to Adjt. Gen., Nov. 22, repeating telegram from Brooke, same date; and Boyd, *Recent Indian Wars*, pp. 221–22.

8. Two Strike's statement (interpreted by Louis Richard), in Thomas A. Bland, *A Brief History of the Late Military Invasion of the Home of the Sioux* (Washington, National Indian Defense Association, 1891), p. 8. Smith to Miles, Nov. 21, 1890. Ruger to Miles, Nov. 21. Reynolds to Belt, Nov. 26. Boyd, p. 226. McGillycuddy to Herbert Welsh, Dec. 4, 1890, in Welsh, "The Meaning of the Dakota Outbreak," pp. 450–51.

horn, in 1876, the Sioux had shot away half this regiment.) Capt.
Allyn Capron and Light Battery E, First Artillery, accompanied
the Seventh. At Rosebud Agency, four companies of the Twenty-
first Infantry from Fort Sidney, Nebraska, joined Lieutenant
Colonel Smith, and Lt. Col. J. A. Poland took command. Orders
went to New Mexico for the Sixth Cavalry to rush north, and to
Fort Leavenworth, Kansas, for a provisional squadron formed
from several cavalry regiments. General Ruger alerted stations
in Montana. Miles ordered the crack Cheyenne scout troop of
Lt. E. W. Casey at Fort Keogh, Montana, to prepare for field
service and authorized Brooke to recruit two troops of Indian
scouts at Pine Ridge. By the 26th, forty progressive Oglalas and
forty of Little Chief's Cheyennes had been enlisted.

Pine Ridge teemed with humanity—Oglalas, a few Wazhazhas
from Pass Creek, soldiers, scouts, and newspapermen. The reporters crammed James A. Finley's tiny hotel to overflowing.
They had rushed to the theater of war only to discover no war
at all. Their editors demanded sensational stories, and they
obliged. Lined up at the counter of James Asay's trading post,
they invented lurid accounts of battle, massacre, and atrocity
that delighted the folks back home. To relieve the boredom,
they draped themselves with guns and ammunition belts, and
posed for the photographers. "So far as my observation goes,"
wrote one, "there are but two correspondents here who are not
round-shouldered because of the weapons and missiles they have
to carry around."[9]

General Brooke was not amused by the antics of the press and
in fact went so far as to have Carl Smith of the Omaha *World-
Herald* recalled. Smith understood the Morse code and discovered that simply by hanging around the telegraph office in
Rushville he could pirate official dispatches denied to his colleagues. Before long, Brooke had alienated most of the reporters.
A rigid, austere, and somewhat unimaginative man, he did not,
in contrast to Miles, make any effort to cultivate the press. The
correspondents tried constantly to learn his plans, but he evaded
their questions or bluntly refused to be interviewed. As time

9. Quoted in Elmo Scott Watson, "The Last Indian War, 1890–91—A Study of
Newspaper Jingoism," *Journalism Quarterly, 20* (1943), 218.

went on and the troops failed to move, the reporters grew increasingly critical of his management of the campaign and in their dispatches bitterly assailed him for appeasing the Indians.

But the general's position was in truth one of extreme delicacy. The Indians had accomplished for him his first task of separating "friendlies" from "hostiles" (a questionable term but nonetheless a convenient distinction). The demeanor of the latter was undeniably hostile, but threats and noisy belligerence did not give him the excuse to march forth and clean out their camp. This would mean war, which he had been instructed to avoid at all hazards. Yet he had to do something. He could not maintain a large army in indefinite idleness while waiting for the hostiles to make the first move. At the same time, given the unpredictable temper of the dancers, he had to step gingerly, for any step could crack the thin ice that separated peace from war. Under the circumstances there was only one course of action open to him—to try to coax the hostile leaders to come in and join the friendlies.

Brooke was on the point of sending a scout, Frank Merrivale, as emissary to the White Clay camp when, on November 23, a familiar figure showed up at Pine Ridge. Valentine T. McGillycuddy, bearing a commission of colonel in the South Dakota militia, rode in to investigate the situation for Governor Arthur C. Mellette. The Oglalas welcomed Wasicu Wakan, who in seven winters of contention had never summoned soldiers, and implored him to have the troops sent away. Promptly upon learning of Brooke's resolve to negotiate, McGillycuddy volunteered for the mission. But the general had received the flamboyant ex-agent with notable coolness and turned down the offer. He sent Merrivale, who returned to report that the dancers had fired over his head. McGillycuddy left in disgust.[10]

A gap in the record leaves the student curious over what happened next. Probably Brooke had more success with other emissaries. The Pine Ridge troubles had attracted many old scouts to the Army payroll once more. They were chiefly mixed bloods who had lived in the years of peace with the Sioux and were well

10. Julia B. McGillycuddy, *McGillycuddy: Agent* (Stanford, 1941), pp. 262–63. See also "Dr. V. T. McGillycuddy on the Ghost Dance," in Vestal, *New Sources of Indian History*, pp. 81–84.

known to the dancers. Among those who turned up were "Young Nick" Janis, Sam Dion, Joseph Bisonette, Oliver Morisette, the three Shangreau brothers, the famous "Big Bat" and "Little Bat" (Baptiste Pourier and Baptiste Garnier), and Frank Grouard.[11] Very likely, some of these scouts, together with the leaders of the friendly progressives camped at the agency, rode down White Clay Creek to reason with the dancers. The awesome mobilization of troops, also, cannot have failed to impress the rebels. Whatever the answer, Brooke reported on November 27 that two of the most recalcitrant chiefs, Little Wound and Big Road, had come in and that their bands were following.[12]

But the fanatical Short Bull and Kicking Bear still held large numbers at the mouth of White Clay Creek, and the erratic Two Strike still hesitated on Wounded Knee Creek. What impelled them to the next move is not apparent; probably the fiery oratory of the prophets proved sufficient. On November 30 the two groups, now largely Brulés, broke camp. Two Strike's people marched down Wounded Knee Creek. En route they plundered the cabins of the friendlies who had gone to the agency, burned their hay, and appropriated their beef cattle. Crossing to the north bank of White River at the mouth of Grass Creek, the Two Strike people united with Short Bull's followers, who had abandoned the White Clay camp and traveled down White River, helping themselves to cattle from the agency herd camp across from the mouth of Willow Creek. The combined force, estimated Royer, numbered 500 lodges, perhaps 600 warriors. The frightened chief herder, whose herd had borne the brunt of the foraging expeditions, put the figure at 1,000 fighting men. They continued a short distance down the river, then turned northward.

A level, elevated plateau, now known as the Cuny Table, separated White River from Cheyenne River. Its sides rose precipitously several hundred feet above the prairie, and it offered

11. Elmo Scott Watson, "Pine Ridge, 1890–91," *Westerners Brand Book* (Denver, 1946), pp. 3–4.

12. Miles to Adjt. Gen., Nov. 27, 1890. For a suggestion of the role of the scouts in negotiations see also James H. Cook, *Fifty Years on the Old Frontier* (New Haven, 1923), p. 233.

few approaches. On its northeast edge the Cuny Table termi-
nated in a curious geological formation—another small table,
shaped roughly like a triangle, about three miles long and two
wide. A narrow land bridge, scarcely wider than a wagon, linked
it with the larger plateau to the south. The Indians called this
small projection the Stronghold. Two springs yielded plenty of
water, and a carpet of good grass provided forage for the stock.
With the stolen beef, hunger was not an immediate problem.
Here the dancers laid out their camp.

The Stronghold afforded a natural fortress that all Brooke's
army would have difficulty taking by assault or siege. Surrounding themselves with pickets to give timely warning of enemy
approach, the faithful threw themselves with renewed frenzy
into a virtually continuous orgy of dancing.[13]

To the division commander and his staff, gathered before the
war map on the wall of Miles' office in Chicago, the policy of
caution and conciliation at Pine Ridge seemed the best approach
for the time being. No Indian village in history was free of
quarreling factions. Delay would give the dancers a chance to
start squabbling among themselves and also afford time for more
troops to converge on the scene of the trouble. Brooke was growing impatient under the newspaper attacks, but Miles restrained
him. Above all, he warned, "Do not allow your command to become mixed up with the Indians friendly or otherwise. Hold
them at a safe distance." In subsequent messages, he reiterated
this injunction. Mutual suspicion and one nervous trigger finger
could touch off fighting that neither side wanted.[14]

One measure under active consideration in Chicago was the
arrest of the dance leaders. Now that the Army could make the
arrests and also bear the brunt of any unhappy consequences or
humanitarian outcry, the Indian Bureau thought this a fine idea.
As early as November 20, Acting Commissioner Belt had in-

13. Royer and Cooper to Belt, Nov. 30, 1890 (two letters), Dec. 1. Brooke to
Miles, Nov. 30, Dec. 1. Williams to Miles and Adjt. Gen., Dec. 1. Royer to Belt,
Dec. 4. For a contemporary description of the Stronghold see William D. McGaa
Interview, Ricker Collection. A map of it is in Miller, *Ghost Dance,* p. 154.

14. Miles to Brooke, Nov. 22, 23, 24, 1890.

structed the Sioux agents to wire him the names of "fomentors of disturbances," in order that "assistance of the military while operating to suppress any attempted outbreak may be had to make arrests."[15]

This request did not long await responses. All the agents promptly made recommendations, Royer alone submitting the names of sixty-five Indians who should be taken into custody. Belt consolidated the lists, and they were turned over to the War Department with the Secretary of the Interior's plea that soldiers seize the individual's named. Miles, too, believed that the troublemakers should be removed, but at Pine Ridge and Rosebud, even though the agents were anxious to get on with it, such a move at this time was fraught with explosive possibilities.

Standing Rock was another matter, for here McLaughlin still retained control. Miles believed Sitting Bull to be at the bottom of the whole trouble and wanted his influence neutralized as soon as possible. Yet, of all the agents, McLaughlin opposed immediate arrests. His list of candidates for military prison, submitted to the Indian Office for the third time on November 21, bore an important qualification: "Everything being quiet here at present with no snow and the weather summer-like, [I] do not think it prudent to make arrests now." He believed that the move should be deferred until the cold and snow had its usual enervating effect upon the Indians. Then, to avoid the turmoil that the appearance of soldiers would excite, Indian policemen should be used.[16] General Ruger and Colonel Drum concurred, though not in writing.

General Miles had only contempt for Indian agents and was inclined to treat their ideas with scorn, if he noticed them at all. At a banquet on November 24 he encountered an old friend. As a scout, William F. Cody—Buffalo Bill—had shared the rigors of Miles' campaign against Sitting Bull in 1876. For a time Sitting Bull had been a featured attraction of Cody's famous Wild West show, and Miles let himself be convinced that, if anyone could capture the Hunkpapa leader, Cody was the man. The general supplied him with an order for the arrest of Sitting Bull and on

15. Belt to Sioux agents, Nov. 20, 1890.
16. McLaughlin to CIA, Nov. 21, 1890.

the back of a calling card scrawled instructions for military commanders to supply such transportation and escorts as Cody might
request. The old scout promptly hopped a train for St. Paul and
Bismarck.[17]

Pausing in Wisconsin to pick up three companions—Frank
Powell (White Beaver), Robert H. Haslam (Pony Bob), and G.
W. Chadwick—Buffalo Bill showed up at Standing Rock on the
evening of November 27 trailing these men and five newspaper
reporters. Still attired in dress suit, silk stockings, and patent
leather shoes, he presented his credentials to a chagrined Mc-
Laughlin. During this same night, McLaughlin's agent at Grand
River, schoolteacher John M. Carignan, reported by letter that
the Indians were quieter and if only left alone would probably
make no trouble. Above all, he advised, keep all strangers away.[18]

Convinced that if Cody tried to carry out his mission, he might
get himself killed and precipitate an outbreak as well, McLaughlin and Colonel Drum acted quickly. The officers at Fort Yates
conspired to lull the great scout and showman with the pleasures

17. Stanley Vestal, *Warpath and Council Fire* (New York, 1948), pp. 298–99.
Williams to Asst. Adjt. Gen. Dept. of Dak., Nov. 28, 1890, informed General Ruger,
somewhat belatedly, of Cody's mission. The visiting card is on display at the
Buffalo Bill Museum in Cody, Wyoming.

Cody's able biographer, Don Russell, contends that neither Miles nor Cody had
any thought of Cody's actually arresting Sitting Bull by force, that "Cody had no
other intention than to have a talk with Sitting Bull and try to persuade him not
to start a war," and "invite Sitting Bull to a conference with General Miles." But
Miles' written orders to Cody, reproduced by Russell, authorize Cody to "secure
the person of Sitting Bull and and [*sic*] deliver him to the nearest com'g officer of
U. S. Troops, taking a receipt and reporting your action." If this was not an order
for Sitting Bull's arrest, certainly McLaughlin, Drum, and anyone else who read
it cannot be blamed for regarding it as such. Despite his friendship for Cody, it
seems improbable that Sitting Bull would have accepted an invitation from him
to leave Grand River at this time. Whether Cody actually would have tried to use
force, no one can say. See Don Russell, *The Lives and Legends of Buffalo Bill*
(Norman, 1960), pp. 358–61.

18. Carignan to McLaughlin, Nov. 27, 1890, in Vestal, *New Sources of Indian
History*, pp. 8–10. This was in response to a letter from McLaughlin sent by
messenger at 4:00 P.M. As Carignan's reply was sent back by the same messenger and
was written at 10:30 P.M., McLaughlin must have received it about 4:00 A.M. on
Nov. 28. Names of Cody's companions are from the Sioux Falls *Argus-Leader*, Dec.
13, 1890; Washington *Evening Star*, Dec. 4 and 29, 1890. Chadwick in the *Argus-
Leader* is authority for Cody's attire.

of the post officers' club, while the agent dashed off a telegram to Washington pleading that Miles' order be rescinded. But Cody's capacity was already legend. Late next morning he walked out of the club, apparently no worse for the night, and prepared to ride for Grand River.[19]

McLaughlin and Drum had foreseen this possibility, and what happened next they had carefully arranged through fast-riding couriers who left Standing Rock during the night. That day, November 28, Cody and his entourage journeyed twenty miles in the direction of Grand River, camping for the night where the Sitting Bull Road crossed Oak Creek. Early next morning, Louis Primeau, returning from Grand River, rode into this camp and asked where Cody was going. When informed, he replied: "Well, you're too late. Sitting Bull has gone into the agency with Jack Carignan. They went over the other trail." The other trail was called Primeau's Road, and it crossed Oak Creek two miles upstream. Cody expressed disbelief, and Primeau suggested that he ride over and check the other road for tracks. One horse was shod, the other unshod, and they were drawing a buggy. On the Primeau road, of course, Cody found the carefully planted trail of the horses and buggy and, crestfallen, returned to the agency.[20]

There he discovered that he had been victimized. But there, too, McLaughlin showed him a telegram that Colonel Drum had received from department headquarters four hours after Cody's departure. Receiving McLaughlin's urgent wire, the Secretary of the Interior had hastened to President Harrison and Secretary of War Proctor. As a result of the conference, the President had suspended Cody's orders and deferred all attempts to arrest Sitting Bull. Confronted with evidence of this decision, there was

---

19. Capt. Peter E. Traub, "The First Act of the Last Sioux Campaign," *Journal of the United States Cavalry Association, 15* (1905), 873–74; McLaughlin to Belt, Nov. 28, in CIA, *Annual Report* (1891), p. 331. Captain Traub's article furnishes the soundest support for the story of the officers' club. E. A. Brininstool, who got his information from another participant, tells the story entertainingly in "How Gen. Miles Blundered in Ordering Buffalo Bill to Arrest Sitting Bull," El Segundo (Calif.) *Herald*, Dec. 28, 1928, copy in files of Order of Indian Wars, American Military Institute, Washington, D.C.; and in "Buffaloing Buffalo Bill," *Hunter-Trader-Trapper*, April 1938.

20. Narrative of Carignan in Fiske, *Life and Death of Sitting Bull*, pp. 38–39.

nothing for Cody to do but leave Standing Rock. He returned to
Chicago, submitted a bill for $505.60 to cover transportation for
himself and three associates, and retired to his home at North
Platte, Nebraska, to recover from a severe cold—the result, perhaps, of a forty-mile horseback ride in banquet-hall attire.[21]

Miles was furious over the interference of the upstart agent,
and knowledge that somehow Colonel Drum had conspired to
thwart the desires of the division commander did not abate his
anger. Since he could not learn the particulars, he contented
himself with rapping Drum's knuckles. "If reports are correct,"
his adjutant general wrote General Ruger confidentially, "the
Division Commander is not entirely satisfied with the action of
the military at Fort Yates."[22] The episode, moreover, led the
President himself to review the whole question of arrests. While
leaving the timing of future arrests to Miles' discretion, he cautioned that "they ought not to be made until there is the amplest
preparations to suppress any outbreak that might result."[23]

The Cody episode strengthened Miles' conviction that the
agents must be brushed aside. The very day the President can-
celed Cody's authority to arrest Sitting Bull, Miles expressed this
conviction in writing. A lasting resolution of the Sioux problem,
he informed his superiors, depended entirely upon placing the
Sioux "under absolute control and beyond the possibility of
doing harm." The agents could not do this. The only answer was
to put "those large powerful warlike tribes, that have been for
years a terror to the north-west States and Territories, entirely
under military control, and at once." He also staunchly advocated another measure. The ration allowance prescribed by
treaty should be granted at once. The Sioux were starving, and
full stomachs would go a long way toward restoring contentment
on the reservations.[24]

21. Belt to McLaughlin, Nov. 28, 1890. McLaughlin to CIA, Dec. 1. Proctor to
Miles, Nov. 29. Schofield to Miles, same date. Williams to Asst. Adjt. Gen. Dept. of
Dak., same date. Letters covering Cody's travel expenses, Dec. 1 to Feb. 6, are sum-
marized in the Register of Letters Received, Hq. Div. of the Mo., 1890, vol. 1.

22. Corbin to Ruger, Dec. 10, 1890. See also Miles to Schofield, Dec. 6, 1890.

23. Harrison to Noble, Dec. 4, 1890.

24. Miles to Adjt. Gen., Nov. 23 and 28, 1890.

On November 28 the general boarded a train for Washington to sell his ideas in person. Possibly with a shrewd appraisal of the effect of public opinion on the outcome of his efforts, he suddenly began to emit declarations of alarm. At trainside in Chicago he told reporters that the situation was grave. "In fact, the necessity for a winter campaign is becoming more and more apparent." At the Ebbit House in Washington he told reporters, "It is a more comprehensive plot than anything ever inspired by Tecumseh, or even Pontiac."[25] In interviews with the press he made much of the necessity for military control of the agencies and restoration of full rations. Thus he drew in public the battle lines of an interdepartmental war. Officials of the Indian Bureau had never let themselves be entirely convinced that the Sioux were starving, and instead of shifting the blame to the House of Representatives, where it properly belonged, Acting Commissioner Belt branded Miles' statements "exaggerated and unfounded." If the Sioux were hungry, he declared, it was because of their own improvidence.[26] The Indian authorities also girded for battle over the military attempt to encroach on the prerogatives of their agents, and Commissioner Morgan opportunely returned to Washington to organize the defense.

Congress had just convened when Miles reached Washington, and the Capitol chambers provided an admirable sounding board for his pronouncements, many of which were quoted on the Senate and House floors. The immediate issue was a bill to provide Federal arms and ammunition to the terrified settlers of the Northwest. But on December 3 Senator Daniel Voorhees, the "Tall Sycamore of the Wabash," rose from his desk and in ringing tones declared:

> I look upon the policy which has been pursued by the administration of Indian affairs as a crime revolting to man and God. I look upon the present outbreak or threatened outbreak—which will bring not merely the destruction of the Indians, but will bathe the snows of the Northwest crimson with the blood of our own brave soldiers and officers—

25. *New York Herald*, Nov. 29, 1890. Washington *Evening Star*, Dec. 1, 1890.
26. Washington *Evening Star*, Dec. 4, 1890.

as something revolting in the extreme, and that instead of sitting here debating Election bills and Force bills, and providing for the issuance of arms to the States in the Northwest, we should be hurrying, anxiously and eagerly, to provide for the feeding of these starving people.[27]

"The speech," reported the *New York Herald*, "created a sensation." At the same time, a bill to appropriate money for rations languished in the House while the people of the Northwest got their arms—1,000 stand each for Nebraska, North and South Dakota, Wyoming, and Montana. But Miles had his way. On December 1 the Secretary of the Interior ordered the Sioux agents to spend money earmarked for the remainder of the fiscal year in order to bring ration issues, for the time being at least, to the level set by treaty. On the same day he awarded Miles partial victory on the other proposal, ordering the Commissioner of Indian Affairs to wire the Sioux agents that "as to all operations intended to suppress any outbreak by force, [you will] cooperate with and obey the orders of the military officer commanding on the reservation in your charge."[28]

The contest between the Interior and War Departments was far from over. Miles had merely won the first round. Nor were the gathering clouds of bureaucratic strife strictly interdepartmental. There were rumblings in Miles' own camp. For many years Army cohesion had been rent by factional bickering. Constellations of lesser officers had clustered around two bright stars, Crook and Miles. The two generals had differed fundamentally on how best to handle the Indian problem. The difference in philosophies and techniques was as deep and irreconcilable as the difference in personalities. The death of Crook had not healed the wounds, for his protégés were scattered throughout the Army hierarchy. Miles' militant utterances to the press, so

27. *New York Herald*, Dec. 4, 1890. For the congressional story see *Cong. Rec.*, 51st Cong., 1st sess., 22, Pt. I, 44–48, 68–74, 167, 200; and *U.S. Statutes at Large*, 51st Cong. (1889–91), 26, 1111–12. Interestingly, it was Senator Voorhees who had secured Hugh Gallagher's appointment as Pine Ridge agent in the Cleveland administration.

28. Noble to CIA, Dec. 1, 1890.

much in contrast to the unpretentious manner of Crook, annoyed many important officers.

No sooner had troops reached Pine Ridge than the Washington *Evening Star* quoted "a prominent army officer" stationed in the Capital as saying:

> Miles is predicting a general Indian war and virtually asks that the command of the entire army be turned over to him. He wants to create a scare and pose as the savior of the country. In fact he is almost in the attitude of a political Messiah, such as the Indians themselves are looking for. I have no doubt in the world that he is honest in his candidacy. He has shrewdly enlisted the favor of nearly every newspaper man in California, and has by his agreeable manners and the expenditure of his means managed to make himself very popular in a certain way in the west. He is one of the most ambitious men in the army and he is pulling his wires shrewdly.[29]

Miles clipped out the article and sent it to General Schofield, asking that the author of this "malicious and unwarranted attack" be identified, arrested, and hauled before a military tribunal. The handling of the protest had its comic aspects. Schofield endorsed it to the Secretary of War "with recommendation that necessary steps be taken to ascertain the identity of the 'prominent officer.' " Proctor endorsed it back to Schofield "for information as to what proof can be furnished in regard to the identity of the prominent officer." Schofield endorsed it back to Miles "for any information he may have to communicate." Miles endorsed it once more to Schofield with the comment that had such an offense occurred in his headquarters, he would have felt an obligation to find out who did it and take action. Here rested the case of the "prominent officer."[30]

That more than one prominent officer entertained such beliefs was revealed by a published interview with Brig. Gen. Wesley Merritt, an old Indian fighter scarcely less distinguished than

29. Washington *Evening Star*, Nov. 21, 1890.

30. Miles to Schofield, Nov. 26, with endorsements dated Nov. 29, Dec. 3, and Dec. 10.

Miles. "A man like General Crook would not have called all the troops from the South in an emergency of this kind," he told a correspondent for the *Army and Navy Journal,* "and he would have been pretty apt to have been master of the situation. . . . It is pretty well understood in Army circles that private ambitions have had more or less to do with the present Indian situation." "Remember that I do not join in this criticism," he added disarmingly. "I have no insinuations to make concerning that mischievous little insect sometimes called the 'Presidential bee.' "[31]

Such criticism was grossly unjust. Although Miles was hardly above exploiting the situation for personal advantage, he certainly had nothing to do with creating it. As it turned out, moreover, he handled it brilliantly. To his credit, he refrained from engaging in a public brawl with his detractors. Besides, upon his return from Washington on December 3, the management of field operations absorbed most of his time and attention.

The two small reservations of Crow Creek and Lower Brulé, separated by the Missouri River but administered by the same agent, had thus far escaped the Ghost Dance infection. The Lower Yanktonais at Crow Creek, on the east bank, had long since been made over in the white image, and they scorned the doctrine. The Lower Brulés, though far more docile than their kinsmen of Rosebud, had yet to be reconstructed. They were unhappy over the boundaries drawn for them by the land agreement and incensed at Commissioner Morgan's obstinate refusal to let them move down to Rosebud and live with the Upper Brulés. The Ghost Dance emissaries from Cheyenne River who came among them late in November found some willing pupils.

On November 27 Agent A. P. Dixon learned that a dance had been organized on his reservation. A man of action, he marched out of the agency the next day at the head of his police force. By evening he had nine dance leaders packed in the agency jail and was complaining to Washington that he needed more prison facilities. In the next few days the number of arrests rose to twenty-two. Soldiers came to take seventeen of the prisoners to

31. *Army and Navy Journal, 28* (Dec. 20, 1890), 279.

Fort Snelling, Minnesota, for confinement in the military prison there. Alarmed at Dixon's initiative in a matter the Interior Department preferred to leave strictly to the Army, Belt quickly clamped down. On December 6 he telegraphed, "Secretary directs that you make no more arrests whatever except under orders of the military or upon an order of the Secretary of the Interior." But the agent's prompt and decisive action had already won the day, and the Ghost Dance movement on the Lower Brulé Reservation collapsed.[32]

With Kicking Bear in the Stronghold, the Miniconjou dancers of Cheyenne River Reservation looked for leadership to Hump and Big Foot. The bands of these chiefs had united in one great conclave on Cheyenne River near the mouth of Cherry Creek. About 600 people kept a dance in progress almost continuously. Residents of the newly founded town of Cheyenne City, less than twenty settlers, cowered in their rude homes on the ceded tract across the river. The mixed-blood agency farmer, Narcisse Narcelle, worked tirelessly at the perilous task of trying to talk the dancers into giving up the foolishness. Hump was already wavering in his belief. Not the unyielding Big Foot, who in council on November 25 urged his people to acquire all the guns and cartridges they could find and stay together in one camp. Friendly Indians told Agent Palmer, who visited the Cherry Creek camps on November 27, that the dancers were spoiling for a fight and intended to have one soon. They also warned Palmer that white traders were furnishing the recalcitrants with rifles.[33]

General Miles thought chances good of detaching Hump from the disaffected and thereby considerably shrinking the size of the Cherry Creek dance center. Hump had surrendered to Miles in 1877, had guided him to Lame Deer's hostile village, and had served him faithfully as a scout in the Nez Percé war of 1877. For seven years he and other recent hostiles were in the charge of one of Miles' officers, Capt. Ezra P. Ewers. Between Hump

32. Dixon to Belt, Nov. 28, 1890. Belt to Noble, Nov. 29. Belt to Dixon, Dec. 6. Dixon to Ruger, Dec. 15. Dixon to Morgan, April 10, 1891.
33. Cheyenne River Agency Clerk to Belt, Nov. 28, 1890; Palmer to Belt, Dec. 1.

and the captain had grown a bond of mutual trust and friendship that Miles believed might now be turned to good advantage. On November 28, as Miles left for Washington, orders sped to the Department of Texas for Captain Ewers to hasten to Fort Bennett. On December 4 Miles sent instructions to him at Pierre, South Dakota. Ewers was to go to Hump, recall old times, tell him that Miles now had charge of all the Sioux and Cheyennes, and ask him to give up the Ghost Dance and come to the agency.[34]

Accompanied only by Lt. Harry C. Hale, Captain Ewers rode up Cheyenne River to the Cherry Creek camp. Hump was absent, but a runner was sent for him. Learning that his old friend wished to see him, Hump at once returned to camp. Aided by Hale and Farmer Narcelle, the captain went to work. Informed that Miles wanted him to take his people away from the dancers and come to Fort Bennett, Hump replied that he would do as General Miles desired. With a large share of his band, Hump arrived at Cheyenne River Agency on December 9. He once more donned the uniform of an Army scout and thereafter, under the watchful eyes of Captain Ewers, threw his influence against the Ghost Dance.[35]

With the defection of Hump the ardor of Big Foot cooled considerably, and he took his people home to their cabins at the mouth of Deep Creek, ten miles below the forks of Cheyenne River. Already he was boxed by troops. To the east, Col. H. C. Merriam and the Seventh Infantry reached Fort Sully on December 7 and prepared to cross the Missouri for a march up Cheyenne River. To the west, Captain Henissee's "camp of observation" had stood near the forks of Cheyenne River since spring. It was now manned by Troops C, D, and I, Eighth Cavalry, Company I, Third Infantry, and two Hotchkiss guns, Lt. Col. Edwin V. Sumner commanding. On December 15 another company of infantry and a detachment of Indian scouts strengthened the command.

34. Special Orders, No. 278, War Dept., *Special Orders, 1890*. Miles to Brig. Gen. D. S. Stanley, Nov. 28, 1890. Corbin to Ewers, Dec. 4.

35. Palmer to CIA, Dec. 9, 1890. Miles to Ewers, Dec. 10. Corbin to Ruger, Dec. 10 (two telegrams), Sec. War, *Annual Report* (1891), *1*, 147.

Parleying with Sumner, Big Foot professed peaceful intentions. Sumner's judgment that he told the truth seems correct. But the militance of his followers had not abated. The tragedy of Big Foot was to repeat a theme familiar in the history of the Indian wars—a chief hurried unwillingly toward disaster by fiery young men he could not control.

At Rosebud all was serene. With the Brulé dancers absent in the Stronghold, only progressives remained at the agency. At Reynolds' summons, they had moved there and laid out an immense temporary encampment. Aside from the routine of bivouac, Colonel Poland's troops had nothing to do but shiver in their tents.

On December 1 George Wright turned up at the agency. He had cleared himself of the charges brought in September by Inspector Cisney and now resumed his old job. Special Agent Reynolds stayed on to help. A welcoming committee of progressive headmen filed into the office to assure Wright of their peaceful feelings. They castigated the Brulés in the Stronghold for bringing calamity upon the Sioux and promised to heed any advice the agent might offer. Only please, they begged, do not let the dreaded bluecoats harm them. Wright quieted their fears and on December 5 wrote Commissioner Morgan, now back from his trip to the Southwest, that "all Indians remaining on the Agency are quiet and will remain so."[36]

The issue now hung on the outcome of General Brooke's efforts at the storm center, and all eyes focused on Pine Ridge.

36. Wright to CIA, Dec. 5, 1890.

8. BROOKE TRIES FOR PEACE

PINE RIDGE AGENCY occupied a low plateau formed by the junction of Wolf and White Clay Creeks. The road running south to Rushville divided the village into commercial and official districts. East of the road stood the Episcopal and Presbyterian churches with their parsonages, three trading posts, and the low log structure that the correspondents dubbed the "Hotel de Finley." West of the Rushville road stood the agency buildings—shops, warehouses, a day school and the rambling 180-pupil boarding school; employee apartments; the long edifice that housed the council room and offices of the agent, chief clerk, and police; and the modest dwelling of Agent Royer, which General Brooke now claimed as his headquarters. Scattered around the fringes of the hamlet were cabins of the half-breeds.

Directly west of the agency, along both sides of White Clay Creek, the cabins of Red Cloud's band clustered around the empty two-story frame house the Government had built for the old chief. Red Shirt's settlement sprawled along the valley a short distance to the south. The tent city of Brooke's soldiers, now housing more than a thousand men, separated the agency from the friendly camps.

Hotchkiss and Gatling guns commanded every approach to the agency. One of the guns frowned upon the camp of old Blue Horse, who resented the implication. "There is no trouble at my camp," he complained, "and it might go off and hurt someone." Brooke declined to turn it in another direction.[1]

The defection from the dance ranks of Little Wound, Big Road, and their followers swelled the Oglala camps around the agency. Many of these people still counted themselves adherents of the Ghost Dance religion but had come in rather than face the probable consequences of Short Bull's provocative policies. Brooke had all those who professed belief in the religion camp apart from the nonbelievers, and the "hostile" camps of these people littered the valley south of the agency.

At one such camp on November 30 the dancers tried a deadly experiment. An Oglala named Porcupine volunteered to test the bulletproof qualities of the Ghost Shirt and ended with a nearly fatal wound in his thigh. News of the episode spread through the camps with faith-shattering effect.[2]

With only a few Oglalas in the Stronghold, nearly all the Pine Ridge people were gathered at the agency. Including the bands of Red Cloud and Red Shirt, there were more than 4,000 Indians. They were restless, suspicious, and afraid, but seemingly determined to do nothing that might anger the soldiers.

In this determination the enfeebled Red Cloud shared. So consistently had he opposed the reforms of past years, however, that many automatically suspected him of complicity in the rebellion, a suspicion that the reporters were not slow in passing on to their editors. "Some of these gentlemen," wrote scout James H. Cook, "informed me that old Red Cloud was at the bottom of all the deviltry that was going on; that he was managing the hostiles who were out in the bad lands, making his headquarters at the fine house which Uncle Sam had so kindly given him in order to make him comfortable in his old age." But neither

1. McGillycuddy, *McGillycuddy: Agent,* p. 262.
2. Colby, "Sioux Indian War," p. 149.

Cook nor his associates among the scouts "could ever discover that old Red Cloud had anything to do with either directing the hostiles or giving them aid and encouragement." Royer, too, could find "no evidence that goes to show that he is connected with the Ghost Dance, and . . . he has given me no trouble of any character." All the creditable evidence supports Red Cloud's own assertion that "so far as the dance is concerned I can truly say that I never had anything to do with or encourage it, never having seen one."[3]

For Brooke, the Brulés in the Stronghold caused greater concern. The first reports of the flight from the White Clay camp had alarmed the general, for they raised the fear that the fugitives were making a break for Canada, thus endangering the Black Hills settlements, especially Rapid City. Had the Brulés in fact wished to go north, they probably could have slipped with little difficulty around the troops stationed at the forks of Cheyenne River. By the end of the first week in December, however, the escape paths to the north had been covered. The Fort Leavenworth Cavalry Squadron (one troop each from the First, Second, Fifth, and Ninth Regiments), under Lt. Col. George B. Sanford, took post along the left bank of Cheyenne River immediately northwest of the stronghold. The Sixth Cavalry, Col. Eugene A. Carr commanding, patrolled east and west from a base camp at the mouth of Rapid Creek. Farther north, units from Montana forts scouted the country south of the Northern Pacific Railroad.[4]

Word from the Stronghold soon made it clear that Short Bull and his associates had no intention of going north or in any other direction. They planned to stay where they were, dance all winter, and in the spring decide upon the next move. They made it equally clear that they would fight to the last if the Army tried to take their badlands refuge. In their present temper, Brooke believed, they meant precisely what they said. He therefore stepped up his diplomatic assault.

3. Cook, *Fifty Years on the Old Frontier*, p. 233. Royer to Belt, Nov. 25, 1890. Red Cloud to T. A. Bland, Dec. 10, 1890, in Bland, *Brief History of the Late Military Invasion*, pp. 19–21.

4. Sec. War, *Annual Report* (1891), *1*, 63–70.

Several large parties of friendlies rode to the Stronghold to try persuasion but turned back when the pickets fired over their heads. Then the thought occurred to Brooke that perhaps Father John Jutz could talk his way into the Brulé camp. The seventy-year-old Catholic missionary had come to Pine Ridge in 1888 to establish the Holy Rosary Mission and School, four miles north of the agency. Staffed by Franciscan Sisters from Buffalo, New York, and supervised by the kindly old priest, the mission had prospered, and its founder had won a secure place in the affections of the Indians. They had assured him that, if war came, his mission and all who sought refuge in it would not be harmed. Father Jutz believed that the rebels would receive him and responded eagerly to Brooke's proposal.

Accompanied by Jack Red Cloud, himself recently a dance leader, Father Jutz left the agency at noon on December 3. The next day, ten miles short of their destination, they ran into the line of pickets that curved around the tableland escarpment. Couriers galloped back to the dance camp and soon returned with orders for the pickets to admit the Father. By 11:00 P.M. the two emissaries were at Short Bull's headquarters.

For most of the night Father Jutz sat through a seemingly endless council. Present were Short Bull, Kicking Bear, Two Strike, Turning Bear, High Hawk, Crow Dog, Eagle Pipe, and several others. The Sioux leaders dwelt at great length on their grievances. They expressed particular anger over Census Agent Lea's enumeration at Rosebud, which had cut 2,000 from the population total. It was false and would not give them enough food to live on. The new boundary between Rosebud and Pine Ridge was also a source of discontent. Jutz' plea that they surrender fell on deaf ears. The name of every headman present was on someone's list of Indians who should be arrested, and they vowed to die fighting rather than be locked in the white man's big iron house. By daybreak, however, Jutz had persuaded several of the leaders to come in for a talk with General Brooke, and they set forth almost immediately.[5]

The delegation consisted of Two Strike, Turning Bear, Big

5. *New York Herald,* Dec. 7, 1890. See also Brooke to Miles, Dec. 4 (two telegrams) and Dec. 5, 1890.

Turkey, High Pine, Big-Bad-Horse, and Bull Dog, together with an escort of twenty-four armed warriors. War paint smeared their faces and arms, and tufts of sacred eagle feathers fluttered from the hair of the riders and the manes and tails of the ponies. Some of the men wore Ghost Shirts. The Indians did not feel so brave as the defiant trappings suggested. They feared that the invitation to parley was really part of a plot to arrest them. Outriders preceded the advance, and the most trivial occurrence threw the column into confusion.

The group camped for the night of December 5 at Father Jutz' mission and the next morning, shorn of paint and feathers and bearing a white flag, moved hesitantly toward the agency. Preceded by the mounted warriors, Two Strike rode with Father Jutz in a buggy. Four times the procession faltered as fear asserted itself. Finally, Father Jutz promised that the warriors could kill him if the soldiers made any menacing move, and the cavalcade marched into the agency. At Brooke's headquarters the Indians dismounted with military precision. The chiefs tied their mounts to the hitching rail and with studied dignity filed into the general's presence behind Father Jutz.[6]

After such a colorful entry, the conference was something of an anticlimax. Flanked by Colonels Wheaton and Forsyth, Brooke sat facing the semicircle of chiefs. For two hours they debated, the general urging surrender, the chiefs responding with long discourses on the iniquities of the white man. To most of their complaints, Brooke replied that there would be plenty of time to adjust grievances after the refugees had come to the agency. As added inducement, however, he promised to provide abundant food and to employ some of the young men as scouts.

Turning Bear answered for the Indians. He did not see how the soldier chief could hire men as scouts when there was no enemy to watch, but all the same they would be happy to be paid for it. As for coming to the agency, they would have to give this matter long and careful thought. For one thing, there was not enough grass and water for their ponies. (This was true; the 5,000 people already at Pine Ridge had seen to that.) For an-

6. Boyd, *Recent Indian Wars*, pp. 245–46. *Nebraska State Journal* (Lincoln), Dec. 7, 1890.

other, even if they did decide to come in, it would take a long time. The old men and women had no ponies to ride; nor were there enough to pull the wagons. Shifting finally to a happier topic, Turning Bear hoped in conclusion that the delegates would be given something to eat before beginning the long journey back to the Stronghold. Brooke consented, and all moved over to the warehouse for a grand feast and, for entertainment, a squaw dance.[7]

General Brooke interpreted Turning Bear's remarks rather more optimistically than the facts warranted. "The result of the council," he wired Miles, "is that they will come in and camp near here at such points as may be agreed upon. . . . The prospect is that trouble with the Indians is in a fair way to speedy settlement."[8] Brooke was elated with the day's work and was more than a little chagrined to learn Miles' reaction: "The Division Commander," telegraphed the assistant adjutant general, "directs me to say that he deprecates any extended council with the hostiles further than to give them to understand that your orders and instructions are to be obeyed implicity. After they do so there will be ample time and opportunity given them to make known any grievances or ask favors."[9]

Brooke was hurt and annoyed. Slightly misrepresenting the situation, he replied that "there was no talk of grievances; the Indians wanted to know my wishes which they heard and promised to obey." But when Miles read the newspapers next day, December 7, he was even more certain that the negotiations had been mismanaged. Again he telegraphed Brooke. The press dispatches, he said, "seemed to indicate that you were not master of the situation at that place." If the newspapers were correct, Brooke had promised food and jobs but said nothing about the

7. Omaha *Daily Bee,* Dec. 7, 1890. Boyd, p. 236 (quoting press dispatches). W. F. Kelley (reporter for *Nebraska State Journal*), "The Indian Troubles and the Battle of Wounded Knee," *Transactions and Reports of the Nebraska State Historical Society, 4* (1892), 36. Brooke to the contrary notwithstanding, these sources all agree and are internally sound.

8. Miles to Adjt. Gen., Dec. 6, 1890, repeating Brooke to Miles, same date. Corbin to Brooke, same date.

9. Miles to Adjt. Gen., Dec. 6, 1890, repeating Brooke to Miles, same date. Miles to Brooke (two telegrams), Dec. 7, 1890.

depredations committed against the property of the friendlies, nothing about the theft of government beef from the herd camp, and nothing about the necessity for the rebels subordinating themselves absolutely to the authority of the Government. "I must call your attention," he emphasized, "to my original order not to allow the command to be mixed up with the Indians in any way or to be taken at disadvantage. This will apply not only in a military sense but in a diplomatic." Brooke protested, and Miles, having made his point, soothed the injured pride. Then he began laying plans to go to Dakota himself and exercise closer control of the situation.

Brooke had not, as he thought, persuaded the Two Strike people to surrender, but he had started them thinking about the comforts of the agency. When the chiefs left Pine Ridge for the journey back to the Stronghold, Louis Shangreau, a half-breed scout, and thirty-two friendlies went along, apparently to gain information and if possible to talk with the other hostiles.[10]

At the Stronghold camp, Shangreau and his escort found a Ghost Dance in full swing. The Indians refused to suspend it even long enough to hold a council, and it continued with unabated fury for thirty hours. Then Short Bull called an intermission to hear what Shangreau had to say. The scout made a strong plea for the dancers to surrender. "The agent would forgive you if you would return now and would give you more rations," he told them, "but [would] not permit you to dance." Crow Dog spoke up in opposition to accepting the proposal. So did Two Strike. In his absence, several warriors of his band had visited a trader's store on Cheyenne River. A group of cowboys,

10. The only detailed sources for the Shangreau mission are press dispatches giving its result, summarized in Boyd, pp. 205–10. The essentials of these accounts are confirmed by several telegrams from Brooke to Miles, which, however, do not mention Shangreau. The scout later stated that he went by Brooke's authority, although what his orders contemplated is hazy. I have assumed that he accompanied Two Strike and his associates, for the timing of later events makes it obvious that, if he did not go with Two Strike, he left within a matter of hours afterward. Supporting sources for the following construction are Brooke to Miles, Dec. 9, 11, 12, 14, and 15, 1890; Colby, pp. 150–51; and Shangreau's statement to T. A. Bland in Bland, p. 9.

trigger happy or simply scared, opened fire on the Indians and killed one. The episode weakened whatever hold Brooke's arguments had gained on the mind of the old chief. Short Bull delivered the answer:

I have risen to-day to tell you something of importance. You have heard the words of the brothers from the agency camps, and if you have done as myself you have weighed them carefully. If the Great Father would permit us to continue the dance, would give more rations, and quit taking away portions of the reservation, I would be in favor of returning. But even if you [turning to Shangreau] say that he will, how can we discern whether you are telling the truth? We have been lied to so many times that we will not believe any words that your agent sends us. If we return he will take away our guns and ponies, put some of us in jail for stealing cattle and plundering houses [all of which was probably true]. We prefer to stay here and die, if necessary, to loss of liberty. We are free now and have plenty of beef, can dance all the time in obedience to the command of Great Wakantanka. We tell you to return to your agent and say to him that the Dakotas in the Bad Lands are not going to come in.[11]

The dance resumed, and for two days Shangreau could not get it stopped for another council, although it is likely that he used the time advantageously to work on individuals. At noon on the third day, probably December 10, the headmen sat down for another talk. Old Two Strike suddenly rose and, inexplicably reversing his earlier stand, announced that he had decided to take his people to the agency. Crow Dog stood up and declared that he, too, believed the time had come to surrender. Shangreau had driven the fatal wedge in the unity of the chiefs, but he had not reckoned on the fanaticism of Short Bull. The apostle sprang to his feet and shouted, "At such a time as this we should all stick together like brothers. Do not leave; remain with us. These men from the agency are not telling the truth;

11. Quoted in Boyd, pp. 207–08.

they will conduct you back to the agency and place you in jail there. Louis is at the bottom of this affair. I know he is a traitor; kill him, kill him!"[12]

Some of Short Bull's warriors clubbed their Winchesters and rushed at Shangreau. The friendlies formed a screen around the scout, and Two Strike's men hastened to the rescue. Instantly the village was a scene of brawling chaos. It had happened before. Many times in past years factional quarrels within a band had exploded in a paroxysm of brief but bloody violence. The pandemonium that now reigned in the Stronghold followed the pattern of past affairs. Mounted and afoot, the warriors raced to and fro, yelling, charging, firing arrows and rifles, swinging clubs. Several went down, dead or wounded. Suddenly Crow Dog—murderer of Spotted Tail, opportunist, master diplomat and dramatist—sat down in the midst of the turmoil and drew his blanket over his head. The din gradually subsided and all eyes turned on the shrouded figure. When the silence was complete, Crow Dog cried out that he could not bear to see Sioux shed their own blood. Then, slowly rising, he announced, "I am going back to White Clay [Pine Ridge]; you can kill me if you want to, now, and prevent my starting. The agent's words are true, and it is better to return than to stay here. I am not afraid to die."[13]

Crow Dog's dramatic intervention restored order. The proponents of peace, now numbering well over half the camp, struck their tepees, loaded their wagons, and set forth with Shangreau and the friendlies on the journey to the agency. This was too much for the dance faction. The defectors had gone only two miles when the rest of the Brulés, having struck camp also, caught up and joined the cavalcade. Plodding along on their ponies, however, Short Bull and Kicking Bear were seized with visions of military prison. Four miles later, they and about 200 die-hards again changed their minds and turned back to the Stronghold.

A courier brought word of Shangreau's triumph to Brooke on the morning of December 11, and joyfully he telegraphed Miles

12. Quoted in ibid., pp. 208–09.
13. Quoted in ibid., p. 209.

the good news. There was now nothing to be done but wait for the Two Strike Brulés to make their tedious way to the agency and hope that they suffered no second thoughts en route. Then the matter of Short Bull and Kicking Bear could be reconsidered.

Brooke's policy of conciliation seemed to be achieving good results, but this did not mollify the correspondents who had come to report a war, and their dispatches condemned him with increasing bitterness. The settlers around the reservation also grew loud in their denunciation of his reluctance to force the issue. Although Brooke would not unleash the regulars, the sixty-two ranchers and cowboys mustered by Col. H. M. Day into the South Dakota militia were spoiling for a fight. Patrolling Cheyenne River on the eastern flank of the Black Hills, they skirmished with the warriors who had returned to the Stronghold after the defection of Two Strike. During the week of December 14, Day's command collided four times with parties of Indians. On the 15th, eighteen of the militiamen crossed the Cheyenne and rode up Battle Creek Draw toward the Stronghold. The Sioux came out in force and drove the intruders back across the river. In another clash, at Phinney's Ranch, between Spring and Battle Creeks, Day and ten men stood off a party of Sioux for four hours. The Indians set fire to the corral and, while the whites fought it, ignited the prairie, too. A fortunate shift in the wind saved the defenders, and the warriors withdrew.

On the 12th, one of the reporters, Will Cressey of the Omaha *Bee,* saw some action. George Cosgrove, a rancher, and twelve cowboys rode into Day's camp to report that a party of Sioux had been seen near Daly's Ranch, at the mouth of Battle Creek, and declared their intention to return to the ranch and lie in ambush. Cressey went along. The cowboys posted themselves behind a woodpile at Daly's Ranch and waited. In half an hour the Indians approached the ranch. One started to ride through the gate, and a cowboy, Fred Thompson, fired. The warrior fell to the ground, and his pony galloped into a nearby field. The other whites instantly poured a volley into the rest of the Indians, and two more were seen to fall from their mounts. The two sides then exchanged fire until nightfall, with two further casualties among the Indians and one cowboy seriously wounded in the shoulder. As the Indians were withdrawing, Colonel Day and two more men rode up and exchanged shots with the departing Sioux.[14]

In Chicago, General Miles prepared to take the field. Before leaving, however, he fired another salvo at the Interior Department. Secretary Noble's order of December 1 merely subordinated the agents to the Army commanders on each reservation in strictly military matters. This was not enough for Miles. Much had been accomplished in Dakota, he wrote his superiors, but the problem had by no means been solved, "and will not in my opinion until action is taken, placing the Sioux nation of five [actually seven] different tribes, together with the Cheyenne tribe under such control and government as to make them cease to desire war, and make it impracticable for them ever to resume hostilities with any hope of success." The solution was obvious: "Nothing but the firm strong arm of the military power can govern them. This will be necessary for several months, if not for a term of years." To avoid division of authority and such "interference with the plans of the military as there has been recently"—a slap at McLaughlin—Miles would replace the civil agents with Army officers backed by a strong force of troops at each agency. These officers, whom he recommended by name, had more than twenty-five years of service each, long experience on the frontier, and outstanding records of Indian management.[15] Dropping his plan in the mail, Miles boarded a train for Dakota. He intended to make his headquarters, for the time being, at Rapid City, on the eastern edge of the Black Hills.

Rattling across the barren prairies of northern Nebraska, Miles received progress reports from Pine Ridge. With Two Strike coming in, Brooke was confident that no more Indians could be detached from the recalcitrants through diplomacy. It now remained to clean out the hostile camp by force. He proposed to have Carr and the Sixth Cavalry move down from Rapid Creek and blockade all escape routes north of the Stronghold, while Brooke himself led the force at Pine Ridge in an assault on the fortress-like table from the south. Miles disliked the idea. He

14. Omaha *Daily Bee*, Dec. 14 and 19, 1890.
15. Miles to Adjt. Gen., Dec. 11, 1890.

scribbled a reply and handed it to the telegraph operator when the train paused at Long Pine, Nebraska. "You may be sure those Indians will not stand a fight with any such force," he informed Brooke, "but would slip out through some pass as they have done many times leaving all the troops far in the rear." Instead, Miles believed that the cavalry should be deployed in three strong columns around the tableland to bottle up the rebels and hold them until winter closed down in earnest. Then, with cold and snow enervating Indians and ponies alike, the troops could much more readily march in and make short work of any opposition that developed.[16]

Brooke was inclined to debate the point, but once more the spotlight suddenly shifted to Standing Rock. On December 15, as the first elements of Two Strike's caravan began straggling into Pine Ridge Agency (the rest arrived on the 16th, for a total of 900 Brulés in 184 lodges), Indian policemen rode into the Grand River settlement with orders to arrest Sitting Bull.

16. Brooke to Miles, Dec. 15 and 16 (five telegrams), 1890. Miles to Brooke, Dec. 16 (two telegrams).

9. THE END OF SITTING BULL

JAMES MCLAUGHLIN believed that if the Standing Rock Indians were to continue their march toward civilization, Sitting Bull and a few other leaders with similar reactionary tendencies would have to be removed from the reservation. The old chief's role in the Ghost Dance only gave the inevitable task a certain immediacy. Now the arrest would have to be accomplished before spring, when the dancers, daily anticipating the prophesied millennium, would rise to new heights of emotionalism, and when Sitting Bull's presence in their midst would be most incendiary. In the balmy November of 1890, however, the arrest was not of compelling urgency; in fact, in McLaughlin's view, delay was essential. Deep snow and freezing temperature vastly extended the limit of provocation Indians would endure when resistance involved the certainty of winter warfare.

McLaughlin desired carte blanche to deal with the matter when and how he saw fit. He felt confident of his ability to confine the Ghost Dance to the Grand River camps throughout the winter. He would wait until the weather became severe, then, on a day of his own selection, send his policemen to Grand River to make the arrest. Meanwhile, as proposed to the Indian Office on November 19, he would open an offensive on the Ghost Dance by cutting off rations to all who refused to admit the error of their ways.

The Indian Bureau did not sanction the plan to withhold rations—in fact, did not even reply to the proposal. And the Army upset the plan for arresting Sitting Bull at a time chosen by McLaughlin.

The President's directive of November 13 assigned the War Department responsibility for suppressing any outbreak among the Sioux. McLaughlin seems to have regarded this as designed chiefly to meet exigencies on the other Sioux reservations and as applying to Standing Rock only in a formal sense. General Ruger and Colonel Drum apparently shared this view, and were inclined to let the agent have a free hand. But General Miles plainly felt otherwise, and in sending Buffalo Bill to arrest Sitting Bull he had announced his own assumption that military authority extended to Standing Rock as well. The assumption gained added force on December 1 when McLaughlin, together with the other Sioux agents, received instructions to "cooperate with and obey the orders of the military officer commanding on the reservation in your charge," instructions that Miles had gone to Washington to advocate.[1]

Nor did the general concur in McLaughlin's desire for delay. He had reports (almost certainly erroneous) that Sitting Bull was caching arms and attempting to unite all the tribes of the Northwest in a grand alliance to make war on the whites, and Miles regarded his imprisonment as a matter of utmost urgency. The abortive Cody mission broadcast Miles' intentions and in his view made a prompt arrest all the more imperative.

Two fears now haunted the Standing Rock agent. The first was that Miles, who made little effort to conceal his hostility toward McLaughlin, would again order the arrest of Sitting Bull without consulting the authorities on the scene and thus choose an inopportune time. From a desk in Chicago, the weather and the temper of Sitting Bull's followers could hardly be gauged

1. See above, p. 128.

with any degree of accuracy. The second and stronger fear was that the general would insist on the soldiers at Fort Yates, rather than the Indian police, making the arrest. Since the arrival of troops at Pine Ridge on November 20, countless rumors of military movements or intended movements had swept the Grand River settlements. The dancers were so wrought up that the mere appearance of bluecoats, regardless of their mission, would in McLaughlin's opinion touch off fighting. Moreover, Sitting Bull's spies kept Fort Yates under constant surveillance, ready to speed warning to him if troops marched in the direction of Grand River, while McLaughlin could have sufficient men in place at any time simply by augmenting the police detachment already stationed in the Grand River district.

In the early days of December, McLaughlin and Drum discussed the problem and agreed upon a course of action. McLaughlin would move the Grand River police into the Sitting Bull settlement at dawn on one of the biweekly ration days, when most of the Indians would be at the agency. Under cover of night, Drum would send a command from Fort Yates to take station within supporting distance. The police would make the arrest, and if anything went wrong the troops would charge to the rescue. As their carefully laid plans might be upset at any moment by General Miles, the two officials immediately and quietly determined to seize the first good opportunity.

Colonel Drum's command consisted of Troops F and G, Eighth Cavalry, and Companies G and H of his own regiment, the Twelfth Infantry. He assigned the supporting mission to the cavalry and briefed Capt. E. G. Fechet and his officers on what was intended. Detachments were designated and drilled in operation of the Hotchkiss and Gatling guns. Rations, grain, extra ammunition, buffalo overcoats, and horse covers were packed and set aside, ready for instant loading into the spring escort wagon and ambulance that were to accompany the command.[2]

McLaughlin promptly strengthened the Grand River force. For several weeks the police had been hauling logs with which

2. Maj. E. G. Fechet, "The True Story of the Death of Sitting Bull," *Proceedings and Collections of the Nebraska State Historical Society*, 2d ser. 2 (1898), 181–82. Reprinted from *Cosmopolitan*, 20 (1896).

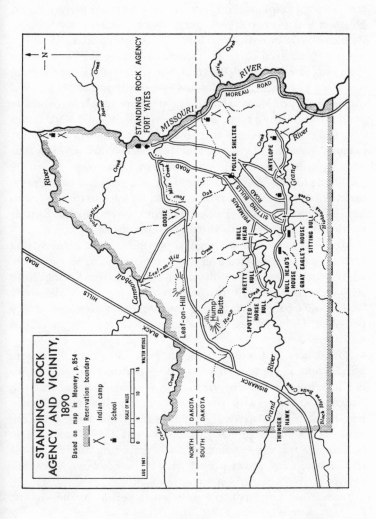

STANDING ROCK
AGENCY AND VICINITY,
1890

Based on map in Mooney, p.854

▨ Reservation boundary

⋏ Indian camp

◼ School

SCALE OF MILES

0   5   10   15

WALTER WEDGE

AUG 1961

to build a halfway shelter where the road from Standing Rock to Grand River crossed Oak Creek. McLaughlin used this project as a pretext for assigning additional policemen to the district. He soon had twenty-one on duty, under Lieutenant Afraid-of-Bear, better known as Bull Head, and Sergeant Shave Head.

Bull Head lived three miles west of Sitting Bull's camp, on the south side of Grand River. A fine specimen of Indian manhood, he was courageous, resourceful, and completely devoted to McLaughlin. Shave Head, too, was thoroughly dependable and had made a big name by killing a bully named Red Thunder. Bull Head took his assignment all the more seriously for personal reasons. There had long been bad blood between him and Catch-the-Bear, Sitting Bull's principal lieutenant. As Sitting Bull had publicly backed Catch-the-Bear, he too had been drawn into the feud. Bull Head rather looked forward to the day when he would receive orders from the agent to arrest Sitting Bull. It would help to quench his thirst for vengeance.[3]

Meanwhile, he and his men kept vigilant watch on Sitting Bull's camp and reported every occurrence to John M. Carignan, whose school stood three miles down the river from Sitting Bull's settlement. Carignan in turn sent frequent reports to McLaughlin by police courier. As Sitting Bull well knew, few events happened on Grand River of which the agent for long remained uninformed.

The dances continued, Sitting Bull presiding over them from a handsome lodge erected several hundred feet in front of his cabin. When not dancing, he and his men held long councils in the cabin he shared with his two wives, his children, and a fluctuating number of relatives. The chief's son Crow Foot, a solemn youth of seventeen, joined all the talks and displayed a wisdom remarkable for one so young. He was preparing himself for the chieftainship and never played with the other boys. "He grew old too early," recalled one who knew him.[4]

Aside from Carignan, the only white person in the vicinity

3. For the details of this quarrel see Vestal, *Sitting Bull*, pp. 251–52, 273–74; and Fiske, *Life and Death of Sitting Bull*, p. 50.

4. Robert P. High Eagle, "Note on Crow Foot," in Vestal, *New Sources of Indian History*, pp. 55–56.

was Mary Collins, the purposeful Congregational missionary. She tried hard to lead Sitting Bull to renounce the Ghost Dance and put a stop to it among his people. As she later remembered it, he admitted his lack of faith in the doctrine but declared that he had gone too far to turn back now.[5] Gall, too, worked against the dance. Once a mighty chief, he had led the Hunkpapas in the shattering assault that overwhelmed Custer. Now, still a personification of dignity and strength, he helped the agent guide the Hunkpapas along the white man's road. At his camp on the Missouri near the mouth of Grand River, he held councils with all who would come, eloquently pleading for an end to the dance and a return to the white man's church and school. His efforts bore fruit when Running Horse and his whole band defected from the standard of Sitting Bull.[6]

The weather at last turned cold, and on December 5 it began to snow. The next day was ration day, when most of the Grand River people would be at the agency. McLaughlin wired Washington: "Everything quiet at present; weather cold and snowing. Am I authorized to arrest Sitting Bull and other fomentors of mischief when I think best?"[7] McLaughlin's request arrived in Washington at a bad time. As we have seen, the Cody affair at Standing Rock and Agent Dixon's wholesale arrests at Lower Brulé had led the President to review the question of arrests.[8] Only the day before, he had passed his decision on to Secretary Noble. Although Acting Commissioner Belt favored giving McLaughlin free rein, Noble, probably with relief, could fall back on the policy set by the White House. McLaughlin had his answer the same day, December 5, and all the other Sioux agents received similar messages: "Secretary directs that you make no arrests whatever except under orders of the military or upon an order of the Secretary of the Interior."[9]

5. Collins, "Autobiography," pp. 68–72. Robinson, "Sidelights on Character of Sitting Bull," pp. 191–92.

6. Gall to McLaughlin, Nov. 29, 1890, in Vestal, *New Sources of Indian History*, p. 40. Williams to Adjt. Gen., Dec. 1, 1890.

7. McLaughlin to CIA, Dec. 5, 1890.

8. See above, pp. 126, 131.

9. Belt to Sec. Int., Dec. 5, 1890. Sec. Int. to CIA, same date. Belt to McLaughlin, same date.

General Miles now held the high cards. On December 10 he had a confidential telegram sent to General Ruger ordering him to "direct the Commanding Officer Fort Yates to secure the person of Sitting Bull, using any practical means. The agent at that post is under his direction and orders for any purpose of this kind or any purpose affecting the police, control and government of these Indians." For some reason, Ruger delayed passing the word to Colonel Drum until December 12, then wired him in cipher to "make it your especial duty to secure the person of Sitting Bull. Call on Indian agent to cooperate and render such assistance as will best promote the purpose in view."[10]

Ruger and Drum were still inclined to follow McLaughlin's lead. Drum took the telegram to agency headquarters, and he and McLaughlin decided to carry out their original plan. The next ration day was December 20, and they set this as the date for the coup.

Events were already shaping that would upset the timetable. Sitting Bull had received an invitation from Short Bull and Kicking Bear to join them in the Stronghold. In council, the Grand River headmen agreed that their leader ought to go. On the 11th a courier brought Sitting Bull a message from the agent ordering the dancers to disperse to their homes. That night the headmen assembled at Sitting Bull's cabin and discussed both matters. Sitting Bull addressed a letter to McLaughlin, dictating it to his semiliterate son-in-law Andrew Fox. Fox had considerable trouble putting the Hunkpapa thoughts into English, but two salient points emerged from the nearly incoherent result. First, McLaughlin should quit meddling in the religious affairs of the Indians—in other words, the people had no intention of giving up the Ghost Dance and going home. And second, "I got to go to Agency & to know this Pray"—in other words, he had to go to Pine Ridge to learn more about the faith from those who best knew its tenets. A member of the chief's personal bodyguard, Bull Ghost, rode to Standing Rock with the letter and handed it to McLaughlin on the evening of the 12th, several

10. Corbin by command of Miles to Ruger, Dec. 10, 1890. Barber to CO Ft Yates, Dec. 12, in CIA, *Annual Report* (1891), p. 333.

hours after Drum had brought over the order for Sitting Bull's arrest.[11]

The very thought of Sitting Bull's presence at Pine Ridge made McLaughlin shudder. Short Bull and Kicking Bear were smalltime medicine men who, as undoubted authorities on the Ghost Dance, had catapulted to fame. The people looked to them as apostles of the religion but accorded them decidedly less respect as temporal leaders. The defection of Two Strike and his people amply demonstrated this truth. A leader with the towering stature of Sitting Bull was another matter. If he succeeded in reaching the Stronghold, the Pine Ridge situation might well blow up in General Brooke's face.

But as Sitting Bull's letter to McLaughlin gave no indication of when he planned to depart for Pine Ridge, there appeared no reason to move the date of the arrest forward. Immediately after reading the letter, however, McLaughlin had his interpreter, Louis Primeau, dash off a quick note to Lieutenant Bull Head. A policeman, White Bird, carried it to Grand River. The message alerted Bull Head that Sitting Bull might try to leave the reservation and cautioned him to keep close watch on the dance camp for any such move. Under pretext of beginning construction of the halfway shelter on Oak Creek, the lieutenant was to gather in all the policemen strung along Grand River. If Sitting Bull tried to leave, "you must stop him and if he does not listen to you do as you see fit, use your own discretion in the matter and it will be all right."[12]

McLaughlin also sent verbal instructions by Sergeant Shave Head, who happened to be at the agency. The sergeant was to inform Bull Head that orders had arrived for the seizure of Sitting Bull. When the time came, McLaughlin would give the word.

11. It is difficult to believe Sitting Bull so naive as to think McLaughlin might grant him a pass to go to Pine Ridge, but it seems clear from Carignan's letter, quoted below, that this was indeed the hope. Stanley Vestal (*Sitting Bull*, pp. 287–90) implies further that Sitting Bull did not plan to go at all unless and until he received a pass. I believe the testimony of Carignan and Bull Head of the active travel preparations in Sitting Bull's camp is adequate contradiction of this assumption. Vestal prints the Sitting Bull letter, pp. 283–84.

12. Primeau to Bull Head, Dec. 12, 1890, in Vestal, *New Sources of Indian History*, p. 12.

If Sitting Bull tried to leave the reservation before that time, Bull Head was to act on his own initiative, for the chief's flight had to be blocked by any means. That same night, Shave Head and a handful of agency policemen started for Grand River. The next morning, December 13, another eight men under Sgt. John Eagle Man left the agency bound for Oak Creek, ostensibly to help build the shelter.[13]

This same Saturday the 13th, Bull Head learned of another council at Sitting Bull's cabin in which the headmen had agreed that their chief should leave for Pine Ridge on Monday the 15th. They immediately began to corral their horses and make other preparations for the trip. On the night of the 13th Bull Head reported these developments to John Carignan, who shortly after midnight drafted a report to McLaughlin. It read in part:

> Sitting Bull has received a letter from the Pine Ridge outfit, asking him to come over there as God was to appear to them. Sitting Bull's people want him to go, but he has sent a letter to you asking your permission, and if you do not give it, he is going to go anyway; he has been fitting up his horses to stand a long ride and will go horseback in case he is pursued.
>
> Bull Head would like to arrest him at once before he has a chance of giving them the slip, as he thinks that if he gets the start, it will be impossible to catch him. He says to send word to him by courier immediately.[14]

Carignan entrusted the letter to Hawk Man, one of twenty special policemen recently authorized as temporary additions to the force. He began the forty-mile ride immediately.

Late the following afternoon, December 14, Hawk Man dashed into the agency on a lathered pony. Colonel Drum saw him rein up at the agent's office and walked over to learn the news. He found McLaughlin reading the letter from Carignan.

13. McLaughlin's annual report, Aug. 26, 1891, in CIA, *Annual Report* (1891), pp. 334–35. This source reproduces practically all the correspondence that passed between McLaughlin and the Indian Office during these critical weeks.

14. Carignan to McLaughlin, Dec. 14, 12:30 A.M., in Vestal, *New Sources of Indian History*, pp. 13–14. See also Carignan's narrative in Fiske, p. 44.

No longer could they hope to defer the arrest until the next ration day. Both agreed that it must be made the following morning, December 15. Together, they drafted instructions for Bull Head:

> From report brought by Scout "Hawk Man," I believe that the time has arrived for the arrest of Sitting Bull and it can be made by the Indian police without much risk. I therefore desire you to make the arrest before daylight tomorrow morning, and try and get back to the Sitting Bull road crossing of Oak Creek by daylight to-morrow morning or as soon thereafter as possible. The Cavalry will leave to-night and reach the Sitting Bull crossing of Oak Creek before daylight to-morrow morning (Monday), where they will remain until they hear from you.
>
> Louis Primeau will accompany the Cavalry command as guide, and I desire you to send a messenger to the Cavalry as soon as you can after making the arrest, so that the troops may know how to act in aiding you or preventing any attempt of his followers from rescuing him.
>
> I have ordered all the police at Oak Creek to proceed to Carignan's school and await your orders. This gives you a force of 42 policemen for the arrest.
>
> Very respectfully,
James McLaughlin,
U.S. Indian Agent.
>
> P.S. You must not let him escape under any circumstances.[15]

At 5:45 that evening Second Sergeant Red Tomahawk galloped out of Standing Rock with two copies of these orders—one in English, the other in Santee Sioux. Another courier left with a similar message for Carignan. At almost exactly the same hour, the officers at Fort Yates were gathering for after-dinner cigars when "officers' call" sent them scurrying to post headquarters. By 11 P.M. the wagons had been loaded, and as the cavalry troopers sat down to a hot dinner, Colonel Drum, Agent Mc-

15. This is reproduced in Vestal, *Sitting Bull*, p. 282, and in McLaughlin, *My Friend the Indian*, pp. 217–18.

Laughlin, and Captain Fechet assembled in Drum's office to go over the captain's orders. They agreed that, instead of halting at Oak Creek, the cavalry should move ten to twelve miles closer to Grand River, in order to be within more effective supporting distance of the police. At midnight, Troops F and G, Eighth Cavalry, moved out behind Captain Fechet. There were five officers and ninety-nine enlisted men, two wagons, a Hotchkiss gun, and a Gatling gun.[16]

Red Tomahawk reached Bull Head's cabin at 10:15 that night, having ridden the forty miles from Standing Rock in only four and one-half hours. Unfamiliar with the roads, he had taken the wrong crossing of Oak Creek and thus had missed Sergeant Eagle Man. Bull Head selected Iron Thunder, who weighed only 135 pounds, to race back to Oak Creek, eighteen miles distant. He was to tell Eagle Man to join the rest of the police at Sitting Bull's house promptly at daybreak.

About 1:00 A.M. John Carignan and two more policemen from downriver came in. Following the road, they had passed directly through Sitting Bull's camp. The nightly orgy of dancing had ended, and the silent camp, dimly lit by the dying embers of the fires, resounded with the clatter of Carignan's buggy. Dogs began to bark, and an Indian came out of his lodge to investigate. In the darkness, he could not make out the identity of the intruders, but accepted their explanation that they were destined for the agency. Thirty policemen had now assembled at Bull Head's cabin.

It was a solemn gathering. Even before Bull Head asked Chaska, the local interpreter, to read the orders brought by Red Tomahawk, the men knew that the moment they had been dreading had come at last. Devoted as they were to Bull Head and McLaughlin, reprehensible as they considered Sitting Bull's recent activities, they could not shake a haunting uneasiness over the role in which they had been cast. They were Sioux, some of them Hunkpapa Sioux. They were about to set forth to challenge other Hunkpapas in the name of the white man and to

16. Fechet, pp. 182–84. Drum to Asst. Adjt. Gen. Dept. of Dak., Feb. 27, 1891, enclosing Fechet to Post Adjt. Fort Yates, Dec. 17, 1890, and Special Orders, No. 247, Fort Yates, Dec. 14, 1890, in Sec. War, *Annual Report* (1891), *1*, 194–99.

perform a mission that few believed could be accomplished without shedding Hunkpapa blood. "We all felt sad," recalled John Lone Man.[17]

After McLaughlin's instructions had been read, Bull Head outlined the plan for taking the chief. They would move first to Gray Eagle's house, a short distance east of Bull Head's. Then, just before dawn, they would ride quickly to a position south of the river across from Sitting Bull's camp. As the dancers would expect any threat to come from the direction of the agency, Bull Head hoped that his column, approaching from the opposite direction, would be less readily discovered. Promptly at dawn, the police would cross the river and quietly surround Sitting Bull's cabin. The officers would enter and make the arrest.

Carignan knew the route proposed by Bull Head. Recalling that McLaughlin had stressed the necessity of taking a light spring wagon in which to spirit Sitting Bull away before his people could rally, the teacher spoke up. "How about the spring buggy you are going to use to take Sitting Bull to the agency? You can't take it over that rough trail on the south side of the river." Bull Head had decided, however, not to use a wagon. Instead, while the officers were inside the cabin, Red Bear and White Bird were to saddle Sitting Bull's favorite horse, an old gray circus animal presented to him by Buffalo Bill, and have it ready for the chief to mount as soon as the arrest had been made.

The police rode over to Gray Eagle's house and waited, passing the time by telling war stories of old. At 4:30 A.M. Eagle Man rode in with nine men. Rather than go directly from Oak Creek to Sitting Bull's, as directed by the lieutenant, he had ridden to Bull Head's, then followed to Gray Eagle's. He had no wish, he explained, to risk another Little Bighorn affair. There, Custer had charged in two parties, and bad timing had led to disaster. This time Sitting Bull must confront his aggressors all at once.

Back at Bull Head's, Carignan brewed a pot of coffee and

17. John Lone Man, trans. Robert High Eagle, "The Arrest and Killing of Sitting Bull," in Vestal, *New Sources of Indian History*, p. 48. My account of the events of the night of Dec. 14 is drawn from this source and from Carignan's narrative in Fiske.

lingered over a cup before climbing into his buggy for the long, cold ride to the agency. At Gray Eagle's the police, now numbering thirty-nine plus four volunteers, knelt in the predawn blackness and prayed to the white man's God, then went outside and mounted. "Hopo," commanded Bull Head, and the column trotted toward the river.

A freezing drizzle made the ride miserable, and the mantle of depression that settled on the horsemen grew heavier as they wound through the icy thickets of the river bottom. Owls hooted and coyotes howled. Even they gave warning, remarked one of the men, "so beware." At 5:30 A.M., in the gray half-light of dawn, the police forded the river behind Sitting Bull's house, then fanned out and rushed into the village at a gallop. Instantly the packs of dogs set up a noisy barking.

At Sitting Bull's the police dismounted and swiftly surrounded the cabin. Red Bear and White Bird ran back to the corral to saddle the gray circus horse. Bull Head, flanked by Shave Head and Red Tomahawk, sprang to the door and pounded on it; Lone Man took station to one side. The knock woke Sitting Bull and he called out, "How, all right, come in."[18] The officers entered. One struck a match, sought out a kerosene lamp, and lit it. Sitting Bull crawled out from under the blankets of his pallet. In the nude, he looked wholly insignificant and breathed none of the defiance that might have been expected under the circumstances.

"I come after you to take you to the agency," said Bull Head. "You are under arrest." The old chief submitted meekly. "How," he replied, "let me put on my clothes and go with you." One of his wives brought his clothing, and he slowly dressed himself. By now Crow Foot was up, too. Sitting Bull told him to go saddle a horse, but Bull Head interrupted to say that this had already been taken care of. As the officers and their prisoner started through the door, the wife began to howl—an Indian custom, said Lone Man, of saying goodbye.

18. Sources for the following paragraphs are Lone Man; McLaughlin's annual report, Aug. 26, 1891; Fechet, pp. 184–89; reports of Drum and Fechet cited in note 16; Fiske, pp. 50–52; and, although my version differs in important respects, Vestal, *Sitting Bull,* chap. 38.

Outside the police were already in trouble. Barking dogs and, finally, the cry of Sitting Bull's wife had roused the whole camp. It bustled with excited Indians, all converging on the cabin of their chief. They pressed tightly on the cordon of police, many of whom, recently recruited, grew frightened and unsure of themselves. From the doorway the officers emerged with Sitting Bull, Shave Head on the left, Bull Head on the right, and Red Tomahawk behind. The prisoner's horse was not ready yet, and the four men stood, waiting, in front of the door. The crowd, bristling with anger, now included most of the camp.

Catch-the-Bear shouldered his way through the mob. Beside himself with hate, he surveyed the scene in front of the cabin. Here was his chief, whom he had sworn to defend and to whom he was personally devoted, being abducted by his mortal enemy, Bull Head. The day of reckoning had come. "Now, here are the ceska maza [metal breasts]," he said scornfully, so all could hear, "just as we had expected all the time. You think you are going to take him. You shall not do it." Turning to the people behind him, he commanded, "Come on now, let us protect our chief!"

Some of the men began to work through the police line and press closer to Sitting Bull. Crow Foot, the youth who had grown up too fast, came out of the cabin and chided his father. "Well, you always called yourself a brave chief. Now you are allowing yourself to be taken by the ceska maza." This was too much for the old man. His people expected more of him; they only awaited his command to fall upon the metal breasts. "Then I shall not go," he declared.

The horse had finally been readied and brought around. Bull Head implored Sitting Bull to go peaceably. "Come now," he begged, "do not listen to anyone." "Uncle," Lone Man added, "nobody is going to hurt you. The agent wants to see you and then you are to come back—so please do not let others lead you into any trouble." But the chief hung back. Bull Head and Shave Head grasped his arms and pulled. Red Tomahawk pushed from behind. The people went wild, shook their fists, cursed the policemen, and shouted, "You shall not take our chief." "The police tried to keep order," recalled Lone Man, but "it was like trying to extinguish a treacherous prairie fire."

At this moment Catch-the-Bear threw off his blanket and shouldered his Winchester. Bringing Bull Head into the sights, he pulled the trigger. The bullet tore into the officer's right side and sent him sprawling. As he fell, he turned his revolver on Sitting Bull and shot him full in the chest. At the same instant, Red Tomahawk fired another bullet into the back of his head. The mighty chief of the Hunkpapas dropped to the ground, dead. Lone Man sprang at the smoking muzzle of the Winchester that had gunned his beloved relative and superior, Bull Head. Again Catch-the-Bear pulled the trigger, but the hammer snapped. Lone Man tore the rifle from Catch-the-Bear's grasp, clubbed him with the butt, and shot him dead.

Infuriated, Sitting Bull's followers swarmed over the metal breasts with knives, clubs, and guns. It was a terrible fight at close quarters. The wounded Bull Head caught three more bullets. Sergeant Shave Head fell before the rifle of Strikes-the-Kettle, another of Sitting Bull's top subordinates. Of the assailants, Chiefs Spotted-Horn-Bull and Brave Thunder, together with three other men, went down with mortal wounds. Four more policemen dropped. In the midst of the melee, with bullets lacing the air, Sitting Bull's old horse sat down and began to perform tricks learned during its days with the Wild West show. The police were scared. Had the spirit of the dead chief entered the sitting horse?

In a matter of minutes, the bloody fight ended as abruptly as it began. The dancers broke away and raced to a grove of trees lining the river behind Sitting Bull's cabin. One fired a parting shot that knocked over another policeman. Red Tomahawk now took command and ordered some of the police to drag Bull Head, still alive, into the cabin and make him as comfortable as possible on a pallet.

Inside, one of the men spied a slight movement in a pile of blankets. Lone Man pulled them aside and revealed Crow Foot. The boy cried out, "My uncles, do not kill me. I do not wish to die." The police asked Bull Head what to do. The lieutenant, four bullets in him, looked up from his pallet. "Do what you like with him," he answered bitterly. "He is one of them that has caused this trouble." One of the men struck the boy a staggering blow that sent him reeling across the room and out the door. There, as he lay dazed on the ground, two more policemen pumped bullets into him. Tears streaming down their cheeks, they killed him.

Red Tomahawk summoned Hawk Man No. 1 (the other Hawk Man lay dead outside the cabin) and instructed him to ride fast and bring the soldiers. Hawk Man mounted the gray circus horse and galloped off on the road toward Oak Creek. As he left the battleground, the Sitting Bull people, having rallied, opened fire from the timber. The police took cover in the sheds and corrals behind the cabin, and the two sides exchanged long-range fire.

About three miles north of Grand River, Hawk Man met Captain Fechet and the cavalry squadron. He told the captain that all the police had been killed, he alone escaping. As the troopers prepared for action, stripping off their overcoats and gloves, Fechet scrawled a message to Colonel Drum, informing him of Hawk Man's report and stating that the squadron would rush to the relief of any police who might still be alive. With this letter, Hawk Man rode up the trail toward Standing Rock.

The cavalry formed in two parallel columns of fours, with the artillery between. Fechet had just ordered the advance when another policeman rode up. He reported, more accurately than Hawk Man, that the police were penned up in Sitting Bull's house by the dancers, were almost out of ammunition, and could not hold out much longer. With mounting excitement, the two columns broke into a gallop.

Climbing the last ridge before reaching Grand River Valley, the Hotchkiss gun lurched in a rut and turned over. The harness broke and the mule pulled free. The ambulance, bringing up the rear, halted at the scene of the accident, and Hospital Steward August Nickel jumped out. A giant of a man, he crawled in the back of the ambulance, braced his feet against the tailgate, and took a firm grip on the shafts of the gun carriage. The driver cracked his whip, and the ambulance moved up the slope, pulling the cannon.

From the crest of the ridge, Fechet surveyed the valley. Some 1,500 yards to his front was the Sitting Bull settlement. To his right front, about 900 yards distant, Indians were firing from the top of a knoll at Sitting Bull's cabin. From the timber beyond the cabin came the sound of more firing. And finally, shots were being directed at both places from the cabin. Fechet could not tell friend from foe. He raised a white flag, the signal that had been arranged with the police. None of the parties responded. At Fechet's command, Lt. E. C. Brooks ran the Hotchkiss gun into battery and dropped a shell into the open space between the cabin and the timber. Shortly afterward, a white flag fluttered in front of the cabin. (The shell exploded uncomfortably close to the police. Lone Man tore the white curtain from a window, tied it to a stick, and rushed out waving it at the soldiers.)

Brooks now opened fire on the timber. A few rounds exploded, and the Indians scattered into the hills south of the river. Next he turned the cannon on the knoll to the right front. With shells bursting nearby, these Indians broke for the valley, then veered west and fled up the river to the northwest. Lt. S. L. Slocum dismounted G Troop and pushed a skirmish line into the valley. Lt. E. H. Crowder led F Troop along the top of the ridge to the right to cover Slocum's flank. G Troop moved at double time to the cabin and united with the police, then continued to the river and cleaned out the few remaining Indians, who ran across the river to join their comrades. Upstream, Crowder gave chase to the Hunkpapas fleeing in that direction, but could not catch them. After searching every cabin for a distance of two miles above Sitting Bull's, he led his men back. Slocum and the police had also returned from sweeping out the timber.

The scene around Sitting Bull's house stamped itself on Captain Fechet's memory. "I saw evidence of a most desperate encounter," he later wrote. "In front of the house, and within a radius of 50 yards, were the bodies of 8 dead Indians, including that of Sitting Bull, and 2 dead horses. In the house were 4 dead policemen and 3 wounded, 2 mortally [Bull Head and Shave Head]. To add to the horror of the scene the squaws of Sitting Bull, who were in a small house nearby, kept up a great wailing."[19]

19. Fechet, p. 186.

Some of Policeman John Strong Arm's relatives, who lived in the Grand River settlement, came to where the troops had gathered. In the stable they saw the body of Strong Arm, and they added their fearful wails to those of Sitting Bull's widows. One of the relatives, Holy Medicine, picked up a neckyoke, walked over to the body of Sitting Bull, and with a savage blow smashed in the face. Pvt. Jerry Hart, one of the soldiers, asked, "What the hell did you do that for? The man is dead. Leave him alone."[20] Sgt. James Hanaghan, fearing that the body, lying in a pool of blood, would freeze to the ground, detailed Pvt. A. L. Bloomer to move it and to stand guard in order to prevent further mutilation.

Fires had been kindled, and the soldiers were variously occupied feeding their horses and preparing breakfast. Just as Captain Fechet raised a cup of coffee to his lips, the police shouted an alarm. From the timber only eighty yards distant burst a single Indian. Mounted on a black horse, brandishing a long staff, and singing a ghost song, he raced at full speed toward the soldiers. (This was Crow Woman, one of the most zealous believers in the new faith. He had donned a Ghost Shirt and was demonstrating to his people, who watched from the hills across the river, that it did in fact turn the bullets of the white man.) The police loosed a volley, and the horseman wheeled abruptly back to the shelter of the timber. He emerged some four hundred yards up the valley, and again the fire of the police drove him back to the trees. A third time he galloped into the open, this time passing between two cavalrymen Fechet had sent out as pickets. They opened fire, but the warrior escaped up the valley unscathed. For many Hunkpapas, here indeed was proof of the magical qualities of the Ghost Shirt.

Fechet's orders contemplated the arrest of Sitting Bull but were silent about his followers. Fearing that any pursuit would stir up the friendly Indians and perhaps drive them into the ranks of the dancers, the captain decided to return to Fort Yates. The guards released Sitting Bull's widows, and Fechet told them to get word to the people who had run away that the troops were

20. Fiske, p. 52.

leaving, and any who cared to return home could do so in safety. He also sent runners up and down the valley to notify all Indians who wished to come into the agency that they could accompany the cavalry. A large number, anxious to get out of the battle area, accepted the offer and fell in with the column.

The three wounded policemen, Bull Head, Shave Head, and Middle, were laid in the ambulance for the journey back to Standing Rock. The dead policemen had to share the single wagon with the corpse of Sitting Bull, an arrangement in which their surviving comrades acquiesced only after the most peremptory order from Sergeant Red Tomahawk. The bodies of the men who fell in defense of Sitting Bull were dragged into the stable, to be buried later by Congregational missionary T. L. Riggs. At 1:00 P.M. the cavalcade pointed north and at 6:00 bivouacked at Oak Creek crossing. Near midnight, Colonel Drum marched in with the two companies of infantry from Fort Yates.

Late on the morning of December 16 a messenger from Colonel Drum rode into Standing Rock with news of the tragic events on Grand River. He dispelled the apprehension that had gripped the agency and military post since noon the day before, when Hawk Man had dashed in on Sitting Bull's horse to report that all the police had been killed. Colonel Drum had moved out two hours later with the infantry, and ever since the people left behind had waited anxiously for more news. Now, Drum sent word that he and Fechet had decided that the troops might do much harm by returning to Grand River. Accordingly, they were on their way back to Standing Rock.

At noon, the soldier-teacher at the little school at Fort Yates gave his pupils the rest of the day off. "No school for us this afternoon! No school, and we can see them bring in Sitting Bull!" Seven-year-old Frank Fiske later remembered the scene vividly. First came the dead-wagon, with the bodies of the policemen piled in on top of Sitting Bull. Next came the ambulance with the wounded policemen. Mounted police rode escort, together with the Indians who had accompanied the troops back from Grand River. As the procession passed the trader's store, where young Fiske stood watching, the women were moaning death songs. About a mile behind rode the cavalry; still farther in the rear marched the infantry. The wagons proceeded through the post and into the agency, while the cavalry turned off and halted at the stables.

The dead policemen were laid out in the agency meeting hall and the body of Sitting Bull deposited in the deadhouse behind the Fort Yates hospital. At the small hospital maintained by Catholic Sisters in the agency boarding school, the agency and Army doctors worked hard to save the wounded policemen. Bull Head and Shave Head were beyond help. The latter's stomach had been torn open, and he knew he would die. "Did I do well, father?" he asked McLaughlin. The agent could only nod. "Then I will die in the faith of the white man and to which my five children already belong, and be with them. Send for my wife, that we may be married by the Black Gown before I die." A messenger rode out to bring Shave Head's wife from her home eighteen miles distant. During the night, Shave Head died in the arms of Father Bernard Strassmaier. Fifteen minutes later, the dead man's wife arrived, and sang the death song at his door.[21] Bull Head lingered into the next day. He struggled, reopened his wounds, then died quietly. Middle, the third policeman, recovered.

On the afternoon of December 17, the Standing Rock Indians crowded into the little frame church of Congregational missionary George W. Reed, south of the agency. They filled the pews and lined the walls. Reverend Reed and Father Strassmaier conducted joint services for the six slain policemen. Then the people walked to the cemetery adjacent to the Catholic mission church at the agency. Five graves had been prepared. (Little Eagle, the sixth casualty, was taken back to Grand River for burial.) A company of infantry snapped to attention and fired three volleys over the graves. As the coffins sank into the ground, the notes of "taps" mingled with the mourning wails of the Sioux.

McLaughlin opened the cemetery gate and walked slowly toward Fort Yates. At the post cemetery he joined three officers

21. Usher L. Burdick, ed., *My Friend the Indian, or Three Heretofore Unpublished Chapters of the Book Published under the Title of My Friend the Indian, by Major James McLaughlin* (Baltimore, 1936), chap. 15.

who stood beside another open grave. On the bottom rested a rough wooden box that contained the canvas-wrapped remains of Sitting Bull. A detail of four soldiers—military prisoners—shoveled dirt into the hole.[22]

It was near the end of an era, not only for Standing Rock Agency but for the whole American West. In the popular mind, no chief so fully personified the spirit of Indian resistance as the old man whose body lay in the coffin. Although the Battle of Wounded Knee Creek two weeks later was still to come, it was the end of Sitting Bull that symbolized the end of the Indian wars.

22. McLaughlin, *My Friend the Indian*, pp. 221–22.

10. BIG FOOT

NEWS OF Sitting Bull's death swept the nation, for few Indian celebrities had enjoyed greater prominence. Westerners applauded his passing, and many of the eastern reform group, regretting the violence of his end, could not suppress a sigh of relief that circumstances had at last rolled this rock of reaction from the path of progress. Yet opinion was hardly unanimous. T. A. Bland, whose National Indian Defense Association waged constant war on the conventional reform theories of the day, led a swelling chorus of denunciation.

"The land grabbers wanted the Indian land," shouted a New York minister, follower of Bland. "The lying, thieving Indian agents wanted silence touching past thefts and immunity to continue their thieving. The renegades . . . among the Indian police wanted an opportunity to show their power. . . . And so he was murdered."[1]

Sensationalist newspapers took up the cry and spread across the land the charge that McLaughlin and Drum had conspired to murder Sitting Bull, that they had quietly instructed the In-

1. Rev. W. H. H. Murray in *New York World*, Dec. 21, 1890, reprinted in Bland, *Brief History of the Late Military Invasion*, pp. 25–27.

dian police to bring in a corpse, and that the soldiers had stood by to make certain the police did not fail in their duty. Eager to believe any rumor, Bland wrote the Indian Office that certain "parties" planned to "make [Sitting Bull's] bones a subject of speculation and perhaps his skin also," and demanded punishment of "any parties" found guilty.[2] McLaughlin patiently collected sufficient evidence to refute this accusation but could not stay the larger criticism sweeping the press.

The storm shook the office of the Secretary of the Interior and justified his worst fears. For a month, ever since arrests began to be talked about, Noble had maneuvered to insulate his department from any possible criticism by shifting all responsibility for arrests to the War Department. Now, Indian police, acting under an agent's orders, had thrust the department into the burning glare of public condemnation.

For a month Noble exerted himself to throw the responsibility back to the Army. Three times he made the agent report at length the authority under which he had sent his police to Grand River. "McLaughlin is so proud of his exploit," the Secretary wrote Commissioner Morgan, "that he rather suppresses the source of his action. But it is necessary that it be shown and understood that this was the act of the *Military, without qualification.*"[3] McLaughlin might write page after page explaining how he had merely obeyed the orders of Colonel Drum, who had obeyed the orders of General Ruger, who had obeyed the orders of General Miles, but the press saw only that the central actors in the tragedy were the agent and his policemen. Although the Secretary surely understood that Colonel Drum had acquiesced in a plan conceived and long championed by McLaughlin, he could hardly deny the validity of the explanation. He could only fume at the agent for embarrassing the department and look forward to the day when he might be quietly replaced. (Enjoying widespread and influential support, McLaughlin was a highly regarded Indian Inspector long after Noble stepped down from the Cabinet.)

2. Bland to CIA, Dec. 27, 1890, with endorsements by Post Surgeon, Fort Yates, and by McLaughlin.

3. Noble to Morgan, Dec. 31, 1890.

McLaughlin could not have been more astonished at the furor that burst over his head, nor more angry at the wild stories hurled back and forth by the press. If he was not in fact so proud of his exploit as the Secretary assumed, he was very proud indeed of the valor and devotion to duty displayed by his policemen. Instead of protesting the outcome, he felt, the public ought to be pouring out its gratitude to the men who had offered their lives in the cause of progress.[4] He began at once a crusade to win pensions for the survivors and the widows of the slain, a crusade in which Colonel Drum, General Ruger, and Commissioner Morgan joined.[5] (The effort, which was to see many years of agitation, was destined to fail.)

Other matters occupied McLaughlin in the days immediately following the Grand River affair. Infuriated at the death of their chief, or simply frightened, or both, nearly 400 of Sitting Bull's followers had stampeded when the troops appeared on Grand River. Aware that these people possessed considerable potential for harm if they succeeded in uniting with Kicking Bear and Short Bull in the Stronghold, or even with the Miniconjous along Cheyenne River, McLaughlin promptly sent out emissaries to coax the fugitives back to the agency.

Fechet's artillery had sent them flying southward toward the reservation line. Destitute, a few wounded, they had not paused until reaching the Miniconjou settlements on the Moreau River, within the Cheyenne River Reservation. Here, McLaughlin's couriers overtook them. In hurried councils, the Hunkpapas heard the agent's promises of kind treatment, and 160 people promptly turned back toward Standing Rock. Another eighty-eight remained indecisively on the Moreau, ultimately to return home, too. The rest faced south, hoping to find asylum with Big Foot on Cheyenne River.[6]

4. McLaughlin's annual report, Aug. 26, 1891, in CIA, *Annual Report* (1891), pp. 334–38.
5. Ibid. McLaughlin to Ruger, Dec. 22, 1890. Morgan to McLaughlin, Dec. 30, 1890. Ruger to Adjt. Gen., Jan. 1, 1891. Morgan to McLaughlin, Jan. 12, 1891. McLaughlin to CIA, March 3, 1891.
6. Ruger to Miles, Dec. 18, 1890. Drum to Miles, Dec. 22, 1890. Ewers to Miles, Dec. 24, 1890.

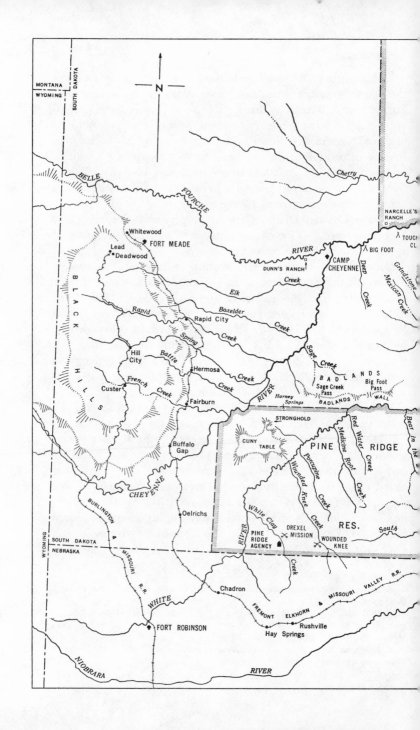

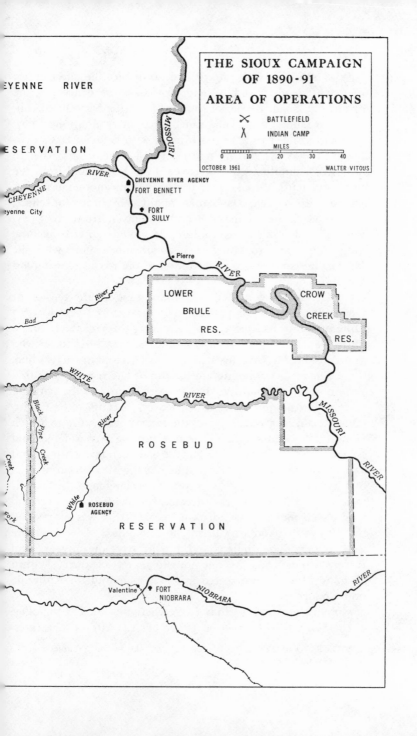

THE SIOUX CAMPAIGN
OF 1890-91
AREA OF OPERATIONS

✕ BATTLEFIELD
入 INDIAN CAMP

MILES
0   10   20   30   40

OCTOBER 1961   WALTER VITOUS

EYENNE   RIVER

ESERVATION

CHEYENNE   RIVER

eyenne City

■ CHEYENNE RIVER AGENCY
● FORT BENNETT

● FORT
   SULLY

● Pierre

RIVER

Bad   River

LOWER

BRULE

RES.

CROW

CREEK

RES.

WHITE

Black Pipe Creek

River

Creek

Creek

fork

RIVER

MISSOURI   RIVER

ROSEBUD

White ▲ ROSEBUD
            AGENCY

RESERVATION

Valentine ✕ ● FORT
               NIOBRARA

NIOBRARA   RIVER

News of Sitting Bull's death had no discernible effect either upon the friendlies at Pine Ridge or upon the dancers in the Stronghold. Small parties of warriors from the Stronghold continued to range through the ranching country along the Cheyenne and to meet in harmless brushes with Colonel Day's cowboy militia. While still trying to persuade a reluctant Miles to authorize a simultaneous offensive on the Stronghold from the north and south, Brooke prepared to mount another peace offensive. Fearing that Day's men might complicate the effort, Miles ordered the colonel to keep his troops north of the Cheyenne. The plan was to send a force of 500 friendlies from Pine Ridge into the Stronghold to negotiate once more with the dancers. Preparations consumed most of the week following Sitting Bull's death.

On December 22 a touch of humor relieved the tension at Pine Ridge. The Indian policemen hauled before Agent Royer a white man they had picked up wandering through the camps, a white blanket draped over his shoulders, preaching to all who would listen. He gave his name as A. C. Hopkins of Nashua, Iowa. The name was not unfamiliar, for he had recently acquired some notoriety by noisily advocating the pansy as the national flower. Now he quietly informed Royer, "I claim to be Christ, the Messiah, in a poetic sense, the same poetic sense in which Hiawatha, Socrates and General Grant are considered and esteemed the world over." In fact, he had been trying for several days to convince the Oglalas that he was the Messiah prophesied by Wovoka. Since he could not speak their language, the Indians were not deceived, but they treated him with the respect and kindness customarily accorded the insane. Royer was less respectful. "Prove that you are Christ," he demanded. "Give me more time among these Indians and I will," was the answer. Said Royer, "I'll give you just one hour to get out of town." Within an hour, Hopkins was seated in a wagon bound for Rushville under police escort.[7]

Hopkins repaired to Sioux City, where he called at the office of the *Sioux City Journal* on December 24. After a long inter-

7. Omaha *Daily Bee,* Dec. 23, 1890. Kelley, "The Indian Troubles and the Battle of Wounded Knee," p. 37.

view with a reporter who had nothing better to do on Christmas Eve, Hopkins left a note and departed. "To America and the world," it read, "greeting: God's peace be with you. The Messiah. Christmas Eve, 1890."[8]

The Miniconjous revered Big Foot (also known as Spotted Elk) as one of the outstanding chiefs in their tribe's history. His distinction rested less upon exploits of war than upon political and diplomatic triumphs. Success at negotiating peace between quarreling factions had earned him a reputation as the great compromiser of the Sioux, and other Teton tribes often sought his aid in patching up internal conflicts. Yet Big Foot was also uncompromisingly wedded to the old life, and this love of traditional ways had led him, in October and November 1890, to embrace the Ghost Dance in hope of restoring the old life. His people pitched camp with Hump on Cherry Creek and threw themselves wholeheartedly into the dance. Hump's defection early in December disillusioned Big Foot, and he took his band home to the cluster of cabins below the forks of Cheyenne River. Thereafter, he shunned the dance, although some of his people proved less willing to surrender a faith that offered so much. The fanatical medicine man, Yellow Bird, kept the Ghost Dance very much alive in Big Foot's band.

Despite the change of heart, Big Foot had already made his reputation. Generals Miles and Ruger duly noted the reports of his defiant behavior on Cherry Creek. On their list of troublemakers, he ranked with Sitting Bull himself, and Miles intended to have him arrested at the first favorable opportunity.

Lt. Col. Edwin V. Sumner had no intimation of the attitude of the generals, even though he was charged with the duty of watching Big Foot. Sumner had assumed command of the "camp of observation," now christened Camp Cheyenne, on December 3, shortly after Big Foot's return from Cherry Creek. In addition to keeping Big Foot under observation, Sumner's orders required him to protect the tiny settlements and isolated ranches on the Belle Fourche and Cheyenne Rivers. For this purpose he had about 200 men, both infantry and cavalry.

8. *Sioux City Journal,* Dec. 25, 1890.

Sumner bore a name illustrious in the annals of the Indian-fighting cavalry for half a century, but he also had genuine respect and sympathy for the Indian. Big Foot discovered in the new soldier chief a warm and genial man. Shortly after the colonel's arrival, Big Foot and his headmen spent two days at Camp Cheyenne getting acquainted. "Without exception," testified Sumner, they "seemed not only willing but anxious to obey my order to remain quietly at home, and particularly wished me to inform my superiors that they were all on the side of the Government in the trouble then going on." In the next two weeks, Sumner and Big Foot exchanged frequent visits, and on each occasion the colonel emerged with strengthened conviction that Big Foot was sincere in his profession of friendship. He saw, too, that many of the villagers did not share their leader's pacifism, but he was "impressed with the idea that Big Foot was making an extraordinary effort to keep his followers quiet." The commander foresaw no trouble with Big Foot.[9]

Sometime in the second week of December, runners brought Big Foot a message from the Oglala chiefs offering "the great compromiser" 100 ponies to come to Pine Ridge and restore tranquillity. After a long discussion with his headmen, who urged him to accept the invitation, Big Foot announced that he would first lead his people to Cheyenne River Agency to draw rations and annuity goods (December 22 was issue day), and after the return he would decide whether or not to go to Pine Ridge.[10] On December 15 (the day Sitting Bull was killed and the day the first of Two Strike's people reached Pine Ridge), the band moved off down the river. Sumner was much relieved, for at the agency the influence of Hump, combined with the warning implicit in the daily activity at Fort Bennett, might have a calming effect on the wilder of Big Foot's people.

Two days later, December 17, Sumner received the first hint that his superiors had designs on Big Foot. A courier from Fort

9. Sumner's report, Feb. 3, 1891, in Sec. War, *Annual Report* (1891), *1*, 223–24. This report reproduces much of the correspondence that passed between Sumner and his superiors, Dec. 8 to 24.

10. Dewey Beard, Joseph Horn Cloud, and Philip Wells Interviews, Ricker Collection.

Meade brought a telegram dispatched the day before from department headquarters in St. Paul: "It is desirable that Big Foot be arrested, and had it been practicable to send you [Capt. A. B.] Wells with his two troops [from Oelrichs], orders would have been given that you try to get him. In case of arrest, he will be sent to Fort Meade to be securely kept prisoner."[11]

This was of course not a direct order, but it did indicate that General Ruger expected Sumner, now or later, to arrest Big Foot. It intimated, also, that Ruger would be very displeased if he knew that Sumner no longer had Big Foot under observation. Later in the day, scouts from downriver brought in another bit of disquieting news. The Hunkpapa refugees from the battle over Sitting Bull were descending Cherry Creek toward Cheyenne River, reportedly with the intention of talking the Miniconjous into joining them in a dash to Pine Ridge. Big Foot, en route to the agency, was now camped in this very area. At the same time, other reports suggested that some of the Hunkpapa fugitives might head for Pine Ridge on trails that ran west of Camp Cheyenne through the settlements fringing the Black Hills on the east.[12]

Sumner faced an uncomfortable dilemma. If he marched for Cherry Creek, he might end up the scapegoat for depredations on the settlements; if he ignored Cherry Creek, he might end up the scapegoat for any explosion ignited by the combination of Sitting Bull Hunkpapas with Big Foot Miniconjous. The colonel vacillated for a day, then, on the morning of the 19th, he sent a platoon of twenty-two cavalrymen, under Lt. R. J. Duff, toward Cherry Creek to find out what he could about the Standing Rock Indians.

Word of the death of Sitting Bull and the flight of his people toward Cheyenne River had also reached Cheyenne River Agency and Fort Bennett. Col. H. C. Merriam, whose Seventh Infan-

11. Barber to Sumner, Dec. 16, 1890, in Sec. War, *Annual Report* (1891), *1*, 229.
12. Sumner to Miles, Dec. 18, 1890; Sumner to Asst. Adjt. Gen. Dept. of Dak., same date; Sumner to Ruger, Dec. 19; Sumner to Carr, same date, in ibid., pp. 229–30.

try had been trying to get across the ice-choked Missouri River since December 7, now commanded all the troops in the vicinity. Merriam's mission was to march up Cheyenne River and join Sumner. As the movement might upset the handful of Miniconjous who still danced on Cherry Creek, he instructed Capt. J. H. Hurst, commanding Fort Bennett, to send an officer to reassure them. Hurst selected Lt. Harry E. Hale, and accompanied by Hump, a policeman named White Thunder, and the post guide, Nolland, the lieutenant set forth on the morning of December 18. Reaching Cheyenne City that evening, they found the settlement all but deserted. The one remaining citizen, crusty old Henry Angell, explained that at noon the day before reports of hostile Hunkpapas sweeping down from the north had stampeded everyone else. He alone refused to abandon his home. The lieutenant promptly sent White Thunder to inform Sumner of the situation, then set about trying to get news of the Hunkpapas from the Cherry Creek Miniconjous at Hump's old camp across the river.

By noon of the 20th he had made little progress and had resolved to cross the river himself when Hump reported the approach of a group of horsemen from the west. A short gallop confronted Hale and Hump with a party of forty-six Hunkpapa warriors. They appeared friendly, and Hale believed that he could persuade them to go to the agency if only he could communicate with them. At this critical juncture Henry Angell joined the council. He understood the rudiments of the sign language, and through him Hale managed to assure the Hunkpapas that if they would camp for twenty-four hours he would ride to the agency and return with Captain Hurst and an interpreter—and no other soldiers. They agreed, and Hale had Angell kill a beef so they could have a feast. Leaving Hump in charge, the lieutenant mounted his horse and raced for the agency. Fearing that in his absence some of Big Foot's people would tamper with the Hunkpapas, he completed the fifty-two-mile ride in six and one-half hours.[13]

The fear was not unfounded. Big Foot had gone into camp

13. Hale to Post Adjt. Fort Bennett, Dec. 26, 1890, in ibid., pp. 200–01.

on the evening of December 17 across Cheyenne River from Cavanaugh's store, twenty miles above the mouth of Cherry Creek. During the night an old Indian brought word to him that soldiers were coming up the river (two companies of Merriam's regiment had finally succeeded in crossing the Missouri). The next day two Hunkpapas, one with a bullet in his leg, arrived in the camp with the news of Sitting Bull's death and the flight of his people southward. The Miniconjous were frightened. Big Foot himself could not decide whether to continue the journey to the agency.[14]

The next day, the 19th, the band moved across the river and made a new camp next to Cavanaugh's store, where the grass was better. Many were armed and painted, and they were holding Ghost Dances—at least so the Cavanaughs claimed. These men, James Cavanaugh and his two grown sons, were understandably frightened by the activity in their front yard. When some of Big Foot's men entered the store and said they were hungry, Cavanaugh lost no time loading them down with provisions. The Indians said they had no beef, and Cavanaugh told them to kill a calf. After they had departed on this mission, he bolted the door and rode swiftly up the river. The two boys watched from the hills for a time, then followed their father. James Cavanaugh ran into Lieutenant Duff's patrol of the Eighth Cavalry about ten miles east of Camp Cheyenne. He reported that he had been robbed by Big Foot's men and that a few Standing Rock people had joined Big Foot. Duff sent Cavanaugh's report to Colonel Sumner, who promptly started his whole command for Cherry Creek.[15]

This same afternoon of the 19th Big Foot selected ten young men to seek out the Standing Rock refugees and offer them his hospitality. Arriving at the mouth of Cherry Creek next day, they found the Hunkpapa women huddled around fires on the north bank of the river. They wore only the clothing in which

14. Dewey Beard and Joseph Horn Cloud Interviews, Ricker Collection.
15. Statements of Lt. R. J. Duff and Capt. E. A. Godwin, encl. to Maj. J. Ford Kent to Asst. Adjt. Gen. Div. of the Mo., Jan. 31, 1891. This is a report of Inspector General Kent's investigation of Sumner's conduct in allowing Big Foot to escape and will hereafter be cited as Sumner Investigation Report.

they had been turned out of bed on the morning of Sitting Bull's death. Some sang death songs; others mourned for those slain in the battle with Bull Head's police. All the men, including the Cherry Creek Miniconjous, were across the river near deserted Cheyenne City, awaiting Lieutenant Hale's return.

The emissaries from Big Foot crossed the river and found the men in council. Hump was urging surrender, and he immediately demanded to know what the newcomers wanted. They explained their mission. Belligerently, he shouted: "You don't have to take them to Big Foot's camp. I will take all these people to the agency. You people want to fight, and I will bring some infantry to help you." Then he formed his warriors, weapons cocked, in a menacing circle around Big Foot's men. But the Hunkpapas intervened, giving Hump to understand that if he meant to fight they would aid Big Foot's messengers. Hump backed down. The upshot of the argument was that 38 Standing Rock Indians and 30 young Miniconjou warriors, former followers of Hump, decided to take refuge with Big Foot, while 166 Hunkpapas and 55 Cherry Creek Miniconjous remained to hear what Captain Hurst had to offer.[16]

Hurst and Hale, accompanied by a sergeant and two interpreters, reached Cheyenne City on the afternoon of the 21st. The captain had two beeves slaughtered, and that night, after a grand feast, he sat down to a council with the Indians. He spoke kindly but firmly. He wanted them to surrender their arms and go with him to Fort Bennett, where they would be fed and clothed. He could make no promises about the future, but he could promise that if they chose to join Big Foot they and perhaps their families too would most certainly be destroyed. The Hunkpapas retired to deliberate. At midnight they laid down their arms and surrendered. The fifty-five Cherry Creek Indians also decided to go to the agency. Early next morning the cavalcade started east. It reached Cheyenne River Agency on the 23d, having en route met Colonel Merriam, at last marching upstream with four companies of his regiment. The Hunkpapas were sent down the Missouri to Fort Sully, where they were held

16. Joseph Horn Cloud and Dewey Beard Interviews, Ricker Collection.

prisoners, and Merriam took station at Cheyenne City to await developments.[17]

On the evening of December 20 Colonel Sumner and his command—C and I Troops, Eighth Cavalry, C Company, Third Infantry, and two Hotchkiss guns—bivouacked at the ranch of Narcisse Narcelle, on the north bank of the Cheyenne, twelve miles above Big Foot's camp. Troop D, Eighth Cavalry, bivouacked six miles in advance. The column moved out next morning and, opposite the abandoned huts of Touch-the-Cloud's village, met Big Foot, one of his lieutenants, and the two Standing Rock Indians who had brought news of Sitting Bull's death. With a show of sterness, Sumner berated the chief for harboring the fugitive Hunkpapas, but moderated when Big Foot pointed out with considerable logic that he could hardly turn away brothers and relatives who came to him hungry, footsore, weary, and nearly naked. Sumner had to agree, for the two Hunkpapas with Big Foot "answered his description perfectly." The colonel then declared that the Miniconjous would have to turn back to their homes. Big Foot agreed. He had already decided on this course anyway, for his people were growing more and more uneasy over the approach of Colonel Merriam's infantry from the east. Escorted by a troop of cavalry, the entire band, together with the Hunkpapa refugees, moved to Narcelle's ranch and made camp, the command forming a chain completely surrounding the Indians. A count showed 333 men, women, and children, including 38 Hunkpapas, of whom 14 were warriors.[18]

The night passed quietly, with the Indians enjoying apparent good humor as a result of the fine feast provided by the soldiers. Early next morning, the 22d, Sumner organized the column for the day's march to Camp Cheyenne, where he planned to hold the Indians under direct observation. He divided the Indian transportation—about fifty wagons with additional travois— into three sections, and had all dismounted people, chiefly wom-

17. Hurst to Asst. Adjt. Gen. Dept. of Dak., Jan. 9, 1891; Merriam to Asst. Adjt. Gen. Dept. of Dak., Jan. 30, 1891, in Sec. War, *Annual Report* (1891), *1*, 209–23.
18. Sumner's report, Feb. 3, 1891, in ibid., pp. 224–25. Statements of Henissee and Capt. Philip Reade, Third Infantry, Sumner Investigation Report.

en, children, and old men, get into the wagons. Each section, escorted by a troop of cavalry, moved out individually. Big Foot rode in a wagon near the head of the column. The mounted warriors, with Interpreter Felix Benoit, accompanied the third section, and Capt. Philip Reade's infantry brought up the rear. This arrangement, which put the Indians thoroughly under control, made all of them uncomfortable. Some of the young men suddenly appeared with painted faces and carried their Winchesters ostentatiously.

As the second section passed through a gate a few miles from Narcelle's ranch, one of the wagons caught on a fence post and the wheels locked. The frightened women struggled to extricate the vehicle but only succeeded in tangling the horses in their harness. An officer commanded the women to quit blocking the gate, which made things even worse. Black Fox, Big Foot's arrogant son-in-law, brandished his rifle at the officer, who retreated.

Now cut off from the head of the column and incensed at the gruff tone of the officer, the warriors could no longer restrain themselves. They raced aimlessly about, and when the gate was finally cleared they poured through and galloped along the column, shouting and waving their rifles. The women began to throw lodgepoles and cooking utensils from the wagons, preparing for flight if necessary. As the warriors neared the head of the column, Lieutenant Duff faced the advance guard to the rear and spread out a skirmish line, carbines pointed at the oncoming horsemen. The warriors reined in and milled gradually back toward the rear. Sumner meanwhile urged Big Foot to calm his people, and the chief sent messengers to assure them that there was no danger if only they did what the soldiers wanted. The crisis passed, but for the rest of the march everyone was nervous.[19]

As the column crossed the river and neared the cabins of Big Foot's village, the people once more grew excited. Some warriors again dashed toward the head of the column. Fearing a collision, Sumner sent word to Lieutenant Duff to let them pass. Big Foot

19. Statements of Duff, Godwin, Henissee, Reade, and Capt. J. B. Hickey, Sumner Investigation Report. Joseph Horn Cloud and Dewey Beard Interviews, Ricker Collection.

came to the colonel and said, "I will go with you to your camp, but there will be trouble in trying to force these women and children, cold and hungry as they are, away from their homes. This is their home, where the Government has ordered them to stay, and none of my people have committed a single act requiring their removal by force." Sumner had to admit the logic of this. Wrought up as the young men were, any attempt to make them go on to Camp Cheyenne involved the gravest risk of violence. "I concluded that one of two things must happen," he later explained. "I must either consent to their going into their village or bring on a fight; and, if the latter, must be the aggressor, and, if the aggressor, what possible reason could I produce for making an attack on peaceable, quiet Indians on their reservation and at their homes, killing perhaps many of them and offering, without any justification, the lives of many officers and enlisted men."[20]

Having settled on the former alternative, he now had to decide what to do with Big Foot personally. General Ruger obviously expected Sumner to arrest the chief at the first favorable opportunity. Yet Ruger's facts were outdated. The danger now resided not so much in Big Foot, one of the most moderate individuals in the camp, as in his headstrong young men. To Sumner, Big Foot himself seemed by far the best instrument for keeping the peace, and to remove his restraining influence at this critical time appeared the height of folly. The colonel therefore told Big Foot that his people could go to their homes, and that he himself could remain with them if he promised to come to Camp Cheyenne the next day for a council and to bring all the Standing Rock people with him. Big Foot gave his promise. By now the column had reached the village, and wagons were already turning off to the various cabins. Sumner saw that he had made the only possible decision, for he could not have re-formed the column by any means short of opening fire. The troops continued to Camp Cheyenne, arriving early in the evening.[21]

General Miles had now set up headquarters in Rapid City and assumed command of all units in Dakota, thus doing away

20. Sumner's report, Feb. 3, 1891, p. 25.
21. Ibid.

with the awkward relationship arising from Brooke's operating in Ruger's department. A wire from Miles reached Sumner by courier from Fort Meade during the night of the 22d. It alerted him to rumors that 200 Indians were loose in western North Dakota, and that they had a troop of cavalry corralled. Miles thought the reports unfounded (they were) but wanted Sumner to screen the settlements on the northern edge of the Black Hills in case the reports turned out to be true. Therefore, directed Miles, "I think you had better push on rapidly with your prisoners to Meade, and be careful they do not escape, and look out for other Indians."[22]

The hard fact, of course, was that Sumner had no prisoners, and he had already, as soon as he reached camp late in the afternoon, admitted this in a message to Miles. Early on the morning of the 23d Sumner sent another dispatch to Miles declaring that if Big Foot did not keep his promise and come in during the day, the cavalry would march down and take him.[23] He sent scouts to find out if all was well at Big Foot's camp. Noon came and went with no sign of Big Foot and no word from the scouts.

The colonel pondered his predicament over lunch. With the possibility of hostiles sweeping down from the north, his command might have fresh work ahead of it, work that would be much hampered by the necessity of watching Big Foot. He could seize Big Foot, as Miles expected and in fact thought had already been done, but this would surely provoke a fight and, even if successful, unleash the impulsive young men to prey on the countryside. He continued to believe that the best insurance against trouble lay in Big Foot's remaining with his people. The only way out of the dilemma, Sumner gradually concluded, was to persuade Big Foot to go to his agency at the mouth of Cheyenne River. Then the garrison of Fort Bennett could have the responsibility of watching him. "All thought of these Indians going south had been abandoned by me," Sumner declared later, "and I supposed they would either go peaceably to the agency or fight."[24]

22. Miles to CO Ft. Meade, Dec. 22, 1890, in Sec. War, *Annual Report* (1891), *1*, 233.

23. Sumner to Miles, Dec. 22 and 23, 1890, in ibid., pp. 233–34.

24. Statement of Sumner, Jan. 25, 1891, Sumner Investigation Report.

While Sumner ate, a rancher named John Dunn came to his tent peddling eggs and butter. Dunn had lived on the Belle Fourche, a few miles from Camp Cheyenne, for ten years and knew Big Foot well. The Indians called him "Red Beard." Sumner asked Dunn to ride to Big Foot's camp and try to persuade him to take the people to Cheyenne River Agency. Dunn demurred but at length gave in to the colonel's entreaties. As the rancher rode off, Sumner had the orderly trumpeter sound "boots and saddles," and soon the whole command was trotting down the valley toward Big Foot's village.[25]

Felix Benoit, the interpreter, accompanied Dunn. As they entered the outskirts of the Miniconjou village, they met the two Indian scouts sent out earlier by Sumner. Benoit stopped to talk with them, while Dunn went on into the village. Benoit asked the scouts why Big Foot had not come in as promised. They answered that the Standing Rock Indians had fled, and Big Foot did not want to face the colonel until he had found them. Accompanied by the scouts, the interpreter rode on into the camp. At Big Foot's cabin they found a throng of excited men milling around Dunn and the chief. "I am ordered to go down to Bennett to-morrow morning," shouted Big Foot to his men. "We must all go to Bennett; if we don't, John Dunn is sent here to tell me that if we don't go the soldiers will come here in the morning and make us go, and shoot us if they have to." Seeing Benoit, Big Foot asked if Dunn told the truth. Yes, replied Benoit.[26]

After Benoit, Dunn, and the scouts had departed, Big Foot and his men heatedly discussed the next move. Some thought they ought to go to the agency; others wanted to accept the invitation from the Oglala chiefs and go to Pine Ridge; still others,

25. Sumner's report, Feb. 3, 1891, p. 225. Statements of Sumner and John Dunn, Sumner Investigation Report.

26. Statement of Benoit, Sumner Investigation Report. Dunn claimed (statement in same source) that he merely passed on Sumner's message. I accept Benoit's version as the more probable not only because of subsequent events but also because both Dewey Beard and Joseph Horn Cloud (Ricker Collection), who were present, remembered that "Red Beard" had warned that the soldiers would shoot if not obeyed. Their statements go into considerable detail, much of it to be discounted, but nonetheless agree with Benoit on the essential point that Dunn said the soldiers would shoot if necessary. Dunn's motives are not clear; probably he just wanted to appear a big man and accordingly embellished Sumner's message.

including Big Foot, favored staying in their homes and awaiting developments. But Sumner's soldiers were approaching from upstream and Merriam's from downstream. This certainly seemed to bear out Dunn's ominous prophecy. ("I know this," Captain Henissee later remarked, "Indians don't care what you say, but are suspicious of actions."[27]) The argument was finally resolved with the decision to move up Deep Creek into the hills and from there to watch to see if the soldiers really were coming.[28]

As the Indians began to round up their ponies and load their wagons for this move, Benoit, glancing back at the village, remarked that the camp must be preparing to start for Bennett right away. Sending one of the scouts back to watch, he and Dunn continued up the river. They found Sumner camped about five miles above the village. Later, the scout came in and reported that the women and children were badly frightened, and it looked as if the band planned to leave for the agency immediately. Sumner promptly sent three scouts to tell Big Foot not to go until morning. One soon returned with word that the Indians had already left, but were moving south. Either they intended to go to Bennett by the ridge road, hoping thereby to avoid Merriam's command on the valley road, or they were breaking for Pine Ridge; he did not know which.[29] Sumner's scouts laced the country during the night, while the colonel hoped against hope that Big Foot would turn east on the ridge road to the agency.

That night, in the hills south of the village, the Indians debated the question in council. The headmen all urged Big Foot to strike south for Pine Ridge, as requested by the Oglala chiefs, and there make the peace that would earn him 100 ponies. Big Foot resisted. He had assured Sumner over and over that his people had no intention of going south. Besides, he did not feel well, and the long journey would be hard for him. As long as they had to leave their homes, he preferred Bennett to Pine Ridge. His advisers, fearing a trap, would not yield. He must go

27. Statement of Henissee, Sumner Investigation Report.
28. Joseph Horn Cloud and Dewey Beard Interviews, Ricker Collection.
29. Statement of Benoit, Sumner Investigation Report.

to Pine Ridge. Big Foot finally gave in, and the band pointed
south. At midnight one of Sumner's scouts, Charging First,
caught up with the procession. Tell Sumner, said Big Foot, that
he, Big Foot, wanted to go to Bennett, but that his people would
not let him. They demanded that he lead them to Pine Ridge,
and lead them he would.[30]

The next morning, December 24, Sumner had this report. He
crossed the river to the deserted village but, still worried about
the reports of hostiles to the north, did not follow Big Foot's
trail. Instead, he returned to Camp Cheyenne. This same day a
courier rode in from Fort Meade with a telegram from General
Miles:

Rapid City, [December] 23d.

To Col. E. V. Sumner,
Commanding Cheyenne:
(Through Commanding Officer Fort Meade.)

Report about hostile Indians near Little Missouri not
believed. The attitude of Big Foot has been defiant and
hostile, and you are authorized to arrest him or any of his
people and to take them to Meade or Bennett. There are
some 30 young warriors that run [sic] away from Hump's
camp without authority, and if an opportunity is given they
will undoubtedly join those in the Bad Lands. The Standing Rock Indians also have no right to be there and they
should be arrested. The division commander directs, therefore, that you secure Big Foot and the 20 [sic] Cheyenne
River Indians, and the Standing Rock Indians, and if necessary round up the whole camp and disarm them, and take
them to Fort Meade or Bennett.

.   .   .   .

By command of Gen. Miles.

Maus,
Captain and Aide-de-Camp.[31]

30. Ibid. Joseph Horn Cloud and Dewey Beard Interviews, Ricker Collection.
31. Reproduced in Sec. War, *Annual Report* (1891), *1*, 231–32.

News of Big Foot's escape touched off a wrathful explosion in Miles' headquarters, and the general's anger resounded in dispatches going to all field commanders. Within a month he had sent his inspector general, Maj. J. Ford Kent, to Camp Cheyenne to assemble evidence with which to bring Sumner before a court of inquiry. Fortunately for the colonel, Kent concluded that the evidence did not warrant court proceedings. Sumner was saved by the fact that he received no *direct* order to arrest Big Foot until December 24, by which time it was too late.

One sympathizes with Sumner. Miles and Ruger assumed that Big Foot was personally dangerous, an assumption that Sumner's experience belied. They assumed, too, that all would be well with the Miniconjous if only Big Foot were withdrawn from their midst, another assumption contradicted by Sumner's firsthand experience. The evidence points to the conclusion that these assumptions were indeed wrong, and that circumstances conspired to frustrate a basically sound policy.

Yet, from December 17 on, Sumner knew without question that Big Foot was his personal responsibility. Thus his decision on the 22d to leave Big Foot unguarded must have been a calculated risk taken in full knowledge that his future career might hang on the good faith of the chief. Even after receiving Miles' telegram on the evening of the 22d, in which the division commander presumed that Big Foot and his people had already been made prisoners, Sumner equivocated for another twenty-four hours, by which time it was too late. Perhaps, as he contended, it would have been folly, with only 200 men, to attempt to interfere with Big Foot and his band. But it was folly, too, to withdraw completely and leave everything to the hope that Big Foot would or could keep his promises. As it turned out, the consequences were indeed tragic.

In military life as in no other, results are what count. Sumner failed to produce.

11. *THE SEARCH FOR THE MINICONJOUS*

GENERAL MILES' anger over the escape of Big Foot is understandable. Consistent with his earlier assumptions about Big Foot, he logically assumed that the Miniconjous were running for the Stronghold, where they hoped to join Short Bull and Kicking Bear. It was an awkward time, for General Brooke's latest peace effort was just getting under way. The friendly chiefs at Pine Ridge had met in council on the 16th and 17th and had decided to send 500 men into the Stronghold for one final, massive attempt at persuading the hostiles to avert bloodshed by giving up. This imposing delegation had just arrived at the destination, and had sent back encouraging reports, when word came that Big Foot had broken away and was heading south. If he succeeded in reaching the Stronghold, war might yet erupt. Accordingly, all energies went into the search for the Miniconjous. The first hope lay with Colonel Carr's Sixth Cavalry, whose three squadrons were ranging east and west from the base camp at the mouth of Rapid Creek.

Full-bearded Eugene A. Carr was a scarred veteran of frontier warfare who traced his career back to the old Regiment of Mounted Riflemen in the years before the Civil War. Few colonels of cavalry in 1890 boasted a longer, more active role in the conquest of the western Indians; none boasted a brighter star on his battle record than his for Summit Springs. The order to move to Dakota had caught the Sixth Cavalry scattered over much of Arizona and New Mexico. Added to the vexations of the journey, the thankless task of patrolling the wintry plains north of White River put Carr in a crotchety frame of mind. Especially annoying were reports of the easy life that the Seventh Cavalry, under Forsyth, "a junior colonel," was enjoying at Pine Ridge Agency. Carr's complaints offer a rare insight into some of the personal sacrifices demanded by frontier service and deserve to be quoted in part:

> I do not suppose any one ever worked harder than I and my Regiment have done since November 24th when I suddenly received a telegram that I was transferred to the Department of the Platte.
>
> This is the fourth week I have been on the jump day and night. My Quartermaster had to stay to turn over [property], and I have done much of his duties.
>
> We packed all our impedimenta in eight days, and were ready always before the Railroad was.
>
> Now we have no station or place for our families.
>
> We were told they could stay at Wingate [New Mexico], but I would not leave any officers or soldiers to care for them, and they would have been lost among strangers; who would be constantly looking for them to vacate quarters, to which the new garrison was entitled, having been moved as suddenly as we were. We were offered some quarters at Forts Snelling [Minnesota] and Randall [South Dakota], which was a mockery! as it would cost more to go there and thence to new posts than to board, so they came on except such as scattered, and some are at Rapid City awaiting developments.
>
> Forgive me for boring you with all this, but my Regiment worked well for you in Arizona, through the heat and sands, mostly without tents, and is ready and willing to work again.

I had similar luck with the 5th Cavalry in '76.

Crook got it "temporarily assigned" to Department [of the] Platte and never let it go.

We lived on horse meat or nothing, and shivered and suffered in this very neighborhood till in the winter, and when we went into quarters they would not even order an officer to see to the bringing of our effects.

I had a trunk broken open, silver stolen, etc. etc.

I hope you will give us a fair show in this scrap. I understand the 7th [Cavalry] has a beautiful camp at Pine Ridge, all laid out according to the Regulations and everything in Apple pie order.[1]

Now Carr had his opportunity to do some serious work. At 10:00 A.M. on December 24, the morning after Big Foot's flight, a courier galloped into the camp at the mouth of Rapid Creek with a message from Colonel Sumner. It alerted Carr that Big Foot was headed south, up Deep Creek, and would probably pass the head of Bull Creek sometime during the night. If Carr marched swiftly to the east, he might get in front of the Miniconjous.[2] Only four troops of the Sixth were in camp, but within half an hour after "boots and saddles" had sounded they were pushing eastward with two Hotchkiss guns bringing up the rear.

By evening the column had reached the middle fork of Sage Creek, on the northern edge of the forbidding, eroded formations of the South Dakota Badlands. Camped in these eerie surroundings, the command passed a memorable Christmas Eve. "The night," recalled one of the officers, "was very cold and the alkaline pools in the vicinity were frozen solid. Those who had brought any food divided with the others as far as possible, but Christmas morning dawned upon a lot of half-frozen, uncomfortable men who had spent a cheerless night, alternately heaping wood on the fires and then trying to sleep on saddle blankets."[3]

1. Carr to Miles, Dec. 18, 1890.
2. Sumner to Carr, Dec. 23, 1890, in Sec. War, *Annual Report* (1891), *1*, 234.
3. Lt. Col. W. H. Carter, *From Yorktown to Santiago with the Sixth U.S. Cavalry* (Baltimore, 1900), p. 260.

Another troop of the regiment rode into camp early in the evening, and still another, having marched from its position at Harney Spring, east of the Stronghold, came in at 2:30 A.M. on Christmas Day. Carr promptly sent its guide, Gus Craven, southward to find the two troops under Maj. Emil Adam patrolling White River Valley. On the chance that Big Foot had already slipped around him, Carr wanted Adam's squadron moved up White River in order to cut off any attempt by the Miniconjous to enter the Stronghold from the northeast. The Badlands Wall, an escarpment some 300 feet high bordering White River on the north for a distance of nearly ninety miles, limited the choice of routes open to Big Foot, for only a few passes afforded convenient exit from the Badlands. Craven descended the Wall by way of Sage Creek Pass and at daylight found Major Adam camped between the mouths of Red Water and Medicine Root Creeks. Upon receipt of the message, Adam mounted his command and marched up White River Valley.

As Sumner had emphasized that Big Foot would probably cross the head of Bull Creek, Carr divided his six troops into two squadrons and on the 25th swept northward on a wide front toward Bull Creek. Crossing this stream, he pushed almost to the head of Deep Creek without discovering any sign of Indians. There could be little doubt that Big Foot by now had dropped far to the south, for he had been on Deep Creek two days earlier. Carr therefore called off the chase and returned to his base camp.[4]

Big Foot had passed to the east of Carr. He had traveled swiftly during the night of the 23d. Dawn found the band on a branch of Bad River; noon, on a second fork of Bad River. The sun shone brightly as the Indian column penetrated the sterile Badlands, but a raw, cold wind whipped clouds of alkali dust across the file of wagons. Big Foot lay in his own wagon, feeling ill, but the pace did not slacken. Late in the afternoon the wagons came to the Badlands Wall at a pass (six miles west of the present headquarters of Badlands National Monument) that had long since fallen into disuse. A tortuous trail, pocked and gullied by ero-

4. Carr to Miles, Dec. 26, 1890. Cornelius A. "Gus" Craven Interview, Ricker Collection.

sion, led down to the valley of White River. The men swarmed
to the front and with axes and spades quickly made the trail
passable. (The pass is still known as Big Foot Pass.) The wagons
wound down the slope, and by nightfall the band was camped
on the south bank of the river.

The Indians had eluded Carr but were camped only a few
miles down the river from Major Adam's squadron of the Sixth.
This threat vanished next morning, however, when Gus Craven
brought Adam the order from Carr to move farther up the river.
Christmas Eve, while camped on White River, Big Foot was pros-
trated by pneumonia, and the flight of the Miniconjous slowed
almost to a crawl. This sudden change of pace further upset the
calculations of the military authorities who were frantically trying to find him.

Leaving three pickets to watch White River for pursuing
soldiers, the band moved slowly to Cedar Spring (now Big Foot
Spring) on the 25th. From here, the failing Big Foot dispatched
three messengers to ride ahead and inform the Pine Ridge chiefs
of his approach. They were to say that he was coming openly
and peaceably and was very sick. The next day the fugitives
traveled only four miles, halting on Red Water Creek.[5]

Units from Pine Ridge had now joined the search. On the
25th, Maj. Guy V. Henry and four troops of the Ninth Cavalry
—Henry's Brunettes—took station at Harney Spring to cover
all approaches to the Stronghold from the east. Only a half-dozen
miles to the west, Little Wound, Big Road, and Fast Thunder,
with Brooke's delegation of 500 friendlies, were trying to persuade the disciples of Short Bull and Kicking Bear to surrender.
Runners to Brooke reported dissension again sweeping the hostiles. Two days after his arrival at Harney Spring, December 27,
Major Henry sent his guide William D. McGaa, with a few
scouts, to work into some point of vantage from which they
could observe the activities in the Stronghold. The scouts came
in that evening to report all tepees struck and the hostiles leaving the tableland in the direction of the agency. The next day
Henry moved down to White River, opposite the mouth of

5. Joseph Horn Cloud and Dewey Beard Interviews, Ricker Collection.

Wounded Knee Creek, but had McGaa go back for another look. This time the scouts found the Stronghold deserted. Short Bull and Kicking Bear were headed for the agency with their entire following.[6]

Big Foot's couriers probably reported to the chiefs at Pine Ridge on the morning of December 26, for Brooke heard around noon that the Miniconjous had crossed White River and were somewhere in the vicinity of Porcupine Creek, destined not for the Stronghold but for the agency. Concluding that Big Foot had given up the attempt to get into the Stronghold, the general immediately ordered out a squadron of the Seventh Cavalry. "I do not think there will be any mistake made with Big Foot if we get him," Brooke wired Miles. "My orders were to dismount [him] and destroy his arms and hold him when caught for my orders."[7]

Miles heartily approved. "Big Foot is cunning and his Indians are very bad," he replied the same day. "And I hope you will round up the whole body of them, disarm [them] and keep them under close guard." Another telegram, reflecting Miles' mounting concern, followed almost immediately: "I have no doubt your orders are all right, but I shall be exceedingly anxious till I know they are executed; whoever secures that body of Indians will be entitled to much credit. They deceived Sumner completely, and if they get a chance they will scatter through the entire Sioux camp or slip out individually."[8]

The mission had been entrusted to capable hands. Seasoned by arduous campaigns against the Apaches, Maj. Samuel Marmaduke Whitside had learned much about Indian fighting. With Troops A, B, I, and K of Custer's old regiment and a platoon of Battery E, First Artillery, two Hotchkiss guns, commanded by Lt. Harry L. Hawthorne, he pitched camp in the evening near the Wounded Knee trading post. The trader, Louis Mosseau,

6. William D. McGaa Interview, Ricker Collection. Brooke to Miles, Dec. 25, 1890 (two telegrams). Miles to Brooke, Dec. 28, 1890.

7. Brooke to Miles, Dec. 26, 1890 (three telegrams).

8. Reproduced in "Proceedings of an Investigation Made Pursuant to Special Order No. 8, Headquarters, Division of the Missouri, in the Field, Pine Ridge, South Dakota, Jan. 4, 1891." Hereafter cited as WKIR (Wounded Knee Investigation Report).

had taken refuge at the agency a month earlier. Now he came back with the soldiers, opened the store, and turned over part of his house, behind the store, to Major Whitside and his officers.

The next morning, the 27th, Whitside sent out a party of Oglala Indian scouts under John Shangreau, chief of Brooke's headquarters scouts, to scour the valleys of Wounded Knee and Porcupine Creeks for signs of Big Foot. They searched diligently, for General Brooke had promised twenty-five dollars to the scout who found Big Foot, and the reporters, exasperated by the lack of good copy, had doubled the incentive. By late in the morning a line of heliographs had been set up to connect the Wounded Knee camp with Pine Ridge, and flashing mirrors brought further instructions from Brooke's aide-de-camp: "I am directed by the Commanding General to say that he thinks Big Foot's party must be in your front somewhere, and that you must make every effort to find him and then move on him at once and with rapidity. There must be a solution reached at the earliest possible moment. Find his trail and follow, or find his hiding place and capture him. If he fights, destroy him."[9]

This same morning of December 27 found the Miniconjous still camped on Red Water Creek, Big Foot's pneumonia growing steadily worse. During the night one of the messengers sent to Pine Ridge on the 25th had returned with news that soldiers were on Wounded Knee Creek, where the road from Pine Ridge to Rosebud crossed the stream. Now, two more Indians rode into camp. They were Bear-Comes-and-Lies, another of the messengers, and Shaggy Feather, an Oglala from Pine Ridge. They reported that the Indians in the Stronghold had at last been persuaded to give up and would reach Pine Ridge in two days, on December 29. Short Bull and Kicking Bear had learned of Big Foot's approach and wanted him to time his marches so as to reach the agency on the same day. The two emissaries also brought word of the soldiers on Wounded Knee and advised Big Foot to avoid them by swinging to the east and south before turning toward the agency. Big Foot replied that he was too sick. The best course was to go directly to the camp of the soldiers.

9. Ibid.

The Miniconjous moved out at noon, paused for supper on Medicine Root Creek where the town of Kyle now stands, then pushed on to American Horse Creek. At midnight they made camp next to the log school building near Little Wound's deserted village.

At sunrise on the 28th the band resumed the journey and by late morning had crossed the divide separating American Horse from Porcupine Creek. Descending the slope to Porcupine, a party of warriors riding in advance spied four of Whitside's scouts watering their horses in the stream. They were Baptiste Garnier (Little Bat), his half-brother, Old Hand, and two Oglala scouts. Taken off guard, they found themselves suddenly surrounded by the Miniconjou warriors. The wagons had now come up, and the people scattered along the stream bank to eat lunch. The scouts were taken to Big Foot, reclining in his wagon. The chief said he wanted Old Hand and one of the Oglala scouts to take word to the commander on Wounded Knee that the Miniconjous were coming directly to his camp.[10]

Old Hand and his companion reached Whitside's camp just as the command was preparing to eat lunch. They told their story to John Shangreau, who went promptly with the report to Whitside. The major had "boots and saddles" sounded and made ready to leave at once. Shangreau objected. "Major," he said, "Big Foot told the men that he was going to come to the camp and we may as well stay here till they come." But Whitside pointed out the Major Henry's squadron of the Ninth was operating somewhere to the north, and the possibility of a collision between these troops and the Miniconjous could not be chanced. Probably, also, Whitside recalled that Big Foot had made a similar promise to Colonel Sumner and while Sumner waited had struck out in the opposite direction. The safest course was to march out to meet the Miniconjous and escort them back to camp.

About noon the four troops moved out at a trot. There were 10 officers and 225 enlisted men, including Hawthorne's artil-

---

10. Sources for this episode are conflicting and somewhat garbled accounts of Dewey Beard, Joseph Horn Cloud, and John Shangreau, Ricker Collection. This seems the most likely reconstruction of what happened.

lery. By 2:00 P.M. they had covered eight miles and had reached
a dry wash, Pine Creek, that meandered among pine-studded
hills at the foot of Porcupine Butte. Beyond the next ridge lay
the valley of Porcupine Creek, where Old Hand had left the
Indians eating lunch. Two horsemen galloped down the slope
toward the column. Little Bat and his Oglala companion had
been released by Big Foot. As they reined up in front of Major
Whitside, the first of the Miniconjou cavalcade crawled into
view on top of the ridge two miles distant. "How does it look
with those Indians?" asked John Shangreau. "They look pretty
tough," answered Little Bat. "We are liable to catch it today."[11]

The squadron continued the march for another mile, then
halted. The Indians had moved part way down the side of the
ridge, mounted warriors to the front. Whitside signaled the
column into skirmish formation, gave the command to dismount,
and ran the two cannon out in front of the line. Horse-holders
grabbed the reins of led horses and withdrew to the rear. The
Miniconjous kept coming. Their men fanned out on a wide
front, forming an animated skirmish line. Some of the warriors
tied up the tails of their ponies in preparation for a fight; others
raced back and forth waving rifles. Behind them, a white flag
fluttered from a pole fixed to Big Foot's wagon.

The Indians stopped, facing the soldiers. Two footmen started
toward the blue line. Shangreau rode out to meet them, then
accompanied them back to Big Foot's wagon. In a moment the
wagon moved through the warriors and drew up next to Whitside. He peered in. Big Foot lay in the bed of the wagon, only
a small part of his face showing from the blankets that swathed
him from head to foot. Blood dripped from his nose, staining
the blankets and collecting in small pools that froze on the floor
of the wagon. The warriors, still in line, milled around nervous-
ly. An occasional metallic click signified the chambering of a

11. The following account of Big Foot's capture is drawn from John Shangreau,
Dewey Beard, and Joseph Horn Cloud Interviews, Ricker Collection; testimony of
Whitside, WKIR; Lt. John C. Gresham, "The Story of Wounded Knee," *Harper's
Weekly*, *35* (Feb. 7, 1891), 106 (Gresham was one of Whitside's officers); and "Lieu-
tenant Hawthorne's Vivid Description of Warpath Life," unidentified newspaper
clipping, ca. Jan. 1891, E. S. Luce Seventh Cavalry Collection.

cartridge. A few warriors on the right flank rode out toward the troops. Big Foot had told them not to be afraid, but to go calmly among the soldiers. Dewey Horn Cloud (later named Dewey Beard) rode right up to one of the cannon and thrust his hand into the muzzle—because, he later explained, he was anxious to die.

As Whitside reached down to shake hands with Big Foot, more warriors clustered around the wagon. With Shangreau interpreting, Whitside told Big Foot that he must bring his people to the camp on Wounded Knee Creek. "All right," was the faltering reply, "I am going there." He also explained that he was headed for Pine Ridge Agency, where he intended to make a peace and earn 100 horses. "John," said the major to Shangreau, "I want the horses and guns." The scout protested: "Look here, Major, if you do that there is liable to be a fight here; and if there is you will kill all those women and children and the men will get away from you." Whitside explained that General Brooke's orders were to disarm and dismount the Indians. "Well, that might be it," replied Shangreau, "but we better take them to camp and then take their horses from them and their guns." Whitside thought a moment, then said, "All right; you tell Big Foot to move down to camp at Wounded Knee." Shangreau translated, and Big Foot answered, "All right, I am going down to camp; that is where I am going."

Again the two men shook hands. Whitside said that the springless wagon in which Big Foot had been riding made the journey too hard, and he motioned an ambulance forward. Soldiers grasped the blankets and gently transferred him to the Army vehicle. The cavalrymen remounted and herded the warriors into a compact group behind the wagons. Two troops of cavalry led the march, followed by the ambulance, the string of Indian wagons, and the mounted warriors. The other two troops and Hawthorne's cannon brought up the rear. The column pointed southwest, toward Wounded Knee.

A courier galloped in advance, headed for camp. He took word for General Brooke that Big Foot and his entire following had been intercepted. There were 120 men and 230 women and children. Whitside suggested that Colonel Forsyth and the rest of the regiment be sent out to Wounded Knee to help in the disarming. "The object I had in view," Whitside later testified, "was that, by their presence, we could overawe the Indians, and so they would submit quietly to be disarmed. I was convinced, from a hostile demonstration at the time of surrender, that otherwise trouble might ensue."[12]

The message, relayed from Wounded Knee by heliograph, reached Brooke late in the afternoon. He at once alerted Forsyth to prepare to march. Then the general, elated at the turn of events, telegraphed the good news to Miles, at the same time suggesting that, as soon as disarmed, the prisoners be marched directly from Wounded Knee to the railroad at Gordon, Nebraska, from where they could be moved by train to Omaha. From Miles came a prompt reply: "All right. Use force enough. Congratulations."[13]

At 4:40 P.M. Troops C, D, E, and G of the Seventh Cavalry, the troop of Oglala scouts under Lts. Charles W. Taylor and Guy H. Preston, and the other platoon of Light Battery E, First Artillery, under Capt. Allyn Capron, formed for the march to Wounded Knee. Colonel Forsyth reported to General Brooke for orders. They were verbal, and as recalled in substance by Brooke were: "To disarm Big Foot's band, take every precaution to prevent the escape of any; [and] if they fought to destroy them." After disarming the Miniconjous, Forsyth and the First Squadron were to return to the agency. Whitside and the Second Squadron were to hold the Indians on Wounded Knee until ordered to march them to the railroad. The command, with an absolute minimum of baggage, faced east and trotted out of the agency.[14]

Shortly afterward, near sunset, Major Whitside and his prisoners reached their destination. The valley here was 300 to 500 yards wide. Wounded Knee Creek meandered northward close to the base of a high ridge bordering the valley on the east. On the other side, marking its western limit, two ridges pointed east. Separating them, a dry ravine snaked eastward across the

12. Testimony of Whitside, WKIR.
13. Reproduced in WKIR.
14. Testimony of Brooke and Forsyth, WKIR.

valley and emptied into the creek. The road from Porcupine Creek, on which the Miniconjous and their escort were traveling, descended the slope on the east and crossed Wounded Knee Creek by means of a bridge, then passed the Wounded Knee Post Office and Mosseau's store and ran southward across the dry ravine before curving to the west, toward the agency. About 150 yards south of the bridge, midway between the store and the ravine, rows of cavalry tents edged the road on the west. They extended to the base of a low hill, the point of the northernmost ridge on the west side of the valley. Bull Eagle lived in a cabin on top of this knob. The Indians killed in the Battle of Wounded Knee were later buried here, and it has since taken the name of Cemetery Hill.

As Whitside's column crossed the bridge, some of the Indians turned aside to Mosseau's store, where they bought candles, coffee, sugar, and a few other supplies. The rest, following the directions of the soldiers, continued down the road past the military camp and halted on the north edge of the ravine. As finally pitched, their tepees extended in an arc from the agency road at the ravine crossing to the southern base of Cemetery Hill, a distance of about 250 yards. Whitside promptly posted Hawthorne's two Hotchkiss guns on top of Cemetery Hill, their muzzles pointed in enfilade at the Indian camp. He also instructed Capt. Myles Moylan, officer of the day, to station his own troop, A, and Capt. Henry J. Nowlan's Troop I as sentinels around the Indian camp. Moylan established twenty posts entirely circling the Miniconjou village, with patrols ranging back and forth between the fixed stations.[15] At the south edge of the cavalry camp, where the scouts had set up their own tent, a large conical affair, Whitside had another erected for Big Foot's use. It was a roomy wall tent, heated by a camp stove. Assistant Surgeon James D. Glennan, with Little Bat interpreting, attended the sick chief.

The rest of the regiment arrived about 8:30 P.M., and Colonel Forsyth assumed command from Major Whitside. The reinforcements took a circuitous route east of the road in order to reach the military camp without alarming the Indians. The additional

15. Testimony of Whitside and Moylan, WKIR.

cavalry, having brought no tents, bivouacked just north of Whitside's camp. Forsyth sent Captain Capron and his two Hotchkiss guns to join Hawthorne on top of Cemetery Hill, and Capron assumed command of the artillery. Lieutenant Taylor's Oglala scouts bivouacked on the south side of the ravine, opposite the Miniconjou camp.

The officers of the Seventh Cavalry had a jolly time that night. James Asay, the Pine Ridge trader, had loaded a keg of whisky on a wagon and had come out with Forsyth. Until late in the night, the officers celebrated the capture of Big Foot. From the reports of this merriment sprang the accusation that the troops were drunk during the battle of the 29th, but witnesses of the evening's festivities pointed out that the enlisted men did not share in the revelry, and that no officer showed any signs of intoxication the next morning.[16] The military camp finally quieted down as all not on duty turned to their blankets. Little Bat and Father Francis Craft, an extroverted Catholic missionary who had ridden out with Forsyth, walked over to Louis Mosseau's house. Next morning, Mosseau awoke to find both men in bed with him.

The Miniconjou slept somewhat less soundly. Although Forsyth had tried to keep them from knowing about his arrival with more soldiers, Taylor's scouts had called across the ravine to their kinsmen and given them the news. Throughout the night the Indians, uncertain about the morrow and deeply suspicious of the soldiers, grew steadily more uneasy. With fear and foreboding, they greeted the chill dawn.

16. See especially Richard C. Stirk and Charles W. Allen Interviews, Ricker Collection.

12. WOUNDED KNEE

COL. JAMES W. FORSYTH had commanded the Seventh Cavalry since 1886. With square chin, piercing eyes under heavy brows, iron-gray hair, and neat mustache, he looked every bit a cavalry colonel. He brought to the regiment a distinguished record in the Civil War—major general of volunteers and a string of brevets in the Regular Army up to brigadier general—but he had very little command experience in Indian campaigning. During the heavy fighting of the 1870s, he had served on the staff of Lt. Gen. Philip H. Sheridan, first as aide-de-camp, later as military secretary. As General Miles was quick to point out after the Wounded Knee catastrophe upset his carefully laid plans, Forsyth "had never exercised command in any engagement with Indians, with the exception of a skirmish between his advance guard and a small party of Bannocks, July 20, 1878."[1] This made no difference to the colonel's officers and men. They liked and respected him, and almost to a man they lined up behind him when he came under fire from General Miles.

On the morning of December 29, 1890, Forsyth's regiment

1. Miles to Adjt. Gen., Feb. 2, 1891.

numbered 413 enlisted men (229 in the First Squadron, 181 in the Second, 3 in regimental headquarters) and 25 officers—a total of 438. The artillery was manned by 20 men and 2 officers; and probably about 30 Oglalas made up Taylor's troop of Indian scouts. In all, Forsyth had a little more than 500 effectives, organized as follows:

SEVENTH U.S. CAVALRY

Regimental Headquarters
    Col. James W. Forsyth
    1st Lt. L. S. McCormick, Adjutant
    1st Lt. Ezra B. Fuller, Quartermaster
    Capt. & Asst. Surgeon J. Van R. Hoff, Medical Director
    1st Lt. & Asst. Surgeon James D. Glennan, Medical Officer
    Veterinary Surgeon Daniel LeMay
    Three Noncommissioned Staff Officers

First Squadron
    Maj. Samuel M. Whitside
    1st Lt. W. J. Nicholson, Adjutant
Troop A—Capt. Myles Moylan; 1st Lt. Ernest A. Garlington
Troop B—Capt. Charles A. Varnum; 1st Lt. John C. Gresham
Troop I—Capt. Henry J. Nowlan; 2d Lt. John C. Waterman
Troop K—Capt. George D. Wallace; 1st Lt. James D. Mann

Second Squadron
    Capt. Charles S. Ilsley
    1st Lt. W. W. Robinson, Jr., Adjutant
Troop C—Capt. Henry Jackson; 2d Lt. T. Q. Donaldson
Troop D—Capt. Edward S. Godfrey; 2d Lt. S. R. H. Tompkins
Troop E—1st Lt. Horatio G. Sickel; 2d Lt. Sedgwick Rice
Troop G—Capt. Winfield S. Edgerly; 1st Lt. Edwin P. Brewer

LIGHT BATTERY E, FIRST U.S. ARTILLERY

    Capt. Allyn Capron, First Artillery
    2d Lt. Harry L. Hawthorne, Second Artillery (attached)
Four Hotchkiss Breech-Loading Steel Mountain Rifles, caliber 1.65 inches; length of bore, 24.72 calibers; weight of tube, 116.6 pounds; weight of carriage, 220 pounds; weight of exploding cartridge, 2 pounds 10 ounces; effective range, 4,200 yards. The battery

was divided into two platoons of two guns each. Capron commanded one, Hawthorne the other.[2]

TROOP A, INDIAN SCOUTS

1st Lt. Charles W. Taylor, Ninth U.S. Cavalry
2d Lt. Guy H. Preston, Ninth U.S. Cavalry

On the whole, the officers were experienced and capable professionals. Six troop commanders of the Seventh Cavalry—Moylan, Varnum, Nowlan, Wallace, Godfrey, and Edgerly—had been in the regiment since Custer's time, and all but Nowlan had fought at the Little Bighorn. Two of the troop commanders, Godfrey and Edgerly (as well as Forsyth and Whitside) later became generals. Allyn Capron, a "huge, powerful man with a voice like a bull,"[3] knew how to get the most out of both men and cannon. The enlisted men were another matter. Except for a hard core of seasoned noncommissioned officers, most of the men had never been under fire. Of the regiment, 81—nearly one-fifth—were recruits, and of these, 38 had joined the regiment at Pine Ridge only two weeks earlier. The soldiers were armed with Springfield single-shot carbines and Colt revolvers. Taylor's Oglala scouts had been enlisted for scouting. At that they were good, but they could hardly be relied upon to do much fighting against their Miniconjou brethren. The command was not, therefore, a force of veteran fighters.

In addition, two other officers, 1st Lt. John Kenzie, Second Infantry, and Assistant Surgeon Charles B. Ewing, had come out from the agency to watch the proceedings. A miscellaneous assortment of civilians rounded out the complement of whites. Among them were Interpreter Philip Wells, attached to Taylor's scouts; Father Francis M. J. Craft; Scouts John Shangreau and Little Bat; and three newspapermen, Charles W. Allen of the

---

2. The gun is fully described in Edward S. Farrow, *Farrow's Military Encyclopedia: A Dictionary of Military Knowledge* (3 vols. New York, 1885), 2, 57.

3. Col. Louis Brechemin to author, March 30, 1949, printed in *Westerners Brand Book* (Chicago), *15* (November, 1958), 71–72. Brechemin served under Capron in 1898.

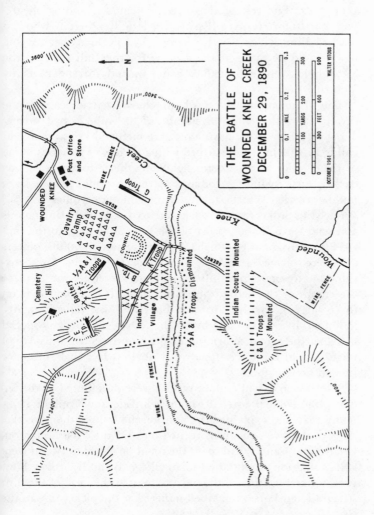

THE BATTLE OF
WOUNDED KNEE CREEK
DECEMBER 29, 1890

OCTOBER 1961   WALTER WITOUS

MILE	0	0.1	0.2	0.3
YARDS	0	100	200	300
FEET	0	300	600	900

Chadron (Nebraska) *Democrat,* William F. Kelley of the *Nebraska State Journal* (Lincoln), and Will Cressey of the Omaha *Daily Bee.* The rest of the correspondents, including the reporter-artist for *Harper's Weekly,* Frederic Remington, who had reached Pine Ridge the day before, had decided that the big news would be made at the agency, for the Indians from the Stronghold were expected to come in and surrender at any moment.

The Miniconjous who awoke in the village adjacent to the cavalry camp that morning numbered the same as had surrendered to Whitside the day before, 120 men and 230 women and children. The men were armed with a variety of weapons, some of them relics of the Custer fight, but the testimony of many participants, including Indians, leaves no doubt that a large number carried Winchester repeating rifles or carbines.

Forsyth's orders from Brooke were to disarm the Miniconjous and send them, under escort of the First Squadron, to the railroad for movement to Omaha. Neither he nor any of his officers considered armed resistance to such overwhelming force anything but a remote possibility. His plan, therefore, was to place the troops of the Second Squadron, mounted, in positions on three sides of the Indians, and hold his First Squadron, dismounted, in reserve close by on the fourth side for any special task that the actual disarming might require. Such a display of might would reinforce the already obvious fact that resistance invited destruction.[4]

After reveille, while more rations were distributed to the Indians, the colonel briefed Major Whitside and Captain Ilsley on his plan and explained the positions he wanted them to take. At 7:30 the two squadrons turned out. Of the First Squadron, two troops, A and I, had spent the night on guard duty and were still in position around the Indian village. B and K Troops, however, formed in front of the officers' tents at the head of the unit streets. Their horses remained tethered at the picket line in the

4. Testimony of Whitside, McCormick, Jackson, Edgerly, and Capron, WKIR; Maj. L. S. McCormick, "Wounded Knee and Drexel Mission Fights," MSS, December 1904, in E. S. Luce Seventh Cavalry Collection.

camp. The Second Squadron formed on horseback at the bivouac north of the tents. Troop E then took station on a hill just
west of the battery and supporting it. Troop G drew up east of
the agency road facing the Indian village. C and D Troops deployed in a long rank across the valley south of the ravine. About
fifty yards to their front, Taylor's scouts formed another mounted line, and in front of the scouts a third line, dismounted
sentinels from the night guard, occupied the brow of the ravine.
This line extended around the west flank of the village and
also around the east flank, on the agency road. The guard reserve, about one-third of A and I Troops, gathered on foot with
Captain Moylan near the base of Cemetery Hill, to the east of
the artillery. As the Indian men were to be assembled at Big
Foot's tent, on the south edge of Whitside's camp, and there disarmed, B and K Troops remained in formation at the head of
their streets waiting for whatever employment the situation
might demand. None of the soldiers was more than 300 yards
from the Indians.

Forsyth had sent John Shangreau to summon the Indian men
to Big Foot's tent, and at the scout's instigation the camp crier,
Wounded Hand, began to circulate among the tepees announcing that the soldier chief wished to have a council with the men.[5]

This intensified the uneasiness that had distressed the people
since the night before, when they had learned that more soldiers
had arrived on Wounded Knee. At no time after the surrender
to Whitside on the 28th, however, had the Miniconjous as a
group considered armed resistance. They wanted only to ap-
pease the soldiers and get started on the final leg of the journey
to, so they believed, Pine Ridge. But now the awful truth dawned
that their guns were to be taken. Even so, there was still no deliberate intent to fight for them. As all could plainly see, such a
course could only result in annihilation. Yet the actual disarming
could be expected to turn loose some intense emotions. Not only
was the rifle numbered among the most treasured possessions of
an Indian, but, one and all, the Miniconjous could not shake the
fear that if they gave up their guns they would be slaughtered

5. John Shangreau and Joseph Horn Cloud Interviews, Ricker Collection.

by the troops. It was an unreasonable and unjustified fear, but a very real one. It explains what was soon to happen.[6]

While the troops were making their way to assigned positions at about 8:00 A.M., some of the Indian men, heeding the camp crier, walked over to where Forsyth stood with a knot of officers and civilians, including the reporters, in front of Big Foot's tent. Inside, Dr. Hoff attended the prostrate chief, whose wife hovered nearby. It was a restless, uncooperative group that confronted the colonel. It fluctuated in size as the men milled back and forth between the village and the council site. Through Shangreau, Forsyth tried to get the men together and settled quietly in one place so that he could state his demands.[7]

Finally, Forsyth, Whitside, and Shangreau herded the men into a rough, crowded line facing the cavalry camp, the center opposite the entrance to Big Foot's tent. With Shangreau interpreting, the colonel spoke pleasantly to them, explaining why their arms must be surrendered and assuring them, in the words of Father Craft, "that they were perfectly safe in the hands of their old friends the soldiers, and that starvation and other troubles were now happily at an end."[8]

The Indians immediately began talking among themselves and at length decided to send two men to confer with Big Foot. Shangreau went along. Inside the tent, they explained what the soldiers wanted and asked what they should do. Give up the bad guns, advised Big Foot, and keep the good ones. Shangreau interceded. "You better give up the guns," he warned, "you can buy

6. See especially statements of Craft, Frog, and Helps-Them, WKIR; Philip Wells, Joseph Horn Cloud, and Dewey Beard Interviews, Ricker Collection; Elaine Goodale to CIA, Jan. 12, 1891; and Elaine Goodale Eastman, "The Ghost Dance and Wounded Knee Massacre," p. 38. Moylan and Robinson both testified (WKIR) that the fact that children were playing in and around the village during the council indicated that the Indians did not expect to fight. Both McCormick and Gresham ("The Story of Wounded Knee," p. 107) later wrote, but did not so testify at the inquiry, that the Indians had planned to fight and had resolved to do so in council the night before. The testimony at the inquiry makes this assumption doubtful.

7. Forsyth's adjutant later gave the clearest picture of this phase of the proceedings: McCormick MSS.

8. Testimony of Craft, WKIR.

guns, but if you lose a man you cannot replace him." "No," answered Big Foot, "we will keep the good guns." The two men returned to the group outside and reported what the chief had said.[9]

Forsyth and Whitside counted off twenty men from the left flank of the Indian line and had Shangreau tell them to go to the village and bring back their rifles. While they were gone the group once more turned unruly, and the disorderly shuffling to and from the village resumed. At length the twenty men returned and laid down two broken carbines—"long used, no doubt, as toys by the children," observed Lieutenant Gresham, "but forming no part of the splendid Winchesters owned by the warriors."[10] These were the only guns they had, the Indians declared. Rapidly losing his patience, Whitside turned to the colonel and said that their purpose could never be accomplished this way, that Big Foot should be brought out and commanded to have his men cooperate. Forsyth agreed that a more positive approach seemed necessary. At his order, the hospital steward, assisted by one of the Indians, carried Big Foot from the tent and laid him on the ground facing the center of the Indian line. He was stiff and weak and bleeding from the nose. The headmen of the band took station behind him and sat on the ground. Dr. Hoff stood nearby.[11]

At the same time, again at Whitside's suggestion, Forsyth decided to put a stop to the traffic between the council and the village, for it was exciting the women. Lieutenant Nicholson, Whitside's adjutant, therefore summoned B and K Troops, a total of 110 men, from their station in the adjacent military camp. K Troop, under Captain Wallace and Lieutenant Mann, drew up about thirty paces behind the Indian line and parallel to it, facing north. B Troop, under Captain Varnum and Lieutenant Gresham, formed at right angles to K Troop and to the

9. Shangreau Interview, Ricker Collection, is the only source for this conversation. Because the men did in fact follow Big Foot's advice as reported by Shangreau, I believe it probably happened substantially as recounted.

10. Gresham, p. 107.

11. Testimony of Whitside and Hoff, WKIR. Joseph Horn Cloud and Dewey Beard Interviews, Ricker Collection.

Indians, on the left flank of both, facing east. About thirty paces
separated the front of this troop from the flank of the Indians;
its left bent slightly and almost reached to Big Foot's tent. At
the apex of the angle formed by the two troops, a gap of perhaps
seventy-five yards intervened between Varnum's right and Wallace's left. As the Indians kept filtering through this exit, sentinels were strung across it at intervals of about twenty-five feet,
and all traffic halted. There were now in the council 106 men,
the other fourteen presumably being in the village. With Forsyth were Whitside, Shangreau, Philip Wells, Drs. Hoff and
Glennan, Lieutenants McCormick, Nicholson, and Robinson,
Father Craft, and the three reporters.[12]

While B and K Troops were moving into these positions under
the guidance of Lieutenant Nicholson, Forsyth was conferring
with the reclining Big Foot. Philip Wells had taken Shangreau's
place as interpreter. Forsyth had him tell Big Foot to direct his
men to give up their guns. Big Foot replied that they had no
guns. All weapons had been seized and burned by the soldiers
at Cheyenne River. After Wells had translated, Forsyth said, according to Wells, "You tell Big Foot that he tells me that his
Indians have no arms when yesterday at the time of surrender
they were well armed. I am sure he is deceiving me." "They
have no guns only such as you have found," answered the chief.
"I gathered up all my guns at the Cheyenne River Agency and
turned them in, and they were all burned up."[13]

Big Foot declining to cooperate, Forsyth and Whitside concluded that there was nothing to do but detail soldiers to search
the village. Wallace and Mann took fifteen men from their left
flank and began at the east end of the village; Varnum broke
fifteen off his right and began at the other end, at the base of
Cemetery Hill. This widened still farther the interval at the

12. This formation is described by all participants, but see especially testimony
of Whitside, Varnum, Nicholson, Hoff, and McCormick, WKIR. McCormick, describing the gap, says, "Each troop being 75 to 100 yards from the apex." Given
the close quarters in which the council was held, this seems much too high an
estimate.

13. Testimony of Whitside and Wells, WKIR.

apex of the angle. Whitside supervised the operation. John Shangreau went with Wallace as interpreter, Little Bat with Varnum. Lieutenant Nicholson and Dr. Ewing accompanied Varnum, while Lieutenant Preston (Taylor's second) and reporter Charles W. Allen accompanied Wallace and Mann.

"Everything found was so hidden that I almost had to dig for it," recalled Varnum. The women tried every stratagem possible to conceal the arms, many of them sitting on the ground and covering rifles with their voluminous skirts. Several had to be bodily removed. "The first rifle I found," testified Varnum, "was under a squaw who was moaning and who was so indisposed to the search that I had her displaced, and under her was a beautiful Winchester rifle." The searchers took everything that could be considered a weapon—knives, axes, hatchets, bows and arrows. Some arms were found in the wall pockets inside the tepees. Soon a sizable pile had accumulated. Captain Moylan brought his small reserve of A and I Troops down from the flank of Cemetery Hill and had the weapons carried up to the battery position. Even the wagons, which the women had packed for the trip to Pine Ridge, were unpacked and searched.

At the other end of the camp, Wallace's pile of weapons also grew. These his men carried to the council and threw in the tent occupied by the scouts. In a letter to his brother, written on his deathbed several days later, Lieutenant Mann described the scene:

> We went through the tents searching for arms, and while this was going on, everyone seemed to be good natured, and we had no thought of trouble. The enlisted men were not allowed to go inside the tents and only took the arms as we [officers] handed them out. The squaws were sitting on bundles concealing guns and other arms. We lifted them as tenderly and treated them as nicely as possible. Had they been the most refined ladies in the land, they could not have been treated with more consideration. The squaws made no resistance, and when we took the arms they seemed to be satisfied. Wallace [a tall, gaunt, fatherly looking man]

played with the children chucking them under the chin and being as pleasant with them all as could be. He had picked up a stone war club, which he carried with him.[14]

While Varnum and Wallace searched the village, the men in the circle, nervous over their separation from the women, grew increasingly restless. Now and then one tried to slip through the barrier of soldiers, only to be turned back. Throughout the morning, the old medicine man, Yellow Bird, attired in the costume of the Ghost Dance, had been gyrating around the crowd of Indians, muttering incantations and occasionally stooping over, gathering a handful of dirt, and casting it into the air toward the soldiers. Suddenly he began to harangue the men, most of whom had squatted on the ground. "Do not be afraid and let your hearts be strong to meet what is before you," he intoned, as Wells recalled it. "We are all well aware that there are lots of soldiers about us and they have lots of bullets, but I have received assurance that their bullets cannot penetrate us; the prairie is large and the bullets will not go towards you; they will not penetrate you." "How," the men, some of whom wore Ghost Shirts, answered in approval. Then Yellow Bird resumed his rhythmic dance around the group.

Wells turned to Whitside, who had come back to the council after starting the search details on their task. "That man is making mischief," he informed the major, and repeated what Yellow Bird had said. Whitside sent him to tell Forsyth. Wells and Forsyth walked over to Yellow Bird and commanded him to sit down. Big Foot's brother-in-law heard the order and said, "He will sit down when he gets around the circle." Yellow Bird soon squatted and lapsed into silence.[15]

About 9:30 A.M. Wallace and Varnum completed the search

14. Sources for the village search: testimony of Whitside, Moylan, Varnum, Nicholson, and Ewing, WKIR; Charles W. Allen, John Shangreau, and Dewey Beard Interviews, Ricker Collection; Gresham, pp. 106–07; McCormick MSS. Mann's letter is printed in full in Lt. Col. Frazer Arnold, "Ghost Dance and Wounded Knee," *Cavalry Journal*, 43 (1934), 18–20.

15. Testimony of Wells, Frog, Helps-Them, and Craft, WKIR. Wells Interview, Ricker Collection. McCormick MSS.

of the village. They had turned up thirty-eight rifles. A few were Winchester repeaters, but most were old pieces of doubtful utility. The Winchesters so much in evidence at the surrender the day before remained concealed. There was now but one place they could be—under the blankets of the men themselves.

With Wells translating, Forsyth announced that each Indian would have to submit to inspection. He did not want to conduct a personal search, he said, but desired the Indians to come forward like men, remove their blankets, and deposit any concealed weapons on the ground. The older men responded with "How," and about twenty got up and moved toward the colonel, who stood just west of Big Foot's tent with Whitside, Varnum, Wallace, and a detail of about six cavalrymen. The young men made no move to comply, and Yellow Bird began to harangue them again.

One by one the old men pulled off their blankets, then were directed to one side. The search revealed no weapons. Next, Whitside and Varnum stood facing each other and began to pass the young men between them. The first three yielded two rifles, one a Winchester, and a quantity of ammunition. Varnum asked Whitside whether the belts should be taken as well as the ammunition. Whitside said to let the men keep the belts. Varnum's first sergeant held his hat while the captain emptied the cartridges into it. Someone went in search of a grain bag to use as a container for the shells.

The young men grew more excited as Yellow Bird continued his harangue. Philip Wells tried to get Big Foot's brother-in-law, a man of some influence, to calm them, but with no success. The tension communicated to the soldiers. Lieutenant Mann, commanding K Troop while Wallace helped with the disarming, observed the young men drifting toward the east edge of the council area. "I had a peculiar feeling come over me," he recalled, "some presentiment of trouble." "Be ready," he cautioned the men, "there is going to be trouble." At the same time, he ordered the troop, standing in four ranks with intervals of about two yards between files, to fall back about twenty-five feet. Executing this movement, the unit involuntarily closed to the left, away from the Indians, thus reducing the intervals and bunching the men together.[16]

Meanwhile, an Indian named Black Coyote had been stalking around holding his rifle in both hands overhead. He was, Turning Hawk later explained, "a crazy man, a young man of very bad influence and in fact a nobody." Joseph Horn Cloud and Dewey Beard added that he was also deaf. Black Coyote shouted that this gun belonged to him; he had paid much money for it; and he would not give it to anyone unless he received pay in return. Two soldiers approached from behind and seized him. There was a brief struggle. Black Coyote brought the rifle down. Pointing to the east and upward at a 45-degree angle, it went off. As Turning Hawk innocently observed, "Of course the firing of a gun must have been the breaking of a military rule of some sort."[17]

At the same instant, Yellow Bird gathered a handful of dirt and threw it into the air. Five or six young men on the east edge of the council area rose as one, threw aside their blankets, turned toward K Troop, and leveled their rifles. Lieutenant Robinson, mounted, was between them and K Troop. Swinging his horse to get out of the way, he shouted "Look out men, they are going to fire!" Captain Varnum, just searching the third young man to pass between him and Whitside, glanced toward the scene of the disturbance. "By God they have broken," he exclaimed. To Lieutenant Mann, the warriors seemed to hesitate an eternal moment. "I thought, 'the pity of it! What can they be thinking of?'" He drew his revolver and slipped through the ranks to the front. The volley crashed into Troop K. "Fire! Fire on them!" screamed Mann.[18]

The explosion of a hundred carbines drowned the lieutenant's command, for by instinct both K and B Troops opened fire. In-

16. Testimony of Whitside, Varnum, Hoff, Wells, Craft, and Frog, WKIR. Mann in Arnold, pp. 18–20. Wells Interview, Ricker Collection. McCormick MSS.

17. Account of Turning Hawk in CIA, *Annual Report* (1891), p. 180. Joseph Horn Cloud and Dewey Beard Interviews, Ricker Collection.

18. Mann in Arnold, pp. 18–20. Wells Interview, Ricker Collection. Testimony of Whitside, Varnum, Nicholson, Wells, Craft, Robinson, Frog, and Helps-Them, WKIR.

dians and soldiers stood face to face and shot it out. "The way those Sioux worked those Winchesters was beautiful," recalled an officer. And another, picturing the response of the troops, said, "I never in my life saw Springfields worked so industriously."[19] Smoke and dust and the din of battle filled the square. Dewey Beard remembered chiefly the glint of brass buttons showing through the murk. The warriors emptied their rifles at Troop K, and every shot that missed a soldier plowed into the village, where women and children scrambled in terrified confusion to get out of the way.

A bullet grazed Lieutenant Gresham's nose; one knocked Varnum's pipe from his mouth; one hit Lieutenant Kenzie in the foot; several riddled Dr. Hoff's clothing; one smashed Lieutenant Garlington's elbow. Stone war club still in his hand, Captain Wallace rushed to his station behind K Troop. He had no sooner reached there than a bullet carried away the top of his head.[20]

Just before the first fire the sun had begun to shine in Big Foot's eyes. Weakly, he rose to a sitting position. When the smoke cleared, White Lance remembered many years later, "I looked [and] I saw Big Foot lying down with blood on his forehead and his head to the right side." He was dead. Most of the headmen, including the elder Horn Cloud, who had scoffed at the Ghost Dance, had been cut down behind him.[21]

"One man," an officer later related, "was hit early in the firing, but he continued to pump his Winchester; but growing weaker

19. Frederic Remington, "The Sioux Outbreak in South Dakota," *Harper's Weekly*, 35 (Jan. 24, 1891), 61.

20. Wells Interview, Ricker Collection. Maj. E. A. Garlington, "The Seventh Regiment of Cavalry," in Theo. F. Rodenbough, ed., *The Army of the United States* (New York, 1896), pp. 265–66.

21. Joseph Horn Cloud and Dewey Beard Interviews, Ricker Collection. Statement of White Lance in James H. McGregor, *The Wounded Knee Massacre from the Viewpoint of the Sioux* (Minneapolis, 1940), p. 118. Charles W. Allen, a reporter, in a Ricker interview, said that as Big Foot lifted himself up, an officer shot him dead. Then, as Big Foot's daughter ran to her father, the officer shot her in the back. This officer, Allen told Ricker in confidence, was Lieutenant Reynolds. There was no doubt about it, for Allen knew him well. Ricker promised never to reveal the name of the murderer of Big Foot. Inasmuch as there was no Lieutenant Reynolds at Wounded Knee, or even in the Sioux campaign of 1890, this statement must remain open to serious question.

and weaker, his shots went higher and higher, until his last went straight up in the air."[22]

With empty rifle magazines, the warriors dissolved into small parties and dashed around the square trying to break through the blue lines. There were individual, hand-to-hand fights.

Dewey Beard rushed a soldier and tried to grab his carbine. The two struggled for a moment. With his right hand, Dewey sank his knife into his opponent's side. The carbine dropped. The soldier seized Dewey around the throat and tried to strangle him. Again Dewey plunged the knife into the man's side. He went down, but tried to rise. Dewey straddled him and, while the soldier screamed, stabbed him again and again in the kidney until he died.[23]

A warrior sprang at Philip Wells with a long cheese knife ground to a fine point. Wells dropped to one knee and threw up his rifle to ward off the blow. The Indian's wrist struck the rifle but the knife sliced deep into Well's nose, which dropped over his mouth, hanging by two shreds of skin. The Indian drew back for another thrust. Wells, now on his back, parried it with his rifle. Again the Indian drew back. Wells smashed him behind the ear with the rifle muzzle. The stunned assailant recoiled, and Wells, jumping to his feet, shot him in the side. He fell. A corporal ran over and shot him again, in the chest. Bleeding profusely, Wells ran for the shelter of trader Jim Asay's wagon. He slipped on the grass and fell. Another Indian jumped on his back with a knife, but only cut his coat. Wells got free and continued to fight. He tried to pull his nose off, but it would not come loose.[24]

Dr. Ewing had crawled in the back of Asay's wagon. As Wells ran toward it, bullets grazed the mules and they stampeded, carrying Ewing around the cavalry tents on the north to the base of Cemetery Hill.[25]

A warrior ran past Father Craft, but paused long enough to drive a knife between his shoulder blades and into one of his

22. Remington, p. 61.
23. Dewey Beard Interview, Ricker Collection.
24. Wells Interview, Ricker Collection. Testimony of Wells, WKIR.
25. Testimony of Ewing, WKIR.

lungs. "The poor fellow did not see that he was stabbing a black robe," Craft later explained. The wound was a bad one, but the priest continued to move among the soldiers, giving first aid and administering last rites to the dying.[26]

Reporter William F. Kelley saw an Indian charging directly at him. He raised his revolver and fired all six shots into the oncoming figure. Then he picked up a carbine and cartridge belt dropped by a soldier and continued to fire at the warriors. He was later credited with killing at least three.[27]

The savage contest at close quarters lasted no more than five minutes before the bulk of the warriors succeeded in breaching the military lines. Some ran to the east, across the agency road toward G Troop. Most, however, broke through and around K Troop and made for the village. Some turned to shoot back at the soldiers, who returned the fire. Again bullets riddled the tepees—and the women and children. Behind, in the council square, more than twenty Miniconjous littered the ground together with more than thirty dead and wounded soldiers of B and K Troops.[28]

Horrified, the troops ringing the battleground had watched the furious melee in the council square. They could not fire because the Indians were mixed up with their comrades. Lieutenant Robinson, who had been caught in the square on horseback, galloped around the rear of B Troop and up Cemetery Hill. Dismounting behind the crest, he scrambled to the top. The artillerymen were standing at their guns, lanyards in hand, waiting for the order to fire. Captain Capron—"a grim old fellow, with a red-lined cape overcoat, and nerve enough for a hundred-ton gun"—noticed that one of the gunners was agitated. Fearing that he would jerk the lanyard before the cavalrymen below had separated from the warriors, he ordered the friction primer removed from the gun. Then the Indians broke from the square, B and K Troops fell back among the tents of their own camp, and Colonel Forsyth made his way to the battery position. At

26. Wells Interview, Ricker Collection. Cook, *Fifty Years on the Old Frontier,* pp. 235–36. Mooney, *Ghost-Dance,* p. 872. Testimony of Craft, WKIR.
27. Watson, "Last Indian War," p. 9.
28. Testimony of Whitside, Moylan, Wells, Nicholson, and Robinson, WKIR.

once the four guns opened up on all groups of Indians that could be seen shooting at soldiers. Firing up to fifty explosive shells a minute, they did their work with deadly effect.[29]

The first clear target that presented itself to Capron's eager gunners seems to have been the warriors who bolted to the east of the council square. Joined by some women and children from the east end of the village, they turned north on the agency road toward the store. The artillery hurled shells into them. Many people scattered from the road into the field southeast of the store and came under the carbines of Edgerly's Troop G, which had dismounted. Those who escaped found safety beneath the banks of Wounded Knee Creek to the north.[30]

At the first fire the Indian village boiled with panic-stricken women and children. Those in the northwest end piled into wagons, already loaded and harnessed, and fled up the road to the northwest in the wake of the stampeding pony herd. Troop E occupied the low hill on the right flank of the battery. Lieutenants Sickel and Rice promptly dismounted the unit and deployed it to cover the road. Seeing that the approaching horde consisted of women and children, both officers shouted orders not to fire at the Indians, but to knock down the ponies. The men opened on the herd. An old women on horseback fired at the dismounted line. "There is a buck," shouted one of the troopers, and aimed his carbine at her. "No, it is a squaw," retorted Lieutenant Rice, "don't shoot on her." "Well by God, Lieutenant, she is shooting at us," growled the soldier, but he turned his weapon back on the ponies. The fleeing women and children escaped unhurt up the road.[31]

By the time the warriors broke from the square toward the

29. Testimony of Capron and Nicholson, WKIR. McCormick MSS. The characterization is from Remington, p. 61.

30. This episode does not emerge clearly from the sources, but see especially testimony of Craft, WKIR; Joseph Horn Cloud Interview, Ricker Collection; and statement of George Running Hawk in McGregor, pp. 111–13. Edgerly's testimony is silent on the role of Troop G in this phase, and his lieutenant, Brewer, did not testify at the inqu..y.

31. Testimony of Rice, WKIR. McCormick MSS.

village, the bulk of the women and children had begun to race for the shelter of the ravine on the south edge of the Indian camp. Captain Nowlan commanded the line of sentinels on the opposite side of the ravine. "Don't fire, let them go, they are squaws," he ordered, and the men up and down the line took up the cry. The women and children poured into the ravine. Close on their heels came the rush of warriors who had freed themselves from the council square. "Here come the bucks," yelled Nowlan, "give it to them." The sentinels opened fire, and the charging warriors responded.

The three lines that confronted the Indians on the south side of the ravine—sentinels, Oglala scouts, and C and D Troops— found themselves in a dangerous position. Bullets from Troops B and K, firing into the rear of the warriors, reached into the soldiers and scouts beyond, and Hotchkiss shells began to burst uncomfortably close. The sentinels fell back on the scouts, who in turn scattered both to the east and the west, as well as to the shelter of the ravine in their front. When a shell exploded directly in front of C and D Troops, they, too, began to shift. C Troop, on the right flank, broke into its two platoons. Lieutenant Donaldson and the platoon on the right galloped around a wire fence in the rear and dismounted. A detail led the horses into a shallow ravine to the south, and Donaldson spread out a skirmish line. Captain Jackson and the other platoon fell back and dismounted on the west side of the wire fence. D Troop, at Captain Godfrey's command, withdrew behind the ridge on his left, then formed a dismounted skirmish line on top of the ridge, facing the ravine.

The warriors kept coming, down into the ravine and up the south bank. Now mixed with women and children, they burst onto the flat beyond, trying to reach the agency road. The carbines of Donaldson, Jackson, and Godfrey opened on them. "I gave the command, 'Commence Firing!'" wrote Godfrey six years later. "They fired rapidly but it seemed to me only a few seconds till there was not a living thing before us; warriors, squaws, children, ponies, dogs—for they were all mixed together —went down before that unaimed fire, and I don't think anything got nearer than a hundred yards. I believe over thirty bodies were found on our front."[32]

A half-dozen women ran at Donaldson's platoon from one side, making signs begging not to be killed. Donaldson motioned them to the sheltered position of the horses, then went down himself and told the corporal in charge of the horse-holders to take care of the women. Returning to the line, he found that the Indians were retreating to the safety of the ravine. He went into the field in front of his line. Dead and wounded Indians littered the ground. A rifle protruded from one blanket-shrouded figure. He lifted the blanket. A man and woman lay side by side, both dead.[33]

In the ravine the Indians ran in both directions. Some of those who went up the ravine paused to fire into the rear of D Troop, on the ridge to the south. Godfrey sent Lieutenant Tompkins and twelve men to stop this fire. The squad charged down the slope and poured a volley into the ravine, knocking over three warriors and flushing the rest. "A party of squaws and children ran up the ravine not over 100 yards from my men," testified the lieutenant. "I immediately gave the order don't fire on the women and children. . . . Behind them, 25 or 30 yards from them, came two bucks, stripped and painted, and my men killed these." Tompkins' squad continued to fire into the ravine.[34]

Most of the action now focused on the fringes of the battlefield, with the troops hunting down the fleeing Indians. But there was also sporadic fighting in the council square and in the village itself. Not all the Indians had left the village. An occasional shot came from the tepees. To stop this, the battery raked the Miniconjou camp from one end to the other. Flying shrapnel shredded the lodges and sought out every living thing. One woman, Blue Whirlwind, received fourteen wounds but lived. Her two little boys were wounded by her side. Another woman, maddened by wounds, crawled from the edge of the village. With a butcher

32. Maj. E. S. Godfrey, "Cavalry Fire Discipline," *Journal of the Military Service Institution of the United States*, 29 (1896), 259.

33. Testimony of Nowlan, Godfrey, Donaldson, and Taylor, WKIR. Paddy Starr and Standing Soldier Interviews, Ricker Collection.

34. Testimony of Tompkins and Godfrey, WKIR.

knife between her teeth, she made her painful way over a distance of ten yards to where a soldier lay on his back, wounded. She raised the knife over him and, as he screamed, plunged it into his breast. Another soldier, in the square, saw the act and sent a bullet into her head. She dropped next to her victim.

The artillery silenced the fire from the village. Later, the troops found Sgt. Maj. Richard Corwin, Quartermaster Sergeant Charles Campbell, and Hospital Steward Oscar Pollack lying with the bodies of Indians amid the wreckage. Campbell was still alive, but Corwin and Pollack were dead. Whether they were shot by Indians or soldiers is not known. Whitside later stated that they had gone to the village without authority.[35]

In the square, Yellow Bird had taken refuge in the Sibley tent belonging to the scouts. Slitting a hole in the canvas wall, he shot down several soldiers before someone noticed the source of fire. A private of K Troop said, "I will get the ——— out of there," and ran toward the tent. "Come back," shouted Lieutenant Mann. The soldier ignored the command and with his knife slashed open the tent. Yellow Bird fired into his attacker's stomach, and he recoiled. "My God," he exclaimed, "he has shot me. I am killed. I am killed." Turning, he staggered toward his lieutenant but fell forward, dead. Cavalrymen riddled the tent, and a Hotchkiss gun pitched two shells directly into it. Some soldiers stacked bales of hay around it and ignited them. The tent burned to the ground, revealing the shattered, charred body of the man who bore the largest responsibility for the Wounded Knee tragedy.[36]

The fighting now centered on the ravine. Of all the images of the battle that the Indian survivors retained to their last days, the experiences in this inferno remained most vivid. Dewey Beard's ordeal, if not typical, was in after years related with greatest clarity.[37]

35. Testimony of Whitside, Nicholson, and Craft, WKIR. Guy Vaughn Interview, Ricker Collection. Record of Events, Seventh U.S. Cavalry, Month of December 1890, E. S. Luce Seventh Cavalry Collection. Mooney, p. 869.

36. Mann, in Arnold, pp. 18–20. Philip Wells and Charles Allen Interviews, Ricker Collection. Testimony of Wells and Frog, WKIR.

37. Dewey Beard Interview, Ricker Collection.

After stabbing the soldier in the council square, Dewey bolted through K Troop and the village to the ravine. The sentinels on the south side fired at him, and a bullet struck him in the arm, knocking him down. Another soldier pointed his carbine, but the hammer snapped on an empty chamber. Dewey tried to shoot back, but his rifle, too, was empty. He got up and ran down the slope into the ravine. Another bullet hit him "in the lap." He sat down, reloaded, and began to fire at the blue figures dimly seen through the smoke on the opposite lip of the ravine. His gun jammed, a shell stuck in the chamber. He struggled to his feet and staggered up the ravine. Soldiers stood on both sides, firing down. (They were sentinels of A and I Troops who had been stationed on the west side of the village, and the detail from Troop D under Tompkins positioned by Godfrey.)

From an old man, Dewey got a cavalry Springfield. With two other warriors, he climbed the south bank and charged some soldiers. His companions dropped. Dewey raced back to the ravine. He came face to face with one of Taylor's scouts, who had sought shelter from the bullets lacing the flats above. Both men fired. Both missed, but Dewey, weak from his wounds, fell on his back. The scout ran away.

For a few moments Dewey watched the women and children surging up the ravine. Many fell as bullets and shrapnel struck them. Hugging the banks, mothers clawed at the sides of the ravine, digging shelter in which to place their infants. Crawling up the ravine, Dewey overtook his mother, badly wounded, holding a soldier's pistol in her hand. "My son," she said, "pass by me, I am going to fall down now." Another bullet hit her and she slumped to the ground, dead.

Now out of cartridges for the Springfield, Dewey obtained a fully loaded Winchester from another old man and continued his painful journey up the ravine, looking for his wife. He found his brother William sitting against the bank. Blood ran from a hole in his chest, but he was still alive. White Lance, Dewey's closest friend, slid down the bank. He was wounded, too. Together the three men went farther up the ravine. At a point where it turned sharply, forming a pocket, they and several other warriors crawled to the brow and began to fire at E Troop and the battery.

They drew a deluge of shot and shell. Bullets, shrapnel, smoke, and dust filled the ravine until the atmosphere was both deadly and suffocating. The bursting artillery rounds churned up the earth and caved in the banks. Dewey saw a Hotchkiss shell punch a six-inch hole in the middle of a man's stomach. Up and down the ravine the people sang death songs. A bullet smacked the earth directly in front of Dewey's face and threw dirt into his eyes, blinding him. He slid down the bank.

The troops remembered well the heroic stand of Dewey and his companions at the pocket. To get better aim on the pocket, Cpl. Paul H. Weinert and several men moved a Hotchkiss gun from Cemetery Hill to the lower hill on the west, where E Troop was formed.

All of the Indians opened fire on us [Weinert wrote]. One of my men went for ammunition and didn't come back. . . . My captain called to me to come back, but I kept moving nearer the Indians, and kept shooting. Lieutenant Hawthorne came toward me and was calling, when suddenly I heard him say: "Oh, my God!" Looking around, I saw him lying on his side, and then I knew he had been hit. Hartzog ran to him and carried him back behind the hill. I said: "By God! I'll make 'em pay for that," and ran the gun fairly into the opening of the ravine and tried to make every shot count. The Hotchkiss was a single-shot affair and had to be pulled off with a lanyard. They kept yelling at me to come back, and I kept yelling for a cool gun—there were three more on the hill not in use. Bullets were coming like hail from the Indians' Winchesters. The wheels of my gun were bored full of holes and our clothing was marked in several places. Once a cartridge was knocked out of my hand just as I was about to put it in the gun, and it's a wonder the cartridge didn't explode. I kept going in farther, and pretty soon everything was quiet at the other end of the line. Then the other guns came down. I expected a court-martial, but what was my surprise when gruff old Allyn Capron, my captain, came up to me and grasped me by the shoulders and said to the officers and men: "That's the kind of men I have in my battery."[38]

At Forsyth's order, Lieutenant Rice took his platoon of Troop E to the northwest and started down the ravine, clearing everything in his front. The pressure of this movement, together with the close-range fire of Weinert's cannon, drove the warriors from the pocket.[39]

Dewey had started up the ravine, still looking for his wife, but had to climb out and flee to the south and west when he ran into Rice's skirmishers moving east. (Dewey's wife, Wears Eagle, was in fact dead. When she was later found, shot in the chest, her 25-day-old infant, Wet Feet, was still nursing at the mother's breast. According to Dewey, the child swallowed so much blood that she died three months later. Besides his wife and baby, Dewey lost his mother and father and two brothers, William and Sherman.)

Lower down the ravine, Philip Wells, his nose still dangling, had walked to the edge of the ravine and cried out, in the Sioux tongue, "All of you that are still alive get up and come on over, you will not be molested or shot at any more." One old man painfully raised up and braced himself with his hands in a sitting position. Paddy Starr, who had come out with Taylor's scouts, watched in horror as, just then, the first of Rice's platoon, relentlessly sweeping the ravine from above, came into view. The troopers had not heard or understood Wells and, seeing the old man move, they instantly cut him down with their carbines.

38. Weinert, in W. F. Beyer and O. F. Keydel, eds., *Deeds of Valor* (Detroit, 1907), 2, 316. See also Harry L. Hawthorne, "The Sioux Campaign of 1890–91," *Journal of the Military Service Institution of the United States*, 29 (1896), 185–87. Col. Louis Brechemin, who served in Capron's battery in 1898, wrote to me in 1949: "Hawthorne was shot through his watch pocket and the works scattered through his anatomy. He had about five operations afterwards. He served in the same battery in later years, and the men said there was no living with him. Kept them at work all the damned time." This letter is printed in *Westerners Brand Book* (Chicago), 15 (November, 1958), 71–72.

39. Testimony of Rice, WKIR.

When they became aware of the situation, however, they called off the operation. One by one, wounded people emerged from the ravine and, guided by soldiers, made their way to the hospital area north of the cavalry camp.[40]

Wells went to the council square, where more than twenty Miniconjous lay scattered around. "These white people came to save you," he called out in the Sioux language, "and you have brought death on yourselves. Still the white people are merciful to save the wounded enemy when he is harmless, so if some of you are alive raise your heads. I am a man of your own blood who is talking to you." About a dozen prostrate figures raised their heads. One, named Frog, called Wells to his side. Pointing to the body of Yellow Bird, he asked, "Who is that man lying burned there?" Wells told him.

> He raised himself a little higher [related Wells], raised his closed fist, pointing it towards the dead Indian, shot out his fingers, which is amongst Indians a deadly insult, meaning I could kill you and not be satisfied doing it, am sorry I could do no more to you, and then used words tremblingly which I could not all catch, but he said this which I did hear, speaking as though to the dead man: "If I could be taken to you I would stab you," then turning to me said, "he is our murderer; only for him inciting our young men we would have all been alive and happy."[41]

Shortly after the close of the heavy fighting at the lower end of the ravine, Major Whitside rode over to confer with Captains Jackson and Godfrey. Crossing the ravine, he met a soldier holding an infant lifted from the arms of a dead mother. The trooper asked what he should do with it. Whitside pointed to a group of women, guarded by a detail of cavalrymen, and told the man to turn over the baby to these women. Continuing, he found Jackson and Godfrey with their troops south of the ravine. Jackson he ordered to go after the pony herd, which was grazing along the road about a mile west of Cemetery Hill. Godfrey he ordered

40. Paddy Starr Interview, Ricker Collection. Statement of Rough Feather in McGregor, pp. 109–10.
41. Wells, corroborated by Frog, WKIR.

to follow the ravine to its head, some two miles to the west, in search of any Miniconjous who had got that far from the battle-field.[42]

Leaving the balance of Troop D with Lieutenant Tompkins on the edge of the ravine, Godfrey took fourteen men and followed up the ravine to the crest of the divide, then descended to the wooded valley of a small creek on the other side. Surmounting a high hill west of this creek, he scanned the country-side without detecting any sign of the enemy. Returning to the valley, he had led his detachment a short distance down it when the advance guard shouted back that Indians were running into a clump of dense brush on the bank of the stream in their front.

Godfrey at once dismounted and pushed a skirmish line cautiously forward. "How, Cola; squaw, papoose, Cola, How, Cola," he shouted. There was no response. The men moved closer. "How, Cola; squaw, papoose," repeated the captain. Still there was no sound or movement. "Ready, Fire," commanded Godfrey, and a single volley crashed into the brush. Someone screamed. "Cease firing," Godfrey shouted. He ran to the brush and parted it. A woman and two children lay thrashing in their death agonies, while a fourth figure, which Godfrey took for a man, lay still on his face.

As the men turned to leave, Blacksmith Carey flicked aside the coat tails of the prostrate form and exclaimed, "This man ain't dead." Instantly he sent a bullet into the back of his head. Turning the body on it back, Godfrey saw a boy of perhaps fourteen or fifteen, although later witnesses contended that he was no more than eight or ten. The detachment headed back toward the battlefield.[43]

42. Testimony of Whitside, Hoff, Jackson, and Godfrey, WKIR.

43. These bodies were found some days after the battle by Capt. Frank D. Baldwin of General Miles' staff. Miles, then in the midst of his attempt to discredit Forsyth, made much of the incident. Baldwin declared that there were no leaves on the brush and that the troops could therefore clearly see and identify their target, leaving the implication, which Miles reinforced, that Godfrey's men had deliberately killed women and children. Many years later Godfrey stated that on December 29 the brush was covered with dead leaves and pointed out that the blizzard that swept this locale on December 31 stripped the vegetation. The limbs were thus in fact bare when Baldwin visited the scene. Godfrey was, as he said, "shocked by the tragedy," although it seems clear that he himself had been

Meanwhile, Captain Jackson and thirty-four men of C Troop had ridden hard after the herd, but passed it by when they spied a movement at the head of the ravine about a mile in advance. It was an Indian sliding into the ravine. There were in fact twenty-five Miniconjous concealed here, eight of whom were men. They had burrowed a shelter under an overhang of the bank. When Jackson galloped up, all he could see amid the brush on the edge were the muzzles of rifles pointing at him. C Troop dismounted and both sides began shooting. Jackson sent Lieutenant Donaldson and a detail down the ravine to seal off the only covered escape path and began to close in.

He soon had reinforcements. Captain Edgerly received orders from Forsyth to round up the Indians who had fled to the west. Lieutenant Taylor and a few of the Oglala scouts went with G Troop. Some scouts and soldiers were dropped off to corral and guard the Indian ponies. Arriving at the head of the ravine, Edgerly reported to Jackson and was instructed to post his troop on the opposite side of the besieged Indians.

After a brief exchange of fire, one of the scouts told Taylor that there were women and children in the ravine, some of them his own relatives. He thought they could be persuaded to come out and give up. Jackson gave the "cease fire," and the skirmish lines pulled back a bit to afford the scouts a chance to negotiate. Three or four went near the Miniconjous and shouted that if they surrendered they would not be harmed. "It took half an hour talking with them," said Jackson, "and I had to withdraw my men before they would come out."

---

a trifle hasty in giving the order to fire. The next morning, at Pine Ridge, he called Carey into his tent and asked him why he had shot the boy. "He was very penitent and began to cry, saying he was scared and only thought of self-defense; that he had been warned not to trust a wounded Indian, or take any chances—that he shot on the impulse of the moment." This interview was interrupted by the trumpet summoning the regiment to the Drexel Mission fight, and Godfrey, satisfied with Carey's explanation, let the matter drop. Godfrey also pointed out that Carey was one of the recruits he had picked up at Chadron on the way to Pine Ridge, and had been a soldier only a few weeks.

Pertinent sources: testimony of Godfrey, WKIR; Godfrey to Chief, Historical Section, Army War College, May 29, 1931, File W–12, Order of Indian Wars, American Military Institute, Washington, D.C.; Sec. War to Schofield, Feb. 12, 1891, with endorsement by Miles, March 2, 1891.

The handful of beleaguered Indians were in no condition to
withstand a siege, and at last they began to file from their refuge.
Soldiers went in and carried out the wounded—four men, three
women, and a child. The aid men dressed the wounds of these
people, and Captain Edgerly himself bandaged the injured
child. The men gathered fifteen to eighteen rifles from the
ravine.

A messenger rode back to the battlefield to summon an ambulance. Edgerly and Taylor left, too, picking up the pony herd
en route. Jackson remained with his prisoners to wait for the
ambulance.[44]

As he waited, Captain Godfrey and the fourteen men of Troop
D, returning to the battlefield after scouting the small creek
west of the divide, rode up the ridge from the west and joined
Troop C. Jackson was just organizing a detail to sweep down the
ravine toward the main battlefield when six mounted Indians
rode up from the west. One wore the badge of an agency policeman. At the same time, Jackson noticed a growing party of
mounted Indians forming on a hill to the northwest. The six
men shook hands with Jackson, Godfrey, and Donaldson, then
turned and rode back toward the other Indians. After riding
about seventy-five yards, they wheeled and, while the policeman
gesticulated in an apparent attempt to stop the act, fired back at
the soldiers. One of Godfrey's men fell, wounded.

The Indians on the hill, now numbering about 150, deployed
rapidly and charged the troops from three directions. At Jackson's order, the cavalrymen abandoned the prisoners and scattered down the east slope of the divide. They rallied some 400
yards below and received the charging Sioux with a well-di-
rected volley that killed one, Flying Horse, and wounded two
others. The warriors turned about, withdrew to the top of the
ridge, gathered up the Miniconjous, and rode off to the west.
Jackson had quickly recognized his attackers for what they were
—Oglalas and Brulés from the agency who had heard the sounds
of battle and rushed to the aid of their Miniconjou kinsmen.
The courier he sent to Forsyth for help took this word. Soon

44. Testimony of Jackson, Edgerly, and Taylor, WKIR.

Captain Edgerly with Troops E and G came galloping to the rescue, only to find that the enemy had retired.

Without their prisoners—indeed, without the C Troop guidon —Jackson and his men returned to the battlefield. They found the rest of the command, alarmed at the report of agency Indians joining the fracas, forming a defense perimeter on Cemetery Hill. A wagon train had arrived from the agency with provisions, and the wagons and their contents were being hastily arranged as barricades around the artillery on the hill. It soon became apparent, however, that the fresh force of warriors had no intention of challenging the soldiers. Everyone relaxed and set about the task of cleaning up the battlefield. It was now close to noon.[45]

During the mopping-up operations, Drs. Hoff, Glennan, and Ewing labored in the field hospital improvised on the site of the Second Squadron's bivouac. The two privates of the Hospital Corps, and later the troop aid men, assisted. Civilian teamsters drove the two ambulances. Although one had abandoned the field in panic, he returned after regaining control of himself. The ambulances moved around the field, collecting wounded soldiers and Indians and taking them to the hospital.

The Indian dead were left temporarily where they lay, together with a large number of wounded. Some of the latter had escaped to hiding places away from the immediate battlefield, and others were in parts of the ravine where resistance was never entirely eliminated because Forsyth did not want to risk further bloodshed.

Exactly how many Indians died in the holocaust is not known. The burial detail later interred 146 on the battlefield: 84 men and boys, 44 women, and 18 children.[46] Fifty-one wounded were

45. Testimony of Jackson, Godfrey, and Ewing, WKIR. Godfrey to Chief, Historical Section, Army War College, May 29, 1931. Philip Wells Interview, Ricker Collection. Three weeks later, still harassing Forsyth, Miles alluded to the sensitive matter of the lost guidon and directed that someone be sent to the battlefield to recover it. Lieutenant Donaldson rode out and found the staff and part of the banner. Maus to CO Seventh Cavalry, Jan. 20, 1891, with endorsement by Lt. L. S. McCormick, Jan. 20, and Capt. Henry Jackson, Jan. 22, 1891.

46. CIA, *Annual Report* (1891), p. 130. William Peano Interview, Ricker Collection.

ultimately admitted to the hospital at Pine Ridge.[47] Of these, at least 7 later died. Thus the known dead totals 153, the wounded 44. To this figure must be added the unknown number gathered up on the night of the 29th by agency Indians, and still others who got away from the field under their own power, either to live or die afterward. It is entirely likely that another 20 to 30 may be counted in this category. Few indeed of Big Foot's people escaped death or injury.

White casualties numbered in killed 1 officer (Wallace), 6 noncommissioned officers, and 18 privates, a total of 25. Wounded were 4 officers (including the visiting infantryman, Kenzie), 11 noncommissioned officers, 22 privates, and 2 civilians (Wells and Craft), a total of 39.[48]

Forsyth rushed word of the conflict to General Brooke, who already knew from the sound of cannon fire that a fight had taken place. Lieutenant Preston, accompanied by Pvt. Nathan Fellman and an Oglala scout, carried Forsyth's message to Pine Ridge in the short space of an hour.[49] Now the colonel gave orders to prepare for the move to the agency.

The two badly wounded officers, Lieutenants Garlington and Hawthorne, occupied one of the spring ambulances, Father Craft and a sergeant the other. The wounded, both white and red, were loaded in the freight wagons that had arrived with supplies late in the morning. Sacks of grain overlaid with loose straw served as mattresses, but the jolting of the springless vehicles made the journey to Pine Ridge a painful ordeal. Late in the afternoon, the Seventh Cavalry and its cargo of wounded moved out on the agency road, leaving the battlefield strewn with the corpses of Big Foot and his hapless people.[50]

47. Royer to CIA, Dec. 31, 1890.

48. Recapitulation in WKIR. "On the 7th of January the body of the gallant officer [Wallace], which had been sent to his home in Yorkville, South Carolina, draped in the flag of his troop, was buried with solemn ceremonies at that place. The schools of the town and many of the people joined in the funeral procession; and when the well-deserved eulogies had been pronounced, the local military body fired a salute over his grave." *Harper's Weekly, 35* (Jan. 17, 1891), 41–42.

49. Mooney, p. 873. General Orders, No. 100, Hq. of the Army, Adjt. General's office, Dec. 17, 1891, in War Dept., *General Orders and Circulars, 1891.*

50. McCormick MSS.

A lone white man preceded the Seventh. Valentine T. Mc-
Gillycuddy had returned to the agency and, hearing the sound
of firing, had ridden out to the battlefield. The fight was over by
the time he got there, and he started back toward the agency.
He met a wagon loaded with Indians. "Don't you know me,
Wasicu Wakan?" one asked. McGillycuddy thought. "When you
were our agent," the man continued, "you made an agreement
with us that if we would give you fifty of our young men to act
as police the soldiers would not come to our agency." Exposing
a bloody, bullet-punctured chest, he said, "Look at that, Father.
I was one of your police. How about the promise?" "A promise,
Thunder Cloud, is of no value," replied McGillycuddy, "when
one ceases to have the power to fill it."[51]

The three correspondents who had accompanied Forsyth
rather than remain with the others at the agency had made a
wise decision indeed. Before their eyes unfolded the biggest
news story yielded by the Indian frontier since the Custer disaster fourteen years earlier. After interviewing survivors, the news-
men repaired to Louis Mosseau's store and wrote up their accounts. By 5:00 P.M. they had finished, and Richard C. Stirk,
who had been hired as a courier, galloped out of the valley bearing the dispatches. Three hours later he was in the telegraph
office at Rushville. The correspondents at Pine Ridge had set up
a schedule by which they took turns sending the first dispatch
of the day out of Rushville. Luck favored Kelley of the *Nebraska
State Journal*, for December 29 was his day to enjoy top priority.
In Lincoln, Kelley's editor put his story on the wires of the
United Press, and next morning people everywhere read of the
bloody encounter between Big Foot's band and the Seventh
Cavalry.[52]

Starved for news of a "Sioux War" that in more than a month
had failed to produce any excitement, the nation's press gave
full play to Wounded Knee. Few journals exhibited moderation
in their editorial judgments. One segment of the press portrayed

51. McGillycuddy, *McGillycuddy: Agent*, pp. 268–69.
52. Watson, "Last Indian War." Kelley's story in *Nebraska State Journal*, Dec.
30, 1890.

the battle as a triumph of valorous soldiers over treacherous Indians plotting another Custer affair. The other vented outrage on a regiment that, thirsting for revenge since the Little Bighorn, had wantonly slaughtered gentle Indians and had found particular glee in butchering helpless women and children. The press thus introduced extremes of interpretation that have persisted in the history of Wounded Knee to this day. Few treatments of the event published since 1890 have failed to reflect one or the other extreme.

Yet, as so often happens, the truth lies somewhere between the extremes. Big Foot's people wanted peace. Fear and suspicion led them to carry passive resistance to disarmament to the point where both sides were so nervous that any incident or misunderstanding could spark a conflict. Even so, they would ultimately have given up their guns had not a few unthinking young men, incited by a fanatical medicine man, lost control of themselves and created an incident. Sucked into the cauldron of battle, their families exposed to the murderous fire of the troops, there was nothing to do but fight.

Once fired upon, the soldiers fought back with a fury inspired by what they deemed Indian treachery. They did not deliberately kill women and children, although in a few instances more caution might have been exercised. Women and children were mixed with men, and smoke and dust obscured the battlefield. It was inevitable that, in the excitement of combat, the troops would shoot noncombatants. Indeed, as we have seen, the warriors themselves upon one occasion poured a destructive fire into their own families.

The vast majority of both Indians and soldiers were—within their differing cultural frameworks—decent, ordinary, people. They suddenly found themselves thrust into battle, and they reacted with behavioral extremes that battle from time immemorial has induced in ordinary people.

It is time that Wounded Knee be viewed for what it was—a regrettable, tragic accident of war that neither side intended, and that called forth behavior for which some individuals on both sides, in unemotional retrospect, may be judged culpable, but for which neither side as a whole may be properly condemned.

13. DREXEL MISSION

IT HAD BEEN an eventful day at Pine Ridge Agency, too. At midmorning, the reports of Capron's guns echoed faintly over the hills to the east, announcing to whites and Indians alike that a fight was in progress.

The great camps of Sioux ringing the agency burst into frantic activity, and none more so than that of Two Strike, whose Brulés had so recently numbered themselves among the followers of Short Bull and Kicking Bear. About 150 warriors painted themselves and rushed to the sound of the guns. It was this force that collided with Captains Jackson and Godfrey on the ridge west of the Wounded Knee battleground.

At the agency, the remaining Brulés struck their tepees and prepared for flight. Some of the white women were assembled around a Christmas tree in the chapel sacking candy for the festivities of the Christmas season. Elaine Goodale watched from the window of the chapel. "Their white camps melted away like snow-banks in April," she wrote. "The brown hills were instantly alive with galloping horsemen and a long line of loaded wagons disappeared in the distance."[1]

1. Elaine Goodale Eastman, "Ghost Dance War and Wounded Knee Massacre," p. 36.

General Brooke, Agent Royer, and their assistants tried hard to calm the excited Indians, but with little success. Their efforts became pointless, at least for the Two Strike people, when the Brulé war party returned from Wounded Knee about 1:00 P.M. with word of the slaughter of Big Foot's band. Angered also by the death of Flying Horse before the carbines of Jackson and Godfrey, the Brulés were bent on trouble. They swarmed menacingly over the ridge southwest of the agency, beyond Red Cloud's house. Finally, a man named Turning Bear decided to cross the creek and set fire to the agency barn. The police turned out to stop him. He fired two shots. The police replied with a fusillade that churned up the soil around the lone attacker and sent him running back up the ridge. With Dr. Eastman, General Brooke raced to the scene of the disturbance. "Stop, stop!" shouted the general. "Doctor, tell them they must not fire until ordered!" Eastman translated, and the police stopped firing.

The Brulés now turned a long-range fire on the agency. Most of the bullets fell harmlessly short of the mark, but two soldiers on the line southwest of the military camp were wounded. Lt. A. W. Corliss, commanding here, went to Brooke and asked permission to return the fire with his Hotchkiss gun. Brooke refused. He still hoped to coax the stampeding Sioux into returning quietly to their campsites. To throw artillery shells in the direction of Red Cloud's house would hardly improve the chance of success. Brooke's belief, as he wired Miles shortly after the first exchange of gunfire, was that "the Indians belonging to this Agency are excited but not hostile in their attitude."[2]

The civilians at the agency did not share the general's optimism. The firing convinced them that hundreds of maddened Sioux were about to attack the agency. "Every married employee was seeking a place of safety for his family," said Dr. Eastman. "My office was full of refugees." He made arrangements with one to secure a horse and get Elaine Goodale through to the railroad and safety. On Christmas Day she had consented to marry him.

2. William Peano and Capt. A. W. Corliss Interviews, Ricker Collection. Eastman, *Deep Woods to Civilization*, pp. 108–09. Brooke to Miles, Dec. 29, 1890 (two telegrams). Miles to Adjt. Gen., same date. Royer to CIA, same date.

But Elaine Goodale refused to go. She had her hands full at the chapel and the mission, now "swamped by a crowd of sobbing, terrified women and children—church members, for the most part of mixed descent. The two Presbyterian missionary women left their more exposed cottage on the brow of the hill and joined us in the rectory, one of them carrying her pet canary in his cage. The solid outside shutters were slammed to, the oil lamps lit, and an effort made to calm the excitement with the help of hot coffee and sandwiches."[3]

The fears turned out to be groundless. Except for the war party that went to Wounded Knee, the Two Strike Brulés had fled northwest, down White Clay Creek. Brooke managed to quiet a large share of the Oglalas, but many went with the Brulés, including the Oglala leaders Little Wound, Big Road, and No Water. About dusk the war party lifted the "siege" and headed north to join their families. From his nearby cabin they abducted old Red Cloud. They "forced me to go with them," he later explained to Thomas A. Bland. "I being in danger of my life between two fires I had to go with them and follow my family. Some would shoot their guns around me and make me go faster." To such depths of humiliation had the mighty chief of the Oglalas fallen in his old age.[4]

About fifteen miles northwest of the agency, in the valley of White Clay Creek, the refugees from Pine Ridge met Short Bull and Kicking Bear journeying with their followers toward the agency. The news of Wounded Knee destroyed their already hesitant resolve to give up, and the combined group, numbering about 4,000 people with 800 to 1,000 warriors, went into camp on White Clay Creek near No Water's abandoned village. Throughout the night survivors of Wounded Knee, many badly shot up, drifted into the camp. There was much crying, mourning, singing of death songs and ghost songs, and even some Ghost Dancing. The leaders went into council. In Red Cloud's words, they "made a law, that no one should go back to the agency. All rather

---

3. Elaine Goodale Eastman, pp. 36–37. See also Eastman, pp. 108–09.
4. Red Cloud to Bland, Jan. 12, 1891, in Bland, *Brief History of the Late Military Invasion*, pp. 21–22.

die together. I tried my best for them to let me go back, but they would not let me go, and said if I went they would kill me."[5]

The Seventh Cavalry rode into the agency at 9:30 P.M. Forsyth turned aside to report to General Brooke while the men headed for camp, cared for their horses, and took to their blankets. For most, however, it was a fitful sleep. No one knew what the stampeding refugees would do. "Just when they would appear again," said Lieutenant McCormick, "and whether as an attacking force or as ration receivers, was a question."[6]

The wounded were taken directly to the field hospital that Brooke's medical director, Lt. Col. Dallas Bache, had laid out. Philip Wells got his nose taped back into position, and it later mended so well that only close inspection could reveal the disaster that had befallen it. Father Craft recovered, too. "The wound he received," wrote James Cook, "would undoubtedly have killed some men. He was laid up for a short time, and if he stopped smoking cigarettes for two days because of that little cut, I have no record of it."[7]

Colonel Bache's military hospital accommodated only sixty patients, and Reverend Charles Cook converted the Episcopal mission chapel into a hospital for wounded Indians. He had the pews torn out and the floor carpeted with straw and quilts.

> There we laid the poor creatures side by side in rows [wrote Dr. Eastman], and the night was devoted to caring for them as best we could. Many were frightfully torn by pieces of shells, and the suffering was terrible. General Brooke placed me in charge and I had to do nearly all the work, for although the army surgeons were more than ready to help as soon as their own men had been cared for, the tortured Indians would scarcely allow a man in uniform to touch them. Mrs. Cook, Miss Goodale, and several of Mr. Cook's Indian helpers acted as volunteer nurses. In spite of all our efforts we lost the greater part of them, but a few recovered,

5. Ibid. Philip Wells and Joseph Horn Cloud Interviews, Ricker Collection.
6. McCormick MSS.
7. Cook, *Fifty Years on the Old Frontier*, p. 236.

including several children who had lost all their relatives
and who were adopted into kind Christian families.[8]

There were thirty-eight wounded Indians in the church hospital and another thirteen in the military hospital. Four were men,
the rest women and children.[9] Those in the field hospital also
cowered at the sight of blue uniforms. With professional detachment the Surgeon General of the Army later reported that "The
wounds of the Indians were mostly severe and difficult to heal,
as all capital operations were refused, notwithstanding repeated
explanation and urging through missionaries, interpreters and
friends. The simplest handling was at first resisted or met with
suspicion. In cases of extensive injury to large bones or joints
septic fever came sooner or later, and finally death."[10]

The pathos of the spectacle in the church deeply touched
Episcopal Bishop W. H. Hare, who dropped in a few days after
the battle:

> On entering the church, two sights presented themselves.
> On the church floor, instead of the pews on either side of
> the aisle, two rows of bleeding, groaning, wounded men,
> women, and children; tending them two military surgeons
> and a native physician assisted by the missionary and his
> helpers, assiduity and tenderness marking all. Above, the
> Christmas green was still hanging. To one of my moods
> they seemed a mockery to all my faith and hope; to another
> they seemed an inspiration still singing, though in a minor
> key, "Peace, good will to men."[11]

As the Seventh Cavalry and its wounded neared the agency on
the night of December 29, Maj. Guy V. Henry's squadron of the
Ninth Cavalry, fifty miles to the north, was preparing to turn in
for the night. During the day, his troopers had ridden a punish-
ing fifty miles, scouting the tableland recently vacated by Short
Bull and Kicking Bear. At 7:00 P.M. they had returned to their

8. Eastman, pp. 109–10.
9. Royer to CIA, Dec. 31, 1890.
10. Sec. War, *Annual Report* (1891), *1*, 601.
11. "The Bishop's Column," *Church News*, January 1891, quoted in Howe, *Life
and Labors of Bishop Hare*, p. 240.

base camp on White River opposite the mouth of Wounded
Knee Creek. Two hours later a pair of Indian scouts rode in
from Pine Ridge with news of the Wounded Knee battle and
orders from General Brooke to hasten to the defense of the
threatened agency.[12]

The soldiers promptly struck camp, loaded the wagons, and
set out on a grueling, all-night journey. They huddled in buffalo
overcoats and muskrat caps as gusts of wind whipped a light
snow down the valley of Wounded Knee Creek. Straining to
reach the agency before daybreak, Henry pushed his exhausted
men and horses to the limit, and finally, leaving Capt. John S.
Loud's Troop I as escort, cut loose from the wagon train. Shortly
before dawn, Henry led the remaining three troops into the
agency and, just as reveille was sounding in the camp of the
Seventh Cavalry, they wearily rolled up in their blankets.

Almost immediately one of Captain Loud's men galloped in
on a lathered horse to report that the wagon train had been attacked by Indians two miles east of the agency. Lieutenant Preston quickly mounted the Oglala scouts and, followed shortly
by the Seventh Cavalry, charged to the rescue. They found the
train corralled for defense. On a nearby hill about half a dozen
warriors scattered in retreat before the approaching relief column. Loud had lost a corporal in the brief skirmish, but suffered
no other casualties. Under the formidable escort of a regiment
of cavalry, the train completed its journey to Pine Ridge in
safety.[13]

The warriors who attacked the wagon train, about forty to
fifty in number, had been sent out by the chiefs from the rendezvous camp fifteen miles north of the agency. The mission of this
party was to observe the strength and activities of General
Brooke's soldiers but not, the chiefs emphasized, to bring on a
fight. It was too much to expect of hot-headed young men in-

12. William D. McGaa Interview, Ricker Collection.

13. John Shangreau Interview, Ricker Collection. McCormick MSS; General
Orders, No. 100, Hq. of the Army, Dec. 17, 1891, in War Dept., *General Orders and
Circulars*, 1891. Cyrus T. Brady, *Indian Fights and Fighters* (New York, 1904), pp.
352–54. Brady, an Army chaplain, got the story from Henry in Cuba during the
Spanish-American War.

censed by the events of the day before, and, chancing upon the
wagon train, they could not resist striking a blow. Frightened
off by the approach of the Seventh Cavalry, the warriors rode
northward toward Father Jutz' Holy Rosary Catholic Mission
—the Drexel Mission—in White Clay Valley four miles below
the agency. About twenty persons who lived in the neighborhood, mostly mixed-bloods, had gathered there, for the Indians
had promised not to harm anyone or anything within the mission enclosure. The Sisters of St. Francis, assisted by Philip Well's
wife, a schoolteacher, stood at the gate handing out meat and
coffee to passing refugees making their way from the agency to
the rendezvous.[14]

When the warriors reached the vicinity of the mission, they
were still in ugly humor. A short distance above the mission,
they spitefully set fire to a small log cabin that Mrs. Wells used
as a schoolhouse, then continued down the valley.

The dense column of smoke rising from the burning cabin
alerted the troops at the agency. Fearing that Drexel Mission
had been fired, General Brooke turned out the Seventh Cavalry
and told Henry to be ready to move also if necessary. Behind
Forsyth, the two squadrons of cavalry and a platoon of Capron's
Hotchkiss guns set out at a gallop, followed closely by Lieutenant
Preston and ten scouts, including Philip Wells, John and Louis
Shangreau, Little Bat, and Joe Merrivale. They quickly discovered the true source of the smoke, then continued to the
mission. While Forsyth and Father Jutz talked at the gate to the
mission enclosure, the hungry soldiers, who had not had time
for breakfast, gratefully accepted the meat and coffee offered by
the Sisters.[15]

While pausing here, Forsyth observed two more columns of

14. Philip Wells Interview, Ricker Collection.
15. Sources for the Mission Fight: Philip Wells and John Shangreau Interviews,
Ricker Collection; McCormick MSS; Garlington, "Seventh Regiment of Cavalry,"
p. 267; and documents in packet labeled "Additional Report on Investigation
into the Battle of Wounded Knee Fought on December 29, 1890," filed in National Archives with WKIR. This packet contains Forsyth's report, Dec. 31, 1890,
and testimony of Brooke, Henry, Preston, Rev. Cook, and John Shangreau taken
by Maj. J. Ford Kent in January 1891. A map of the battleground is in Sec. War,
Annual Report (1891), *1*.

smoke rising over the valley to the north. Father Jutz supposed that another log schoolhouse and a shed were also in flames. As no Indians were in sight and the direction taken by the Brulé party could not be ascertained, the colonel decided to return to the agency. He sent word of his intention to General Brooke, advising also that there was now no need for Henry's squadron to follow.

Shortly after the messenger had left, however, Little Bat reported that he thought he heard sounds of firing down the creek. Forsyth knew that the hostile camp lay in that direction, and, somewhere beyond, there would be more troops from the line north of White River. Suspecting that a fight was in progress, he decided to push down the valley in a reconnaissance in force.

The valley below the mission spread out some 300 yards in width. Steep bluffs about 200 feet high on the east and 50 on the west broke into a jumble of hills that rose to the ridge lines 600 feet above the valley floor. The creek hugged the west side for about three-quarters of a mile, then turned abruptly and made a wide loop to the east and back. On the west, the bluffs gave way to a low table, which the road, after crossing the creek on a bridge, ascended. At this point the command ran into trouble.

Preston's scouts flushed a handful of warriors on the table. "You scouts turn back," shouted one, "we don't want to fight you; we want to fight the soldiers." The scouts did not argue the point, but fell back to Preston. "Let's count them," suggested the lieutenant. "Count nothing," replied Louis Shangeau, and led the scouts hastily back to the head of Whitside's squadron.

Only one man, a Cheyenne scout, stayed with Preston. The scout held Preston's horse while the lieutenant ascended the slope to the crest of the table. He saw a score or more mounted warriors on a ridge about 100 yards in his front and fired two shots at them. Forsyth was now behind him with Whitside's squadron and sent a dismounted troop to hold the position. The rest of the squadron, also dismounted, formed a skirmish line below. The led horses were sent to sheltered pockets eroded in the bluffs to the left and rear. For about two hours, both sides exchanged an ineffective, long-range fire. A stray bullet shattered a trooper's foot, but no other damage was done. Forsyth sent Little Bat back to the agency asking for the Ninth to come to the support of the Seventh. By 1:00 P.M. Henry's squadron was in the saddle.

Unaccountably, Forsyth had failed to send out flankers to secure the bluffs on either side of the valley. It was a serious omission, for the warriors worked into positions above him and on both flanks. Their fire was at long range and for the moment not very dangerous, but the valley had every prospect of becoming untenable.

Leaving two troops under Captain Ilsley to tie down the Indians and cover the retreat, Forsyth pulled back the rest of the regiment and stationed it on a low tableland about 200 yards south of the mission. Before he could extricate the covering force, however, he came under fire from three directions—from the bluffs on the east and west, and from the south, toward the agency. Sending Preston to hurry up Henry, Forsyth fought back. To neutralize the fire coming from his right, he had a Hotchkiss gun wheeled into position. As shells began to burst on the bluffs east of the valley, he deployed a skirmish line at the foot of the bluffs on the west and pushed it up the slope toward the enemy. As the line neared the top, however, the Indians opened a grazing fire that wounded two troopers and caused the rest to retreat to the foot of the ridge.

Lieutenant Preston rode about one mile toward the agency before meeting Henry and his "Brunettes," followed by the other two guns of Capron's battery. Henry was "coming at a trot," said Preston, but "his stock was so badly knocked up [as a result of the hundred-mile ride the day before] that he was unable to come much faster." The squadron reached Forsyth at 1:30 P.M., and Henry handed Forsyth a note from Brooke: "I send you Henry and his battalion. We are not yet ready to round up the Indians unless you see your way clear to making a clean sweep. I have sent a messenger to Red Cloud and others to return here."

Just then, Forsyth was not giving much thought to making a clean sweep. He had taken casualties of one killed, five wounded, and an officer, Lieutenant Mann, down with wounds that would prove fatal within a month. Some of the troopers were demoralized by the hot fire of the Indians and cowered behind a rude shack that stood on the low hill. And Ilsley's two troops, the covering force, still occupied the earlier position, unable to withdraw because of the inability of the other six troops—pressed as they were from three sides—to cover the movement.

Major Henry acted swiftly to retrieve the situation. He flung out a mounted skirmish line composed of I and K Troops (Capt. Henry H. Wright and Lt. A. W. Perry commanding) supported by a Hotchkiss gun, up the slope to the east, and another, dismounted, composed of D and F Troops (Capts. J. S. Loud and C. A. Stedman commanding) up the bluffs to the west. With artillery fire clearing the way, the lines advanced expertly into the hills—the warriors everywhere falling back. Forsyth mounted and pushed down the valley to free Ilsley from his precarious position. With D and F Troops of the Ninth driving the enemy from his front, Ilsley had no trouble pulling back across the bridge.

Simultaneously, Loud and Stedman withdrew their skirmish line from the bluffs and took new positions in the valley. Followed by this covering force, the Seventh crossed the valley, ascended the slope on the east, and, passing through Wright's and Perry's lines, headed for the agency on the reverse side of the ridge. Wright and Perry abandoned their positions and took new positions successively along the crest of the ridge. But the warriors had already called it a day and returned to camp. The troops reached the agency around dark.

The Drexel Mission affair reflected little credit on Forsyth. Ignoring an elemental maxim of tactics, he marched an entire regiment of cavalry into a cul-de-sac manned by no more than fifty Indians. Then, after battling all day, he had to be rescued by an exhausted command half his own strength. General Miles wrote indignantly to the Adjutant General:

> The facts appear that a Colonel, with eight troops of cavalry, and two pieces of artillery, numbering about 400 men, allows his command to be drawn into a pocket; marches in the presence of the enemy down a valley, and proceeds to take an untenable position where his troops are commanded

by hostile Indians occupying the adjacent hills and bluffs.
. . . Whether this is the result of incompetency and inexperience or whether it is misconduct in the presence of the enemy, I leave to the General of the Army or higher authorities to determine.[16]

That night the cavalrymen sat around their camp stoves dis-
cussing the events of the past two days, writing official reports,
and relating their stories to the newspaper reporters. Near midnight, they turned out to watch a strange procession enter the
agency. Herded by Oglala scouts on the flanks and rear, seventy-
three Indians filed down the agency street. The men—eighteen
in number—carried no arms; these had been turned over to the
women. In the van, sitting his horse with quiet dignity, rode
Standing Soldier, first sergeant of Lieutenant Taylor's scouts,
former lieutenant of police, and later judge of the Indian court.
His arrival at Pine Ridge came as a fitting climax, and also as a
fitting contrast, to the two days of violence and bloodshed. For,
without violence or bloodshed, without even unpleasant incident, Standing Soldier had brought in the Hunkpapa fugitives
from the battle of Grand River. It was an accomplishment that,
at least in retrospect, puts to shame the efforts of the generals
and colonels of the Army and the agents, special agents, and inspectors of the Indian Bureau.[17]

As we have seen, the thirty-eight Hunkpapa refugees had
abandoned Big Foot on December 23 rather than submit themselves as prisoners to Colonel Sumner. They had fled toward the
Missouri River, but had encountered more Hunkpapas, also
refugees from the battle with McLaughlin's police. Now numbering seventy-three, they turned southwest, probably alarmed
by the march of Colonel Merriam's Seventh Infantry up Cheyenne River, and headed for Pine Ridge. Scouts reported the
movements during the 24th and 25th of Colonel Carr and the
Sixth Cavalry, so the Indians kept well to the east, crossing White
River and reaching Medicine Root Creek by the 27th.

16. Miles to Adjt. Gen., Feb. 4, 1891.
17. Standing Soldier Interview, Ricker Collection. Royer to CIA, Dec. 31, 1890.

Meanwhile, on the 25th, Lieutenant Taylor had sent Sergeant Standing Soldier and fifteen scouts from Pine Ridge Agency to help in the search for Big Foot. On the 27th they sighted the Hunkpapas. As the scouts approached, the Hunkpapas made ready to fight, but calmed down when they discovered that the strangers were not bluecoats. Standing Soldier, an able diplomat, took in the situation at a glance. Instead of demanding their guns, he listened sympathetically to the tale of woe related by the refugees. Then he informed them that he came as a friend to lead them to Pine Ridge, where they would be protected and fed. They agreed to do as the sergeant directed. He ordered his men to share their tobacco with the people and, as they were hungry, to kill several cattle from an abandoned ranch nearby.

Next day, moving southwest, the scouts and Hunkpapas cut the trail of Big Foot. Standing Soldier promptly sent three couriers to tell Big Foot to halt and wait. Camping on the second branch of Medicine Root Creek, the caravan crossed the divide to the third, or west, branch of the same creek on the morning of the 29th. About midmorning, the sound of gunfire echoed over the hills from the south. Suspecting the truth, the Hunkpapas grew frightened. Standing Soldier also suspected the truth but, thinking fast, passed around word that it was the custom of the soldiers to salute their officers with gunfire and that this was doubtless what they were now doing.

That afternoon one of the three couriers sent out on the 28th returned. Reporting to Standing Soldier, he told of the conflict at Wounded Knee. The soldiers had killed all Big Foot's people, he said, slaughtering everyone in sight. One of the scouts had been killed, and Philip Wells had had his nose cut off. The other two couriers had got scared and gone right on to the agency. Lieutenant Taylor had sent him back to tell Standing Soldier to disarm his prisoners and break up their guns.

The Oglala sergeant dismissed this piece of foolishness and instructed the courier to ride to the agency with the reply that he would bring in the Hunkpapas and turn them over to General Brooke, who could then disarm them himself if he wished. Meanwhile, would Taylor please send out some food and tobacco for the destitute prisoners? Ordering his men not to breathe a word of the Wounded Knee affair to the Hunkpapas, he led the procession across the divide to Porcupine Creek, camped for the night of the 29th at the upper crossing of Wounded Knee Creek, above the battlefield, and on the 30th headed for the agency.

During the morning's march, Chief Red Shirt and thirty scouts met the cavalcade and distributed meat and tobacco. Late at night, at the crossing of Wolf Creek, three miles east of the agency, Standing Soldier had Red Shirt ride ahead and alert Taylor and Brooke of his approach. A half-mile out he halted the Hunkpapas and faced them. Raising his right hand, he prayed to the Christian God: "God, our Father, help us that we may make peace and friendship with the Oglalas tonight." Then he said that way back in the treaties the Great Father had told the Sioux that they must live in peace with the white people. For this reason the Oglala scouts had gone to a great deal of trouble to conduct the Hunkpapas safely to the agency. They must now show their good will by turning all guns over to the women and doing just as the soldiers asked. Forming the men in line, he placed scouts on each flank and in the rear and marched into the agency.

The column drew up in front of Brooke's headquarters. Lieutenant Taylor met them and went around shaking hands with the men. Then Standing Soldier and two of the Hunkpapa leaders went to see Brooke. The Hunkpapas expressed their willingness to give up their guns and do whatever the general desired. Brooke said that he was very glad to hear this and ordered Taylor to pass out rations. The Hunkpapas moved down near the camp of the scouts and set up their own camp. They never returned to their homes at Standing Rock, preferring instead not only to "make peace and friendship with the Oglalas" but to become Oglalas in name, too. Their descendants still live at Pine Ridge as part of the Oglala tribe.

On December 31, 1890, General Miles and his staff rode into Pine Ridge Agency. They had taken the train from Rapid City to Chadron, Nebraska, and ridden from there to the agency. Headquarters, Division of the Missouri in the Field, was now set up at Pine Ridge. Miles assumed direction of the campaign against the fugitive Brulés and Oglalas. He also mapped out a campaign against Col. James W. Forsyth.

Miles had learned of the Wounded Knee fight before boarding the train in Rapid City. From Hermosa, South Dakota, on the 30th, he wired a long report of the battle to the Adjutant General, expressing annoyance at the turn of events. That Big Foot got "so near Pine Ridge Agency just at this time," he said, "has complicated the surrender of all the hostiles in the Bad Lands . . .; still the severity of their loss at the hands of the troops may possibly bring favorable results." His ire was directed not at Colonel Forsyth but at Colonel Sumner for letting Big Foot escape in the first place.[18] By the time Miles reached Chadron, however, he was beginning to have doubts about Forsyth's conduct and by the time he reached Pine Ridge Forsyth had definitely replaced Sumner as the villain.

At Chadron Miles had received a telegram from General Schofield in Washington with instructions to "Give my thanks to the brave 7th Cavalry for their splendid conduct."[19] By January 2 Miles had learned enough about Wounded Knee to reply:

> Your telegram of congratulation to the 7th Cavalry is received, but as the action of the Colonel commanding will be a matter of serious consideration, and will undoubtedly be the subject of investigation, I thought it proper to advise you. In view of the fact, do you wish your telegram transmitted as it was sent? It is stated that the dispositions of the 400 soldiers and 4 pieces of artillery were fatally defective; large number of troops were killed and wounded by fire from their own ranks, and a very large number of women and children were killed in addition to the Indian men.[20]

Schofield promptly authorized Miles to withhold the congratulatory telegram. At the same time, he sent another wire containing sentiments direct from the President. From the beginning, Harrison had been particularly sensitive to the pressures of In-

18. Miles to Adjt. Gen., Dec. 30, 1890.
19. Schofield to Miles, Dec. 30, 1890.
20. Miles to Schofield, Jan. 2, 1891.

dian reform groups. Now the sensational reports of Wounded Knee had brought the wrath of the humanitarians down upon him, and he was very unhappy. Schofield's telegram conveyed the President's regrets at failure to solve the Sioux troubles without bloodshed and directed that "an inquiry be made as to killing of women and children on Wounded Knee Creek."[21]

Miles lost no time. On January 4, "by direction of the President," he relieved Forsyth of command of the Seventh Cavalry and issued orders convening a full-scale court of inquiry to find out if Forsyth had disposed his troops so that they shot one another, and if his men had killed noncombatants indiscriminately.[22]

This was not, however, what the President had meant by "inquiry." "It was not the intention of the President," Schofield wired on January 6, "to appoint a Court of Inquiry." Miles was not supposed to have relieved Forsyth by direction of the President or anyone else. "You were expected yourself first to inquire into the facts and in the event of its being disclosed that there had been unsoldierly conduct to relieve the responsible officer."[23]

Now everyone was confused. "General Miles did it," Secretary of War Proctor told reporters. "It is a very mixed up matter and I may explain it later."[24] But Miles had already published his orders, and in the absence of explicit instructions he had no intention of reversing them. The very next day, January 7, Maj. J. Ford Kent, division inspector general, and Capt. Frank D. Baldwin, acting assistant inspector general, constituted themselves a court of inquiry. Miles' orders had also named Col. E. A. Carr a member of the court, but he was in the field. Kent and Baldwin therefore began taking the testimony of the officers of the Seventh Cavalry.

On both specific questions at issue, the witnesses almost to a man supported Forsyth. They demonstrated convincingly, not

21. Schofield to Miles, Jan. 2, 1891 (two telegrams).
22. Miles to Forsyth, Jan. 4, 1891. Special Orders, No. 8, Hq. Div. of the Mo. in the Field, Pine Ridge, Jan. 4, 1891, in WKIR.
23. Schofield to Miles, Jan. 6, 1891.
24. Washington *Evening Star*, Jan. 5, 1891.

only to the court but to the objective student who reads the transcript today, that the officers and soldiers of the Seventh, with one or two exceptions, made supreme efforts to avoid the killing of women and children. The efforts failed only because the noncombatants were mixed with the combatants and in the heat of battle could rarely be identified as such.

The witnesses also argued that Forsyth's disposition of troops had not been faulty, stressing that no one even remotely anticipated that fighting would break out, and that for the purpose of disarming the Indians the units were placed to good advantage. These arguments sounded somewhat less convincing, for no officer could quite deny that, no matter how remote the possibility of a fight, the possibility should nonetheless have been considered in deploying the troops. To nail down the point, Miles had his three orders enjoining field commanders never to let their troops mingle with Indians introduced in evidence.[25] Questioned about whether he passed on this warning to his subordinates, however, General Brooke took refuge in an evasive explanation. It appears that he did not in fact transmit them so forcefully as Miles intended. But although it was apparent that on occasion troops had been endangered by the fire of other troops, it could not be shown that friendly fire had caused a single casualty.

Major Kent and Captain Baldwin faced an unhappy dilemma. One cannot read their opinions, especially Kent's, without gaining the impression that they wanted to clear Forsyth and forget the whole unpleasant affair. Their hearts were patently not in the goal Miles had set of placing the blame on Forsyth. For Miles did not, as law and propriety demanded, remain aloof from the proceedings. He had made up his mind before the court convened that Forsyth had blundered at Wounded Knee, he made

25. Nov. 18: "One thing should be impressed upon all officers, never to allow their command to be mixed up with the Indians, or taken at a disadvantage."

Nov. 22: "Do not allow your command to become mixed up with Indians, friendly or otherwise. Hold them all at a safe distance from your command. Guard against surprise or treachery."

Dec. 7: "I must call your attention to my original order, not to allow the command to be mixed up with the Indians in any way, or to be taken at disadvantage. That will apply not only in a military sense, but in a diplomatic."

no secret of his opinion during the proceedings, and he tried various devices while the court sat to influence its final decision.[26] Kent and Baldwin, members of the general's staff, could not have failed to perceive which way the wind blew, and it is interesting to speculate upon how much the attitudes of General Miles shaped their written opinions.

The two officers quickly disposed of the first question. They agreed that "under the circumstances all care was taken after the Indians made the first break to preserve the lives of non-combatants," and that casualties among women and children "could be ascribed only to the fault of the Indians themselves and the force of unavoidable and unfortunate circumstances."[27]

As for the second question, Kent and Baldwin tried to straddle the issue. They made many excuses for Forsyth and praised the behavior of the regiment. Then they censured (Kent mildly and Baldwin severely) the placement of B and K Troops in such close proximity to the Indians.[28]

Miles was not satisfied and had the court reconvene to probe more deeply into the question whether Forsyth had received and obeyed the orders prohibiting commanders from mixing their troops with Indians. Kent and Baldwin got the idea and, after a thorough ventilation of the matter, turned in supplementary opinions condemning Forsyth much more sharply for his troop dispositions. Thus Kent: "Colonel Forsyth's command was not held at a safe distance," and "the attack of the Indians resulted in a complete surprise." And Baldwin: Miles' injunction "was entirely disregarded and lost sight of by Colonel Forsyth."[29]

The court handed down its final opinion on January 18 at

26. I am led to this conclusion by the language of the telegrams that Miles sent to Schofield before the court convened; by his own (instead of, more properly, the court's) action in sending for Forsyth's military record; by his refusal to accept the first opinion of the court and the coaching that he obviously did to secure evidence that led to the second opinion; and by the extreme censure, far transcending the censure of the court, in the forwarding endorsement. Finally, Philip Wells (interview in Ricker Collection) relates several personal experiences that demonstrate that Miles was throwing his weight around in order to get the kind of opinion he wanted.

27. WKIR.

28. Ibid.

29. Ibid.

Pine Ridge, and Miles, now in Chicago, forwarded it to Washington on the 31st, with a long endorsement which in harshness of judgment went far beyond anything Kent and Baldwin had written. First, Forsyth had "received repeated warnings as to the desperate and deceitful character of Big Foot's band," and also "repeated orders as to the exercise of constant vigilance to guard against surprise." Second, "these warnings and orders were unheeded and disregarded by Colonel Forsyth, who seemed to consider an outbreak of the Indians as being beyond the pale of possibility." Third, the battle map and testimony showed "conclusively that at the beginning of the outbreak not a single company of troops was so disposed as to deliver its fire upon the warriors without endangering the lives of some of their comrades. It is in fact difficult to conceive how a worse disposition of troops could have been made." Conclusion: Forsyth not only disobeyed explicit orders but also demonstrated "incompetence" and "entire inexperience in the responsibility of exercising command where judgment and discretion are required."[30]

Both General Schofield and Secretary Proctor thought otherwise. The evidence alone may have guided their decision, but it is not unlikely that hostility toward Miles and a fervent wish to be rid of a politically explosive issue also exerted an influence. Schofield finished reading the transcript with the judgment that "the conduct of the regiment was well worthy of the commendation bestowed upon it by me in my first telegram after the engagement," and that "the interests of the military service"—here perhaps was the key to his thinking—"do not . . . demand any further proceedings in this case." Secretary Proctor concurred verbosely and decreed that, "by direction of the President, Colonel Forsyth will resume the command of his regiment."[31]

While the documents in the Wounded Knee investigation were working through channels, Miles launched another investigation of Forsyth, this one aimed at indicting him for mismanagement of the Drexel Mission fight. The Seventh Cavalry had returned to Fort Riley by the time this investigation got under way early in February, but the statements of General

30. Reproduced in ibid.
31. Reproduced in ibid.

Brooke, Major Henry, Lieutenant Preston, and Father Jutz were taken, which provided an opportunity for Miles, in forwarding them, to loose another condemnation of Forsyth. But the supporting testimony, which did not include any statements by the participating officers of the Seventh Cavalry, was obviously inadequate. Schofield and Proctor dismissed these charges, too.[32]

By 1895 Miles had risen to the top Army command, but his hostility appears not to have had much effect upon the career of Forsyth, who by 1894 was wearing the star of a brigadier general and who three years later rose to major general. As a further irony, when Forsyth moved up from regimental command, he was replaced as colonel of the Seventh Cavalry by Edwin V. Sumner, the officer who had let Big Foot escape and had also suffered through an investigation instigated by Miles. As the crowning rejection of his attitudes, three officers and fifteen enlisted men were awarded Medals of Honor for heroism at the Battle of Wounded Knee Creek.

On April 12, 1920, a white-mustached old man of 81, still militarily erect but displaying the wandering mind of approaching senility, called at the office of the new Commissioner of Indian Affairs, Cato Sells. With him was a delegation of Pine Ridge Sioux. Lt. Gen. Nelson A. Miles, U.S. Army Retired, explained that the survivors of the massacre at Wounded Knee Creek and the heirs of its victims, too, deserved "some remedial measures on the part of Congress," and he wanted to urge that the claim be seriously considered. It was a view he had advocated for nearly thirty years. "The action of the commanding officer," he wrote to Sells' predecessor, "was most reprehensible . . . and I have regarded the whole affair as most unjustifiable and worthy of the severest condemnation." As luck would have it for the old general, the matter was referred for report to the one official in the Interior Department who knew something about the subject —and about General Miles also—Indian Inspector James McLaughlin.[33]

32. The record of this investigation is filed in the National Archives with WKIR.
33. Sells to Sec. Int., May 4, 1920. Sells to Miles, May 7, 1920. Miles to CIA, March 13, 1917, quoted in Elaine Goodale Eastman, p. 39.

McLaughlin's adverse report did not end the matter. For another twenty years it came before Congressional committees time
and again for exhaustive and mostly uninformed discussion. The
proposal never got beyond the discussion stage and in the end
proved just one more in a long series of bitter disappointments
for the Sioux.[34]

34. 75th Cong., 3d sess., *Sioux Indians, Wounded Knee Massacre:* Hearings before
the Subcommittee on Indian Affairs on H. R. 2535, May 7 and 12, 1938.

14. TIGHTENING THE RING

THE BATTLE AT WOUNDED KNEE changed the entire complexion of the Pine Ridge campaign. As we have seen, on the very day of the battle Short Bull and Kicking Bear, with the die-hard remnant of the Ghost Dancers, were within a day's march of the agency, where they planned to surrender. Wounded Knee not only reversed this intention but added to their ranks the frightened Brulés of Two Strike and the Oglalas of Little Wound, Big Road, and No Water—all of whom, with the un-willing Red Cloud, had stampeded from the agency at the time of the battle. The aggregation—some 4,000 people, about 800 to 1,000 warriors—set up their camp in the valley of White Clay Creek near No Water's village, about fifteen miles north of the agency.

General Miles had about 3,500 soldiers in the immediate area of operations, including nearly half the infantry and cavalry of the Army. Further removed, but participating in the campaign and subject to his orders, another 2,000 stood poised for action. Miles had already begun to pull in his lines in an attempt to con-tract the operational zone and prevent the Indians from return-ing to the Stronghold north of White River. By the early days of January 1891, the units had moved into new positions and had bottled up the refugees, once more termed hostiles, in White Clay Valley.

White River, curving around White Clay Creek on the west and north, defined the deadline for the encircled Indians. Lt. Col. R. H. Offley, with seven companies of the Seventeenth Infantry and Capt. A. B. Wells' two troops of the Eighth Cavalry, had moved down from Cheyenne River and taken station below the mouth of White Clay Creek. En route, Offley had left a force to occupy the Stronghold. His command held the center of the White River line. On his left Col. E. A. Carr and the Sixth Cavalry, which had marched from the mouth of Rapid Creek, spread down White River and up Wounded Knee Creek a short distance. Farther up Wounded Knee, Capt. F. A. Whitney, with two troops of the Ninth Cavalry and a company of the Eighth Infantry from Rosebud Agency, camped near the battleground of December 29. On Offley's right, the Fort Leavenworth Cavalry Squadron, Lt. Col. George B. Sanford commanding, held White River above the mouth of White Clay Creek. On his right, Maj. Guy V. Henry's squadron of the Ninth Cavalry and the entire Second Infantry under Col. Frank Wheaton covered White River almost to the Nebraska line. Col. William R. Shafter and five companies of the First Infantry extended along the Nebraska border south of the agency. Two more companies of the First, together with the Seventh Cavalry under Major Whitside, garrisoned Pine Ridge Agency. General Brooke placed himself with Colonel Offley at the mouth of White Clay Creek and took direct command of the White River line. Miles exercised supreme command from his headquarters at the agency, communicating with Brooke by telegraph and courier through Oelrichs.

Had they tried, the Indians would have encountered great difficulty in breaking through this formidable ring. Had they tried and succeeded, they could have fled in no direction without running into more troops. To the north and west, Col. H. M. Day and 200 South Dakota militiamen patrolled Cheyenne River as a screen for the Black Hills settlements. To the north and east, Col. H. C. Merriam's Seventh Infantry and Lt. Col. E. V. Sumner's command of the Eighth Cavalry and Third Infantry covered the upper reaches of Bad River and the lower part of Cheyenne River. Still farther north, a strong column from Fort Keogh, Montana, under Lt. Col. A. K. Arnold, and another from Fort Lincoln, North Dakota, under Maj. Henry Carroll, threw a net across southern North Dakota. East of Pine Ridge, Lt. Col. J. A. Poland's command still garrisoned Rosebud Agency. And to the south, in Nebraska, the Nebraska National Guard, under Brig. Gen. L. W. Colby, had been mobilized in regimental strength and strung along the Fremont, Elkhorn, and Missouri Valley Railroad to protect the Nebraska settlements.

The Sioux needed only one experience to demonstrate that they were tightly hemmed in and that their freedom of movement was severely restricted. On the afternoon of January 1 a party of more than fifty warriors, still wrought up over Wounded Knee and perhaps emboldened by the success at Drexel Mission two days earlier, rode out on the bluffs overlooking White River five miles above the mouth of Wounded Knee Creek. The Sixth Cavalry had passed down the valley and gone into camp at the mouth of Wounded Knee. But the regimental train of the Sixth, guarded by Capt. John B. Kerr's Troop K, was making its way slowly down the valley on the other side of the river.

Whooping the war cry, the Sioux swept down the slope, crossed the ice-choked stream, and attacked the train. Captain Kerr promptly corralled the wagons and opened fire. The sound of battle carried to Carr's camp down the river, and Maj. Tullius Cicero Tupper and two troops, followed closely by Carr with the remaining five troops, charged to the rescue. Caught in the flank by the relief column, the warriors hastily called off the attack and scattered into the hills south of the river. Firing at the retreating Indians, the cavalrymen killed or wounded six. Another three, who had dismounted and worked into positions close to the besieged train, were cut off by the sudden appearance of Carr and Tupper. Frantically, they fled afoot, trying to dodge the heavy fire of the troops. Although they succeeded in crossing the river, the Cheyenne scouts later found them in the hills, wounded, and dispatched them without formality. Kerr's losses were one horse killed and another wounded.[1]

1. Carter, *Yorktown to Santiago*, pp. 261–62. Carter, "Sixth Regiment of Cavalry," in Rodenbough, *Army of the United States*, p. 249. Maj. Gen. Charles D.

Also on New Year's afternoon, Henry Miller, a cook for the
agency herders at the mouth of White Clay Creek, decided to
ride into the agency. En route he met some Oglalas, who warned
him that the main Sioux camp lay between him and the agency
and that as the young men were in ugly humor he should not
attempt to pass. Miller scoffed at the warning and continued on
his way. Shortly, he encountered a small party of Brulé warriors.
One, Kills-the-Enemy, pointed his rifle at Miller and told him
to dismount. Miller obeyed. The Brulé next ordered him to
throw his revolver and cartridge belt on the ground. Miller did
so. Kills-the-Enemy then calmly pulled the trigger and shot his
prisoner dead.[2]

Now that fighting had broken out, Miles fortified Pine Ridge
Agency. He had trenches dug and earthworks, reinforced with
logs, constructed around the agency. Two companies of the First
Infantry manned the defenses, and artillery commanded all the
approaches.

Miles did not plan to fight, however, unless he had to. He
understood Indian psychology as few other officers did, and he
knew that a carefully devised policy combining gentle persuasion
with a display of overwhelming force would, if not upset by rash
subordinates, ultimately achieve the objective. Thus he had
charged Brooke with erecting a solid blue wall along White River
and Wounded Knee Creek. The military cordon was close
enough to make the Indians terribly uncomfortable, but not close
enough to stampede them. Miles next turned to diplomacy, sending, on January 1, a conciliatory letter to Red Cloud and another
to the rest of the errant chiefs. In the next few days he sent more

Rhodes, "Diary of the Brule-Sioux (Pine Ridge) Indian War" (MSS, 1940, East
Search Room, National Archives). Carr to Miles, Jan. 2, 1891. Brooke to Miles, same
date. Carr to Asst. Adjt. Gen. Div. of the Mo., Jan. 14, 1891. "The award of several
Congressional Medals of Honor was recommended," remarked General Rhodes,
then a lieutenant in the Sixth, "and some were actually awarded for this rather
inoffensive, long-range engagement . . . which excited much controversy in army
circles, as well as bitterness by officers who had won the Medal of Honor in
hazardous engagements."

2. W. R. Jones Interview, Ricker Collection. Statement of Wounded-Brother-
of-White-Deer, in Lt. G. M. Williamson to Asst. Adjt. Gen. Dept. of the Platte,
March 13, 1891.

such messages, each promising kind and fair treatment but making abundantly clear that the Sioux must do exactly as told.[3]

As a matter of fact, the Sioux leadership had split wide open even before Miles' letters began to arrive. The camp had no sooner been laid out on December 29 than the Oglalas began to repent their hasty flight from the agency. By uniting with the followers of Kicking Bear and Short Bull, the Oglalas had automatically acquired the label of hostile, and the maimed survivors of Wounded Knee were vivid reminders of what could happen to hostiles. Moreover, the new soldier chief at the agency was not to be trifled with. Many of the Oglala leaders had surrendered to him on the Yellowstone back in the 1870s. They remembered him as a man who spoke with a straight tongue. In 1876 he had given them a choice—surrender with the certainty of just and humane treatment, or war with the certainty of swift and terrible punishment. They had discovered then that "Bear's Coat" meant what he said; those who gave up and those who held out received exactly what had been promised. Now it was the same story. "A great many troops are on all sides," he reminded them, "but not a shot will be fired or a hand raised against any [Indians] if they do as I direct them." "I know all the wrongs that have been done the Indians and the wrongs the Indians have done. If they do whatever I tell them it will be best for all the Indians."[4] Red Cloud, Little Wound, Big Road, and other Oglala chiefs needed no more coaxing. They were ready to trust Bear's Coat.

The Brulés were not. They stubbornly refused to recognize the hopelessness of their position. They proposed no constructive alternative to surrender and seemingly gave the matter little thought. They knew only that surrender was out of the question. In daily councils, the chiefs wrangled bitterly and inconclusively. At one council, called to consider Miles' first

3. Miles to Red Cloud, Jan. 1, 1891. Miles to Red Cloud, Little Wound, Two Strike, Big Road, Little Hawk, Crow Dog, Knife, No Water, Turning Bear, Calico, White Face, Yellow Bear, Kicking Bear, Short Bull, He Dog, and all Indians away from their Agencies, same date. Miles to All Chiefs on or Near White Clay Creek, Jan. 2. Miles to Red Cloud, Jan. 4.
4. Miles to Red Cloud et al., Jan. 1, 1890.

letter, the debate grew so heated that a "crazy boy," as Red
Cloud termed him, tore up the letter, and the old chief had to
get word out to Miles to send another. Kicking Bear and Short
Bull, as spokesmen for the defiant young men, angrily denounced
the Oglala chiefs for even suggesting surrender and vowed that
no man should desert the cause. The Brulé warriors reinforced
this injunction by turning back all who attempted to escape from
the camp. Factional quarrels broke out, and at least two Indians
were killed in altercations. On January 4 Red Cloud announced
that he intended to start for the agency the next day and would
fight his way out if he had to. Although nothing came of this
resolve, five other leaders (Big Road, He Dog, Little Hawk, Jack
Red Cloud, and High Hawk) slipped out on the 3d and spent
several days conferring with Miles. The words they took back
from him further strengthened the determination of the Oglalas
and even weakened somewhat the resolution of the Brulés.[5]

The Cheyenne scouts from Colonel Sanford's camp on White
River maintained constant observation of the hostile camp.
There were two troops, one under Lt. Louis H. Strother, enlisted from Little Chief's Cheyennes at Pine Ridge, the other
under Lts. Edward W. Casey and Robert N. Getty, enlisted at
the Tongue River Reservation in Montana. The latter was a
crack outfit. Lieutenant Casey was widely regarded as one of the
Army's most promising junior officers. Both a student and a
friend of the Indian, he had won authorization to organize the
scout troop over the opposition of Commissioner of Indian Affairs Morgan, who believed military service incompatible with
progress in civilization. At Fort Keogh, Casey had brought his
scouts to a peak of efficiency, discipline, and morale, and since
joining Sanford's command on December 24 they had performed
outstanding service.[6] Almost daily some of Casey's scouts met

5. Miles to Adjt. Gen., Jan. 3, 1891. Miles to Red Cloud, Jan. 4. Memo of Con-
versation, Miles with Sioux chiefs, Jan. 5. Miles to Big Road, Little Hawk, Jack
Red Cloud, and High Hawk, Jan. 6. Account of events within the Indian camp
is chiefly derived from intelligence reports submitted by the Cheyenne scout units.
See Lt. E. W. Casey to Capt. M. P. Maus, Jan. 2, 1891; Maus to Brooke, Jan. 2;
Casey to Maus, Jan. 3; Miles to Casey, Jan. 4; Brooke to Miles, Jan. 7.

6. A good picture of the scouts is given by Frederic Remington, "Lieutenant
Casey's Last Scout," *Harper's Weekly*, 35 (Jan. 31, 1891), 85–91.

warriors from the hostile camp and exchanged news in a friendly manner. On January 6 a half-dozen or so men from the camp
visited Casey at his bivouac. Their reports of the sentiment in the
camp led him to believe that he might accomplish much by
personally conferring with some of the Sioux leaders.

The next morning, January 7, Casey and two scouts set forth
up the valley of White Clay. They met a small party of Sioux
butchering a cow and chatted pleasantly for a time. Here one
of the Cheyennes turned back. Casey and the other, White Moon,
rode up the valley. Soon they met another Indian, Bear-Lying-
Down, and stopped to talk. The lieutenant asked Bear-Lying-
Down to ride back to the Indian camp and request one of the
chiefs to come down for a parley. If none would do so, he was to
ask Red Cloud himself to come. At the camp, Bear-Lying-Down
told his story to He Dog, who went to Red Cloud's lodge. There,
a number of Oglala chiefs were in the midst of a council. They
had just decided to try to slip out of camp later in the morning
and go to the agency for a talk with General Miles. He Dog relayed Casey's message, and Red Cloud called Bear-Lying-Down
into the tepee to tell his story personally. After he had finished
talking, Red Cloud instructed him to go back to the officer and
tell him that he must leave the area immediately for there were
hot-headed young men all around who might try to kill him. As
Bear-Lying-Down turned to depart, He Dog also asked Red
Cloud's half-breed relative, Pete Richard, who could speak English, to go. The two men, Pete and Bear-Lying-Down, hastened
back down the creek. They met Casey and White Moon a mile
and a half from camp, riding up the valley with two Brulés,
Broken Arm and a Carlisle graduate named Plenty Horses.

Richard shook hands with Casey and asked where he was
going. General Brooke had sent him, answered the officer, to
confer with the chiefs. Richard explained that Red Cloud was
going in to talk with Miles and had sent word for the lieutenant
to turn back. The young men were dangerous, just as if they were
drunk or crazy, and one might take a shot at the blue uniform.
Casey reluctantly agreed to give up his plan and return to White
River. Both Richard and the lieutenant were just turning their
mounts when Plenty Horses, astride his horse four or five feet to

the left and rear of Casey, raised his Winchester and shot the officer through the back of the head. Casey fell to the ground dead. The murderer sauntered off toward the camp. White Moon, the Cheyenne, started to flee, but Richard called him back and told him to take Casey's gear to camp. The Cheyenne refused and at the same time signed to Bear-Lying-Down, "Why don't you shoot Plenty Horses?" "Why don't you shoot him yourself?" Bear-Lying-Down signed in answer. White Moon took Casey's horses but left the body lying on the road. Lieutenant Getty, who succeeded to command of the scouts, rode out with the troop in the afternoon and recovered the body.[7]

Red Cloud failed in his plan to break away from camp that day. But the police measures adopted by the Brulés to prevent defections had begun to disintegrate under the pressure of Miles' blandishments. That day, seventy Oglalas managed to elude the Brulé pickets and escape to the protection of Miles' fortifications. They reported more coming in the next day. Late at night, while the rest of the camp slept, Red Cloud, He Dog, Jack Red Cloud, and White Hawk gathered up their families and stole away. They successfully reached Pine Ridge on the morning of January 8, and throughout the day another seventy-five Oglalas made good their escape.[8]

Either on the 7th or the 8th, Young-Man-Afraid-of-His-Horses, one of the most influential of Sioux chiefs, arrived at Pine Ridge. With some of his people, he had been visiting the Crows in Montana for the past two months. Miles had sent an officer to intercept the return march of the party at Newcastle, Wyoming, and hasten the chief by rail to Rushville. As soon as he reached the agency, Miles sent him into the hostile camp to exert his influence in behalf of peace.[9]

7. Statements of Bear-Lying-Down and Pete Richard in Lt. S. A. Cloman to Camp Adjt. Pine Ridge, Feb. 21, 1891. Getty to Asst. Adjt. Gen. Dept. of Dak., April 13, 1891. Philip Wells Interview, Ricker Collection.

8. Miles to Adjt. Gen., Jan. 7, 1891. Corbin to Brooke, Jan. 8. Red Cloud to Bland, Jan. 12, in Bland, *Brief History of the Late Military Invasion,* pp. 21–22.

9. O'Connell to Miles, Jan. 6, 1891. For assessments of Young-Man-Afraid's role in the hostile camp see Miles to Adjt. Gen., Jan. 27 and March 13, 1891; CIA, *Annual Report* (1891), p. 181; Kelley, "Indian Troubles and Battle of Wounded Knee," pp. 46–47.

The rising number of Oglala defections, combined with the influence of Young-Man-Afraid and the other Oglala chiefs still in camp, Little Wound and Big Road, began to confuse the Brulé leaders. They were no longer so certain of the correctness of the course they had adopted, and gradually their opposition to surrender broke down. But they still could not bring themselves to make the final plunge. It was time, Miles perceived, to reinforce diplomacy by drawing the military cordon a shade tighter. On January 7, as the Oglala defectors began to reach the agency in increasing numbers, he alerted General Brooke to prepare plans for moving the White River–Wounded Knee line toward the agency. Two days later, receiving a report from Young-Man-Afraid that the Brulés had reluctantly consented to move the camp a little closer to the agency on the 10th, Miles gave the order for Brooke to move at the same time.[10]

Very slowly, on the morning of the 10th, the Indians crawled up White Clay Valley, arguing all the way over the advisability of moving at all. Very slowly, Brooke, with Offley and Sanford, followed. The next day, January 11, the camp moved again, this time halting at Drexel Mission, five miles north of the agency. Again Brooke pushed in behind the Sioux. "The situation is so delicate," he reported to Miles, "that any premature move might cause a stampede [and] I have been exceedingly cautious and at the same time watching them closely."[11]

The Ghost Dance leaders and the Brulés had not really given in. They still opposed surrender. But each morning, disconcertingly, they awoke to find a sprawling military camp in their rear and the Oglalas packing for the day's journey. Unwillingly but irresistibly, they were being drawn slowly toward the agency. They broke camp at noon on the 12th and traveled two miles. Brooke marched to the mission and went into camp just as the last Indians were leaving. White Tail, a Brulé subchief, came back and begged Brooke not to follow too closely. That night, at Brooke's order, Wheaton's Second Infantry and Henry's

10. Miles signed Corbin to Brooke, Jan. 7, 1891. Corbin to Brooke, Jan. 9 (two letters). Corbin to Brooke, copy to Carr, Jan. 10. Colby, "Sioux Indian War," pp. 166–67.

11. Brooke to Asst. Adjt. Gen. Div. of the Mo., Jan. 11, 1891.

squadron of the Ninth Cavalry strengthened the command at the mission, and one of Carr's squadrons of the Sixth Cavalry took station a few miles east of the Indian camp. In the next two days, while the Indians mustered courage for the final march, the whole Wounded Knee line—Carr and Whitney—closed in on the Sioux from the east while Wheaton and Henry blocked all escape to the west. Shafter marched the First Infantry to within three miles of the agency on the south. The stage had been expertly set for the final act.[12]

The surrender on January 15 was something of an anticlimax, with none of the ceremony befitting the end of the biggest military operation in the United States since the Civil War. The surrender, in fact, had been going on for a week as defectors from the fugitive village streamed into the agency. Even so, the display of aboriginal might, the last in the long history of Indian warfare, was impressive enough. "It was a spectacle worth beholding," recalled one officer. "They moved in two columns up White Clay Creek, one on each side, about 5500 [closer to 4,000] people in all, with 7000 horses, 500 wagons, and about 250 travois, and in such good order that there was not at any point a detention on any account. . . . The rear and right flank of this mass was covered during the movement by a force of infantry and cavalry deployed in skirmish order, and moved with a precision that was a surprise to all who witnessed it."[13]

With the Sixth and Ninth Cavalry on the east, the Seventh Cavalry on the south, the First and Second Infantry on the west, and the Seventeenth Infantry and Fort Leavenworth Cavalry on the north, the hostiles, once more within the fold, pitched an immense camp that stretched for three miles on both sides of White Clay Creek. Capt. E. P. Ewers, whom Miles had summoned from Cheyenne River Agency, took charge of the "prisoners of war." Big Road sent word that he was collecting rifles—there would be no repetition of Wounded Knee if the Indians could help it

12. Brooke to Miles, Jan. 10, 1891. Brooke to Asst. Adjt. Gen. Div. of the Mo., Jan. 11 and 12. Miles to Brooke, Jan. 12. Brooke to Asst. Adjt. Gen. Div. of the Mo., Jan. 14 (two letters). Corbin to Brooke, Jan. 14 (two letters).

13. Capt. W. E. Dougherty, "The Recent Messiah Craze," *Journal of the Military Service Institution of the United States, 12* (1891), 577.

—and he soon turned in 200 stand of arms. Miles knew there were more, but knowing also that it was impossible to keep an Indian weaponless for very long, he did not press the matter. The only formal surrender came when Kicking Bear, rifle in hand, faced Miles. The two stared at each other for a moment, a hint of defiance in the eyes of the Ghost Dance apostle, a trace of determination in the eyes of the general. Perhaps they recalled a similar scene in 1877, when Kicking Bear had once before surrendered to Miles. Kicking Bear laid his weapon at Miles' feet, and the Ghost Dance uprising was over.[14]

Three days later, while the Indians were still uneasy and a bit suspicious of military intentions, news reached the agency that very nearly caused another stampede.

On the evening of January 10, a small party of Indians returning from a hunt near Bear Butte camped on the Belle Fourche at the mouth of Alkali Creek, halfway between Fort Meade and Colonel Merriam's camp at the forks of the Cheyenne. There were two Oglala families—Few Tails and his wife Clown, and One Feather and his wife Red Owl. The latter couple had two daughters, one thirteen years old and the other an infant. The hunt had been successful, and the two wagons were loaded with close to 1,500 pounds of meat. The Indians picketed their ponies and put up two tepees. They were preparing dinner when a soldier rode up. He was Sgt. Frank Smith, Eighth Cavalry, in charge of a courier station at Quinn's Ranch, seven miles away. He asked what they were doing off the reservation. Few Tails produced a written pass, signed by Agent Royer,

14. Kelley, p. 47. Boyd, *Recent Indian Wars*, pp. 274–79. Miles to Adjt. Gen., Jan. 15, Feb. 3 and 9, 1891. Ultimately, by gentle prodding, the Indians were induced to give up additional arms. By the end of January, the number of surrendered rifles had risen to 600 at Standing Rock, Cheyenne River, and Pine Ridge. "Those I have seen," Miles reported on Feb. 3, "were mostly Winchester, Springfield, and Sharp's rifles. A few of little value were turned in, and much has been said in the public press about that class of arms, but very little about the former." "I may say," he added, "that I have no faith that the Indians will remain disarmed. . . . Some of the Sioux Indians have been disarmed three times, and many of them twice to my knowledge."

authorizing the group to hunt near Bear Butte. Satisfied that the Indians were an inoffensive hunting party, Smith returned to his station.

Next morning the Sioux packed and resumed their journey toward Pine Ridge. They had driven only 300 yards when, from a sage-covered knoll in front of them, a burst of rifle fire stopped them. Few Tails and Clown, riding the lead wagon, caught the first volley. Few Tails slumped dead in the driver's seat, a bullet through his face and one in his chest. Bullets cut down both horses. Clown jumped out of the wagon. A bullet hit her in the leg and another in the breast, and she sprawled on the ground next to the wagon.

One Feather frantically turned his wagon around to flee in the opposite direction. A bullet struck his wife, wounding her. His two daughters cowered amid the meat in the wagon bed. One Feather lashed his horses. The attackers, three white men, mounted and raced to cut off the speeding wagon. Blocked, One Feather turned around again. With the pursuers firing from close behind, he veered from the road and bounced across the prairie, up the slope of the divide between the Belle Fourche and Elk Creek. At the top, he turned over the reins to his wounded wife and with his rifle jumped from the wagon. Several shots delayed the white men long enough for him to catch one of the loose horses and climb on it. As the wagon rattled down the other side of the divide, he conducted a vigorous rear-guard action that kept the assailants at a safe distance. At Elk Creek One Feather made a stand, and the whites, now numbering only two, dismounted to take cover.

Back at Quinn's Ranch, Sergeant Smith had left for the day, but four privates were on duty. Andrew Culbertson, a nearby rancher, arrived with several other cowboys. He reported that he and his two brothers, Pete and Nelson, had been fired upon by some Sioux engaged in a horse-stealing expedition and asked the soldiers to help catch them. Accompanied by Culbertson and the others, two of the soldiers rode swiftly to Elk Creek. Pete and Nelson Culbertson were still there, exchanging shots with One Feather. The reinforcements joined the battle. One Feather had started his family southward in the wagon and soon followed them. Whenever the whites drew too close, he turned and shot at them. One Feather decided to abandon the wagon in order to make better time. He placed the two girls on one pony, and he and his wife mounted the other. "After a while," he later explained, "the mounted men came to where the wagon was, and commenced shooting and shouting, and that was the last I saw of them."

Nearly two weeks later, on January 24, the family made its way into Rosebud Agency. Red Owl was weak from the effects of her wound, and the infant had died of starvation and exposure on Pass Creek, but their very presence at the agency, alive, testified to the courage, skill, and endurance of the One Feather family.

Clown, wife of the dead Few Tails, had suffered an even more fearful ordeal. Through the day and night of January 11 she had lain on the ground, wounded in the leg and chest, next to the wagon containing her dead husband.

And then I got up [she later told the story], and saw that one horse was not killed, and I got on him, and came to a house on Elk Creek, and I knew the people living there, and they opened the door for me. . . . When they opened the door there were two men inside and they got their guns and one of them loaded his gun, and they pointed their guns at me, and the white girls inside said something I don't know what it was, and they took their guns off me. One man came to me, and motioned to me to go away, and I hurried as fast as I could to get away.

After I left the house, which was about evening, I saw a wagon track and I knew it was One Feather's wagon, and I saw tracks of horsemen right behind it, and that evening I came to the mouth of Rapid Creek, where there is a store, at which I traded a great deal, but I was afraid I would cause trouble again, so I did not go in the store. I travelled all that night, resting occasionally, and then came to the foot of the Bad Lands and heard wagons rattle, and listened and the wagons came right near me, and when the wagons passed they were only a short distance away. . . . After that I

> travelled every night, resting day time until I got here at
> the beef corral. Then I was very tired.

It was the morning of January 18, and she had reached the
beef corral east of Pine Ridge Agency, 100 miles from the Belle
Fourche. The Sixth Cavalry was camped at the corral, and that
morning Gus Craven, Carr's civilian guide, found Clown lying
on a hill behind his tent. He summoned some troopers, and they
carried the woman, nearly dead from wounds and exposure, to
the hospital tent. The regimental surgeon dressed her wounds
and had her transferred to the Indian hospital in Reverend
Cook's chapel at the agency. Here, almost miraculously, she was
nursed back to health.

Word of Few Tails' death spread through the great camps of
Sioux at Pine Ridge, for Few Tails was an important man and
a relative of Young-Man-Afraid-of-His-Horses. While the camps
bustled with activity, scores of men began to saddle their ponies
and round up cattle. Miles quickly summoned Young-Man-
Afraid and tried to pacify him, but made little headway. Only
the greatest persuasive efforts on the part of Miles and his officers
succeeded in restoring order and averting serious trouble. Fortunately, official reports of the investigation of the murder arrived from Colonel Merriam that same day, and the chiefs were
shown that civilians, not soldiers, had perpetrated the deed.

Colonel Merriam had started an investigation at once, sending
Lt. F. C. Marshall to examine the scene of the action and interview the participants. The Culbertson brothers claimed that the
Few Tails party had stolen horses from them and had opened
fire when approached. But Marshall's careful reconstruction of
the event, based on the position of the wagon and of Few Tails'
wounds in relation to the piles of cartridges that identified the
site where the three brothers had waited in ambush, cast grave
doubt on the explanation. Pete Culbertson, an ex-convict, himself gave away his motives when he boasted to Sergeant Smith,
"I have shot one of those damned Government pets, and if any
more of them want to be fixed, let them come this way." Maj. J.
Ford Kent later conducted another investigation that supported
Marshall's findings. Kent, Marshall, Merriam, and Miles all

branded the act unprovoked murder, and after One Feather, Red Owl, and Clown told stories that confirmed the military reports, there could no longer be any question that it was indeed murder.[15]

General Miles moved quickly to set the machinery of justice in motion, to prosecute the murderers not only of Few Tails but also of Lieutenant Casey and Herder Henry Miller. Few Tails had been killed when off the reservation, in Meade County, South Dakota, so Miles turned over all the papers in the case to Governor Arthur C. Mellette and recommended that the Culbertsons be tried in the state courts. At the same time he ordered the arrest of Plenty Horses for the killing of Casey, and the arrest of a Brulé named Young Skunk erroneously accused of killing Miller. These crimes had been committed on the reservation and thus came within the jurisdiction of the United States courts. Asked to help apprehend these men, Young-Man-Afraid replied, "No, I will not surrender them; but if you will bring the white men who killed Few Tails, I will bring the Indians who killed the white soldier and the herder; and right out here in front of your tepee I will have my young men shoot the Indians, and you have your soldiers shoot the white men, and then we will be done with the whole business; they were all bad men."[16] The charges against Young Skunk were dropped, but Plenty Horses was arrested on February 18 and immediately sent to Fort Meade for confinement until court convened.

The plight of Plenty Horses aroused the sympathy of most of the high-ranking officers in Dakota, who believed that his deed, occurring in time of war, did not properly come under the criminal law. He had no money to hire a lawyer; his relatives at Rosebud, although they tried, could not raise the necessary money; and the Indian Bureau had no funds for such a purpose. Finally, Plenty Horses' jailor, Lt. Col. E. V. Sumner, brought the matter

15. Merriam to Asst. Adjt. Gen. Dept. of Dak., Jan. 14, 1891, with encl. Marshall to Merriam, Jan. 13. Kent to Asst. Adjt. Gen. Div. of the Mo., Jan. 25. Capt. F. E. Pierce to Actg. U.S. Ind. Agt. Pine Ridge, Feb. 21. Pierce to CIA, Feb. 24. Carr to Roe, Aide-de-Camp, Jan. 18. Miles to Adjt. Gen., Jan. 21. Boyd, pp. 306–09, citing press releases, Pine Ridge, Jan. 19. The above narrative is constructed from these sources, which contain the narratives of Clown and One Feather.

16. IRA, *Ninth Annual Report* (1891), p. 43.

to the attention of the Indian Rights Association, which hired a defense counsel.[17]

The Federal Grand Jury met at Deadwood in March 1891, with V. T. McGillycuddy as foreman. In his testimony, the young Brulé explained why he had killed Casey and at the same time unwittingly delivered a bitter commentary on the efforts of the eastern idealists to rush the Indian down the road to civilization. "I am an Indian," he said. "Five years I attended Carlisle and was educated in the ways of the white man. I was lonely. I shot the lieutenant so I might make a place for myself among my people. Now I am one of them. I shall be hung and the Indians will bury me as a warrior. They will be proud of me. I am satisfied."[18]

Plenty Horses had admitted his crime, and the Grand Jury had no choice but to indict him. The trial took place in the Federal District Court at Sioux Falls, South Dakota, in April. The jury could not agree on whether the offense should be murder or manslaughter. In another trial, in June, the judge ruled that Plenty Horses had acted as a combatant during a state of war and could not be held liable under criminal law. The jury therefore returned a verdict of not guilty, and Plenty Horses went home to Rosebud, a free man.[19]

The Culbertsons, too, were finally brought to trial, although it took considerable prodding from the local United States Attorney, who in turn was being pressed by the United States Attorney General to use every proper means to secure justice. The States Attorney, Alex McCall, wrote Commissioner of Indian Affairs Morgan on March 18, "While the views of our people, and those expressed by you are wide apart touching the question of public policy in dealing with these semi-barbarous offenders against peace and dignity of the nation [the Sioux], yet public sentiment here is well nigh universal in favor of a vigorous prose-

17. John H. Burns (Deadwood lawyer) to Capt. Charles G. Pierce, March 27, 1891. Sumner to Herbert Welsh, March 29. Welsh to CIA, April 3, with encl. Burns to Welsh, March 28.

18. Quoted in McGillycuddy, *McGillycuddy: Agent*, p. 272.

19. U.S. Atty. W. B. Sterling to Adjt. Gen., May 1, 1891. IRA, *Ninth Annual Report* (1891), p. 44.

cution of the perpetrators of this apparently unwarranted attack and cold blooded slaughter of Few Tails." But, he said, Meade County was poor, and the United States Departments of Justice and the Interior would have to help bear the cost.[20]

Although a few Black Hills newspapers and some influential citizens such as McGillycuddy spoke out for energetic prosecution, public sentiment was by no means so widespread as McCall represented it. The trial began in Sturgis on June 22 and, despite overwhelming evidence of the guilt of the Culbertsons, ended on July 2 in acquittal. As McCall explained a year later, when another Sioux fell victim to a rancher's rifle, in Meade County "a white man cannot be convicted for the killing of an Indian."[21]

The campaign, and with it the last Indian war, had finally closed. It had been expensive. In less than two months, more than 350 people had lost their lives, and another 50 to 100 or more nursed wounds received in the fighting. Total expenses, public and private, that were recorded amounted to nearly $1,200,000—"a significant commentary," remarked James Mooney, "on the bad policy of breaking faith with Indians."[22]

At Pine Ridge, the great army assembled by General Miles remained patiently in camp for a week after the surrender. At last, on January 21, assignment of the regiments to new stations had been made, and the general held a grand review of his troops. On the 15th, the Indians had paraded in martial splendor for the last time in the Indian wars. Now it was the Army's turn, and the correspondent for *Harper's Weekly* did it justice.

> There were many stirring and grandly picturesque scenes at Pine Ridge during the closing of the late campaign against the ghost-dancing Sioux, but the one of most absorbing interest was the final review by General Miles of his 3500 soldiers, who had marched through sand-storms and blizzards in order to complete the cordon of bayonets that was to slowly drive the savages to unconditional surrender.

20. McCall to CIA, March 18, 1891.
21. CIA to Sec. Int., March 26, 1892.
22. *Ghost-Dance*, p. 892.

The night before the review, haranguers, with little medicine bags tied about their strange garments, went through
the villages of the hostile and sullen Brules and the peaceable Ogallalas, telling their people of the military demonstration which was to take place in the morning.

When the sun came up, the ridges skirting the agency to
the east and west were fringed with Indians, who looked
like Arab sheiks in their white sheets and hooded heads.
Not a squaw was to be seen among all these ghostly figures,
so distinctly outlined against the horizon. Statuesque and
haughty, the warriors stood watching the flying columns of
cavalrymen and the explosive efforts of the cannoneers as
they urged their animals into line. Down in the same valley,
where the troops were hurriedly preparing for their man-
euvres, but nearly a mile away to the north, were the great
Indian villages, with the squaws corralling their thousands
of ponies, as a precautionary measure against any possible
hostile demonstration on the part of the army.

General Miles was not in uniform as he sat astride a big
coal-black horse, which stood on the crest of a knoll on the
right flank of the advancing column of soldiers. Even his
three-starred epaulets [two-starred], the only evidences of
his rank, were beneath a great overcoat which was buttoned
almost to his ears. Just as the column, with screaming trum-
pets, began to pass General Miles, a furious sand storm
swept through the valley. It cloaked the silent Indian villages in a yellow, swirling shroud, and then tearing along
as though blown from a funnel, pierced the most compact
lines of infantrymen who were marching with a swinging
stride behind Colonel Shafter. From their perches on the
summits of the snow-flecked buttes, the hooded warriors
must have thought that the long line of men and horses
below had stampeded, for that terrible torrent of sand completely cloaked the army to the vision of those who were
above the phenomenal current of air.

There was no cheering during all the time the great column passed in review. Now and then General Miles' black
hat went off to the flash of a saluting sabre held by a muffled

figure that was crouching before the choking blast, but it was not until the Sixth Cavalry, with grim old General Carr at its head, passed in review that the idol of the Indian fighters showed the keen interest he was taking in the demonstration. Again and again his black sombrero fell as Carr's sword gleamed from his fur cap to his spurs. And when the black scowling faces of the Ninth Cavalry passed in close lines behind the glittering carbines held at a salute, General Miles waved his gloved hand to Colonel Henry, whose gaunt figure was almost lost in the folds of his buffalo overcoat. Three weeks before, these black troopers rode 100 miles without food or sleep to save the Seventh cavalrymen, who were slowly being crushed by the Sioux in the valley at the Catholic Mission. Then they dashed through the flanks of the savages, and after sweeping the ridges with carbine and pistol, lifted the white troopers out of the pocket with such grace that after the battle was over the men of both regiments hugged one another on the field.

When the trumpeters of the Seventh Cavalry got in front of General Miles they blew a shrill blast, and passed on into the blinding storm. Then the musicians from Angel Island [First Infantry Band] played "Garryowen." This was Custer's charging music, and as the famous regiment came over the yellow knolls in company front and carbines at a salute, the horses began to dance to the irresistible melody. Major Whitside was in command. He had no sword, but he waved his hand. General Miles' emotion was now so intense that he hung his hat on the pommel of his saddle and let the storm toss his gray hair as far as it pleased. The capes of the troopers were flung back, exposing the lemon-colored linings, and the fur caps were tied in such a way under the chin that they gave the wind-tanned faces a peculiarly grim expression. The scars of three days' fighting were plainly visible in this grand regiment.

There were men missing in every troop, and poor Captain Wallace and brave Lieutenants Mann and Garlington were also gone. A second lieutenant, with a bandaged head, was the only officer of little K Troop; and bringing up the rear was B Troop, with one-third of its men either in graves or hospital cots.

The column was almost pathetically grand, with its bullet-pierced gun-carriages, its tattered guidons, and its long lines of troopers and foot soldiers facing a storm that was almost unbearable. It was the grandest demonstration by the army ever seen in the West; and when the soldiers had gone to their tents, the sullen and suspicious Brules were still standing like statues on the crests of the hills.[23]

23. Charles G. Seymour, "The Sioux Rebellion, the Final Review," *Harper's Weekly, 35* (Feb. 7, 1891), 106.

15. THE FINAL RECKONING

GENERAL MILES left Pine Ridge for Chicago on the evening of January 26. He took with him twenty-five Ghost Dance leaders, including Kicking Bear and Short Bull, whom he intended to confine at Fort Sheridan, Illinois, until passions had subsided enough for them to return to their people. Buffalo Bill Cody, who had turned up at Pine Ridge in the last days of the campaign as a colonel on the staff of the governor of Nebraska, asked to employ the prisoners as part of the troupe of his Wild West show, which was about to embark on a European tour. The chance to get these troublemakers out of the country for a year, and at the same time to relieve the Army of their support, appealed to Miles, and he heartily endorsed Cody's application. But Commissioner of Indian Affairs Morgan regarded circus life as demoralizing and had publicly announced that no more Indians would be permitted to leave the reservation for exhibition purposes. Cody went to the Nebraska congressional delegation and had sufficient pressure applied to Secretary Noble to get the ban lifted, and the prisoners, together with other Sioux recruited at Pine Ridge, joined the show for a profitable trip across the great waters.[1]

Before leaving Pine Ridge, Miles had issued orders disposing of the Indians from other agencies who had gathered there during the campaign. Capt. Jesse M. Lee, who had been military agent for the Brulés in 1876 and 1877, left Pine Ridge on January 31 with 635 Brulés and escorted them across the reservation to Rosebud Agency. Another 141 had already gone of their own accord a week or so earlier. A sergeant of the Sixth Cavalry conducted to Cheyenne River Agency a miscellaneous assortment of seventy-one Indians—largely Miniconjou survivors of Wounded Knee but including also a few Hunkpapas and Brulés. Capt. E. P. Ewers took all of Little Chief's Cheyennes, about 500 in number, to Tongue River Reservation in Montana. These Indians had been residents of Pine Ridge since 1878. Miles believed that they belonged with their kinsmen and, pleading military necessity, had beaten down the protests of the Indian Bureau and transferred them to the north. In May, 254 Hunkpapa prisoners at Fort Sully, refugees from the Grand River fight, were finally released and shipped up the river to Standing Rock.[2]

Still at Pine Ridge were the seventy-three Hunkpapas brought in by Sergeant Standing Soldier after Wounded Knee. They refused to go back to Standing Rock, and although Colonel Shafter, commanding at Pine Ridge, recommended that they be forcibly returned, Brooke and Miles viewed their attitude with more compassion and permitted them to stay at Pine Ridge.[3] Another 600 to 800 Brulés also remained as prisoners of war. They were the Wazhazhas from Pass Creek who were still waiting for a settlement of the Rosebud–Pine Ridge boundary problem to see

1. Miles to Cody, Jan. 16, 1891. Miles to Adjt. Gen., March 14, 17, and 19. Senators C. F. Manderson and A. S. Paddock, Reps. G. L. Laws and G. W. Dorsey to CIA, Feb. 26. Cody to CIA, same date (on U.S. Senate stationery). Morgan to Manderson, March 2. Morgan to Cody and Salsbury, March 9.

2. Special Orders, No. 28, Hq. Div. of the Mo., Pine Ridge, Jan. 26, 1891. Lee to CO Troops in the Field, Jan. 31. Palmer to CIA, Feb. 14. Miles to Adjt. Gen., Jan. 9. Morgan to Sec. Int., Jan. 13 and 20. Barber to CO Ft. Sully, May 12. McLaughlin to CIA, May 13.

3. Lt. G. H. Preston to CO Troops in the Field, Pine Ridge, Feb. 17, 1891, with endorsement by Shafter, same date, Brooke, Feb. 23, and Miles, Feb. 26.

which agency they belonged to. They were restless and hard to control, and they vowed never to return to Rosebud.

The departure of General Miles from Pine Ridge did not end his concern for conditions among the Sioux. Any other general sent to Dakota to suppress the Sioux outbreak would have accomplished this superficially military mission and then withdrawn, leaving the civilian administrators to put things back in order. Not General Miles. He did not trust civilian adminstrators, and he regarded himself as the top expert on the Sioux in the country. With an attitude of smug superiority that infuriated officials of the Indian Bureau, he invaded their preserve and sought to push through his own program for the salvation of the Sioux.

As a matter of fact, he probably *was* the top expert on the Sioux, and his program was rooted in a sounder appreciation of realities than any the Bureau had been able to devise. First, he believed it essential for the Government to win the confidence of the Sioux. A good start could be made by immediately fulfilling the promises of the Crook Commission. "Congress has been in session several weeks," he telegraphed Senator Dawes as early as December 19, "and could if it were disposed in a few hours confirm the treaties [i.e. agreements] that its Commissioners have made with these Indians, and appropriate the necessary funds for its part of the compact."[4] Second, it was patently all wrong to try to starve Indians into learning to support themselves. Rations had to be restored to adequate levels and kept there until the Indians had actually become self-supporting. Third, the soil and climate of Dakota would always prevent agriculture from furnishing the means of subsistence, and the cherished farming program ought to be junked in favor of stock raising. "I do not think any one thing would please those Indians more," he wrote in March 1891, "than to give each family, as far as possible, the Angus or Galloway cattle, which come nearer to their dream of the restoration of the buffalo than anything else."[5] Finally, the Sioux and Cheyennes should be placed

4. Miles to Dawes, Dec. 19, 1890.
5. Miles to Adjt. Gen., March 20, 1891.

under authoritarian rule, which meant military rule. Even before leaving for Dakota in December, Miles had recommended the assignment of Army officers as agents on the Sioux and Cheyenne reservations.[6] By press interviews, by an article in the January issue of *North American Review*,[7] and by correspondence both in and out of proper channels, General Miles vigorously championed his views.

The first item on the program, action intended to instill confidence, was accomplished even before Miles left Pine Ridge. As Little Wound later explained it, "We could not make our Great Father hear us, until we all got out and made a *big noise*."[8] If the newspapers could be credited, the Indians had indeed made a big noise, and Congress was impressed. On January 19, 1891, the President fixed his signature to hastily enacted legislation designed to make good the promises of the Crook Commission: for educational purposes, $165,000; for compensating the Indians of Standing Rock and Cheyenne River "deprived by the authority of the United States of ponies in the year 1876, at the rate of forty dollars for each pony," $200,000 (the Oglalas had already been compensated for their losses); and, at long last, "To enable the Secretary of the Interior to purchase for the Sioux Nation of Indians additional beef required for issue, the rations having been reduced on account of reduced appropriation for the fiscal year ending June 30, 1890, $100,000." A month later, the national lawmakers demonstrated that they remembered the big noise in Dakota. In the Indian Appropriation Act for fiscal 1892 they appropriated $1,100,000 for subsistence and civilization of the Sioux, $100,000 to compensate the "friendly Sioux" for property destroyed by the Ghost Dancers during their dash to the Stronghold in November, and $6,000 to negotiate a settlement of the Pine Ridge–Rosebud boundary problem.[9]

6. See above, pp. 78–79.

7. Miles, "The Future of the Indian Question," *North American Review*, *152* (1891), 1–11.

8. "Rev. William J. Cleveland's Investigation of the Cause of the Sioux Trouble," IRA, *Ninth Annual Report* (1891), p. 31.

9. *U.S. Statutes at Large*, 51st Cong. (1889–91), *26*, 720–21, 1001–02.

With Congress acting kindly toward the Sioux, General Miles decided that it would be fitting to send a party of chiefs to Washington. They could present their grievances to the President and the Secretary of the Interior, and in turn be assured of fair treatment in the future. He requested authority for his plan on January 13, before the final surrender, and set about putting together a delegation that would represent all the agencies and both progressive and nonprogressive factions. Although Miles planned to have the chiefs escorted to Washington by an Army officer, much to his annoyance the Indian Bureau stepped in and won the President's permission to manage the excursion without military participation.[10] Commissioner Morgan sent a subordinate, T. W. Blackburn, to conduct the chiefs to Washington. On February 4 thirty checked in at two Third-Street boarding-houses.

As Miles had conceived it, the conference was supposed to put the chiefs in a happy frame of mind. It had the reverse effect. For the Sioux, a council with officials in Washington was a solemn and portentous occasion. It required, as councils on important matters always had, much oratory and unhurried discussion of the issues. But the Washington officials were busy men and could not find time for the sort of council the chiefs had in mind.

The delegation was escorted to the White House to hear the President make a brief and somewhat threatening talk, then was ushered into the presence of Secretary Noble. It was, reported a correspondent, "a curious and suggestive gathering. . . . The room was small, and crowded to its capacity. There was a desk at one end, and behind it sat the venerable Secretary of the Interior, with white hair and an expression of alternate amusement and concern. Behind and around him was grouped a distinguished array of men and women—high officials and their wives and daughters." The chiefs sat facing Noble. "They looked absurdly out of place and out of harmony. They were in an office in the midst of civilization, sitting on office chairs ranged in rows as at a town-hall meeting. . . . They wore cheap,

10. Miles to Adjt. Gen., Jan. 14, 1891. Adjt. Gen. to Miles, Jan. 13 and 23. Schofield to Miles, Jan. 16.

ill-fitting store-clothes, white shirts, old-fashioned collars, curious neckties. They held in their hands white men's hats."[11]

The Indians had elected John Grass, American Horse, Young-Man-Afraid-of-His-Horses, Hump, Two Strike, High Hawk, and Hollow-Horn-Bear to do the talking, and they had prepared long speeches to make to the Secretary. But the Secretary explained at the beginning that the speeches must be brief. "Did you ever know," American Horse asked indignantly, "of a man who had prepared himself to make a long speech and then be told that his speech would have to be cut short? Did such speech ever amount to anything?" "It is a good thing to make a short speech," the Secretary replied curtly. Well, then, said American Horse, "Is there any possibility of seeing you, say three, four or even five times?" "No," answered Noble. "If you cannot do it in a reasonable time you will have to settle it on the agency, and I wish you would address yourself to the subject of this conference."[12] And so it went throughout the week that the delegation remained in Washington. The chiefs could not say what they wanted to say because no one had the time or patience to listen. They returned home in an angry mood, but not before Young-Man-Afraid had asked some embarrassing questions:

> The troubles spring from seed. The seed was sown long ago by the white man not attending truthfully to his treaties after a majority of our people had voted for them. When the white man speaks, the government and the army see that we obey. When the red man speaks, it goes in at one ear and out of the other. The Indian is for eternity interested in the subject, the white man only when he comes into office for two or three years. I am not an old man, but I have seen many Great Fathers and his headmen.
>
> Why was not the late treaty fixed promptly by the Great Council? Why were our rations cut down a million of pounds? Why have not our winter annuities come? Why was the whole Sioux nation called to account for dancing

11. David Graham Phillips, "The Sioux Chiefs before the Secretary," *Harper's Weekly*, 35 (Feb. 21, 1891), 142.
12. Quoted in Bland, *Brief History of the Late Military Invasion*, pp. 11–14.

a religious dance? Why are the agents always being changed? Why was Agent Gallagher discharged when he wrote that our crops had failed, and our rations must not be cut down? . . . And why does not the blame for what followed belong to the white men?[13]

In March, after the chiefs had gone home, General Miles pointed out that the purpose of sending the delegation to Washington was "to restore and promote confidence and loyalty." "The result," because of the way they had been treated, "has been just the reverse."

> I consider it most unfortunate that these men have been ignored, discouraged and disaffected, and believe that prompt and immediate action should be taken by the Government to correct what has been done, and I earnestly recommend it in the interest of peace in the future. The danger is not now from the hostile element, the leaders of which are either dead or under military surveillance, but from those who have heretofore been loyal, and were represented by the men I originally selected to go to Washington.[14]

The other items on Miles' Sioux program were closely interrelated. He championed military rule of the agencies not only because he was convinced of the necessity for authoritative government but also because he was convinced that military agents could best advance the Sioux toward self-support. The advocacy of military rule stirred up violent controversy, as it had before, notably in the 1870s. It aroused powerful opposition because it threatened the prerogatives of the Interior Department and the patronage of congressmen, and because it struck at the fundamentals of enlightened Indian policy as conceived by reformers in and out of government. But it also won powerful support from those who believed that only military agents could rescue

---

13. Quoted in editorial, "Indian Truth and Eloquence," *Harper's Weekly,* 35 (Feb. 21, 1891), 131. See also Washington *Evening Star,* Feb. 5 and 7, 1891.
14. Miles to Adjt. Gen., March 13, 1891.

Indian administration from the corruption and inefficiency that had burdened it from the beginning.

The press reflected the points of view. Thus the Omaha *Daily Bee:* "The army is not a civilizing agency. Its contact with the Indians has always been demoralizing to the soldier and brutalizing for the red race. The military in charge of the Indian would simply emphasize the frontiersman's motto, 'A dead Injun is a good Injun.' "[15] And the *Chicago Tribune:* "Quaker government has been tried and failed. Church government has been tried and failed. Indian trader and agent government has been tried and worse than failed, for greed, ignorance, and dishonesty have been the outcome of political appointments. Government by the impracticable ideas of visionaries and enthusiasts, a thousand miles away, who never saw an Indian, has been tried, but it is the same old story of failure. What remains now but the government 'just and strong'?" (The words were borrowed from Miles' article in *North American Review*.)[16] Commissioner Morgan expressed the view of the Indian Bureau without equivocation. Asked by Secretary Noble whether the Sioux agencies should be turned over to the Army, Morgan wrote, "To this I answer unhesitatingly—No. . . . The one great and all important object which the nation has set before itself is to civilize and make [the Indians] intelligent, self-supporting citizens. This is essentially a civil process, to be brought about by civil measures and agencies."[17]

Miles enjoyed two significant tactical advantages—first, that the agents, especially D. F. Royer, had spectacularly failed to contain the Ghost Dance mania; and second, that he himself was actually, if not theoretically, running the Sioux reservations. As soon as he reached Pine Ridge on December 31, with Wounded Knee still fresh in the minds of the nation, he began agitating for appointment to the Sioux agencies of the candidates he had recommended on December 11. A master at deliberately misunderstanding instructions and at exceeding authority just

15. Dec. 21, 1890.
16. Dec. 31, 1890.
17. Morgan to Sec. Int., Dec. 23, 1890.

enough to get his way without provoking more than a reprimand from his superiors, he won a fuller victory than anyone in Washington intended.[18]

Pine Ridge presented no problem, for not even the Indian Bureau was prepared to defend Royer. In fact, Commissioner Morgan had recommended his removal on December 12. Thus the President and the officials of the War and Interior Departments were willing to let Miles have an officer for agent at Pine Ridge but were not, despite his ominous predictions of trouble, going to suffer through the open interdepartmental war that his proposal in full would set off. General Schofield informed Miles on January 7 that the military agent at Pine Ridge would have complete control, but that no other officers would be appointed agents. Those nominated by Miles could be assigned temporarily to the other agencies, but only to exercise, in keeping with the President's directive of November 13, such military control as might prove necessary. "This conclusion," said Schofield with intended finality, "is regarded as a final settlement of the question."[19]

Miles' protest—"The authority is not sufficient, and may complicate and embarrass matters"[20]—fell on deaf ears, so he went blandly about attaining his ends anyway. His officers were all strong personalities and could be expected to dominate the civilian agents, with the exception of McLaughlin. Even though the agents were nominally in control, Miles knew who would actually manage the reservations. If the officers failed to perceive what he expected of them, he spelled it out in the order of January 12 that assigned them. Most of General Order No. 2 dealt

18. We have seen (above, p. 245) this technique used to get a court of inquiry for Colonel Forsyth. Miles also used it to have the Cheyennes transferred from Pine Ridge to Tongue River, and he used it in 1886 to have Geronimo and the Chiricahua Apaches sent to a Florida prison after the President himself had ordered otherwise. On this occasion, Miles succeeded in so confusing the issue that the President could only reprimand him for what in fact had been deliberate disobedience of presidential instructions.

19. Morgan to Sec. Int., Dec. 12, 1890, with endorsement by Asst. Commr. Belt, Dec. 20, 1890. Schofield to Miles, Jan. 7, 1891. See also Miles to Schofield, Jan. 6, and Schofield to Miles, same date.

20. Miles to Schofield, Jan. 7, 1891.

with the military surveillance contemplated by Washington, but three paragraphs carried significant implications:

> VI. As idleness and insufficient food are frequently the causes of discontent and hostility, they [the officers] will ascertain to what extent the Indians are occupied, and whether or not rations are sufficient. They will also report the number engaged in civil occupation and the number acting as police or scouts.
>
> VII. As occupation is one of the best measures for the promotion of peace, they will ascertain and report what additional occupation could be afforded these people on the reservation, or in the immediate vicinity, and also whether means of occupation cannot be devised and developed in addition to agriculture and pastoral pursuits, and whether or not they could manufacture all the clothing, leather, agricultural implements and tools required—in fact any industries that would promote their comfort and welfare, and encourage them in peaceful pursuits.
>
> VIII. They will also ascertain whether they realize from the means of occupation afforded them the full benefits, and whether any improvements can be made in that respect.[21]

The order named Capt. E. P. Ewers to Tongue River Reservation in Montana, Capt. Jesse M. Lee to Rosebud, Capt. Joseph H. Hurst to Cheyenne River, and Capt. F. E. Pierce to Pine Ridge. Significantly, for McLaughlin's supporters had rallied to his defense, nothing was said about Standing Rock. The President had suspended Royer on January 8, and Captain Pierce assumed the full duties of Pine Ridge agent on January 12. He fell seriously ill, however, and was replaced a month later by Capt. Charles G. Penney.[22]

21. General Orders, No. 2, Hq. Div. of the Mo., Pine Ridge, Jan. 12, 1891.

22. Pres. Harrison to Sec. Int., Jan. 8, 1891. Capt. F. E. Pierce to CIA, Jan. 13. For evidence of activity by McLaughlin's supporters see correspondence in Vestal, *New Sources of Indian History*, pp. 78–80. Royer told a reporter on Jan. 8: "It [removal from agency] is largely the result of mischief making and strong pressure brought to bear by the democratic press, printing so many falsehoods, gross slan-

Foreseeing immediately that divided responsibility at Rosebud and Cheyenne River Agencies might well produce chaos,
Commissioner Morgan protested Miles' actions. But the general
was ahead of him. On January 30, having returned to Chicago,
he issued an amendment to General Order No. 2, assigning Lt.
Col. W. F. Drum, commander of Fort Yates, to perform the
duties at Standing Rock that Hurst and Lee were charged with
at Cheyenne River and Rosebud.

McLaughlin blew up. "I have been in the Government service
amongst the Indians for 20 consecutive years," he wrote to the
Commissioner. "I am a bonded officer under which I am responsible to the Government and my Commission gives me full control of these Indians and the reservation under the orders of the
proper Department, and in the absence of any just cause I protest
against my authority being thus interfered with, as the unlimited
powers regarding agency management given to officers of another
Department will certainly lessen my influence as agent over the
Indians and cannot be otherwise than detrimental to the service." He and Colonel Drum got along fine, but officers did get
transferred. Drum could be pulled out of Fort Yates "and an officer specially selected by General Miles sent here to assume command, and any officer exercising the powers contemplated in
the order, with General Miles' aggressive views in this respect,
could not be otherwise than detrimental to the welfare of the
Indians and the inevitable result will follow." Therefore, "in
the interests of peace, in justice to myself, and to prevent serious
trouble which I foresee will arise from conflict of authority, I
most earnestly and respectfully request that the Indian Bureau
take the proper steps to cause the revocation of the order of
January 30, so far as relates to this Agency."[23]

It was a telling argument, at least as applied to Standing Rock
and its able agent, and Morgan seized the occasion to reopen the
whole question. He understood the intention behind Paragraphs

---

ders, and infamous matter generally concerning the administration of affairs and
I will add this, in connection, that I do not think the republican press has done
its duty toward me in not helping me to fight the unequal battle which I have
been compelled to face." Omaha *Daily Bee,* Jan. 9, 1891.

23. McLaughlin to CIA, Feb. 4, 1891.

VI, VII, and VIII of General Order No. 2. The responsibilities they contemplated, he pointed out to Secretary Noble, "are not in any sense military functions but belong peculiarly and exclusively to the civil agents. . . . It must be, that General Miles in an excess of zeal has exceeded entirely his authority in thus attempting to take into his hands, to so large an extent, the control and oversight of these Indian agencies." The whole matter should be laid before the President.[24]

Miles had his response ready when the query came from Washington. He recognized the perils of divided authority, he replied, and the solution was simple: turn the Indians over entirely to the control of the Army and thus "end the division of responsibility now existing."[25] Dealing with General Miles, Schofield must have reflected, could be frustrating indeed. He did nothing, probably because he looked to an impending Army shake-up to solve the problem. By a reorganization announced on July 2, 1891, the military divisions were abolished and the department commanders made responsible directly to Washington. The Division of the Missouri became the Department of Missouri, and Miles lost his authority over the Departments of Dakota and the Platte, and thus over the Sioux. A military agent continued to administer Pine Ridge, under General Brooke's command, but the other agencies reverted entirely to civilian management.[26]

Three issues remained unresolved. One was the complaint of the Crow Creek Indians on the Missouri River that their little reservation contained insufficient acreage in relation to population to carry out the allotment program. The Crook Commission had recommended cash compensation as the solution, and the Indian Bureau had repeatedly urged Congress to appropriate the necessary money. But the Indians at Crow Creek were progressive, peace loving, and incapable of making a big enough noise to

24. Morgan to Sec. Int., Feb. 14, 1891.

25. Miles to Adjt. Gen., March 20, 1891.

26. General Orders, No. 57, Washington, July 3, 1891, War Department, *General Orders, 1891.*

be heard in the halls of Congress. They never received their compensation. The noisey Brulés farther west had more success.

Two related issues concerned the Brulés. One was the petition of part of the Lower Brulés, who had gone down to Rosebud in the summer of 1890, to be transferred to the Rosebud rolls and permitted to live with the Upper Brulés. The other was the petition of Lip's Brulés (Wazhazhas) at Pine Ridge to be transferred to the Pine Ridge rolls and permitted to live with the Oglalas.[27] The latter were being held and fed by the Army as prisoners of war pending a settlement, and were giving their military keepers a rough time.

By the Indian Appropriation Act of March 3, 1891, Congress appropriated $6,000 to finance negotiation of the Brulé difficulties. A commission consisting of Charles E. Pearce of St. Louis, A. R. Appleman of Columbus, Ohio, and George H. Harries of Washington, D.C., was formed to conduct the negotiations. Only Harries, who had covered the Pine Ridge campaign for the Washington *Evening Star*, knew much about Indians. The Pearce Commission visited Pine Ridge in June 1891 and quickly found that the only acceptable solution to the problem of the Wazhazhas was to transfer them to Pine Ridge, for they vowed to fight rather than go back to Rosebud. The Oglalas were willing, and more than three-fourths of the adult males signed an agreement to the transfer. A number of Indians from other agencies were also at Pine Ridge and refused to go home, so the agreement embraced them, too. The total number transferred was 811 —635 from Rosebud, 77 from Cheyenne River, 92 from Standing Rock, and 7 from Lower Brulé.[28]

Negotiations at Rosebud went less smoothly. Although the Upper Brulés were perfectly willing to receive the 530 Lower Brulés who wished to move to Rosebud, they conditioned their formal agreement upon a series of unrelated and unacceptable

27. See above, pp. 78–79.
28. Penny to CIA, Aug. 7, 1891. The files of the Indian Bureau and Army contain voluminous correspondence on the Brulé difficulties. Most of the background is given in the terms of reference of the Pearce Commission (Morgan to Pearce, Appleman, and Harries, April 28, 1891) and in Morgan's brief of the commission's report (Morgan to Sec. Int., Nov. 10, 1891).

demands (e.g. moving the Pine Ridge boundary westward to Pass Creek, a proposition the Oglalas had already refused to entertain). The commission had to disband, therefore, without disposing of this matter. The obstinance of the Rosebud chiefs brought into the open the real force behind the desire of the Lower Brulés to move. Several Indians and half-breeds on the Lower Brulé Reservation had been working assiduously to persuade all the Lower Brulés to move, promising that at Rosebud they could forget about farming and live a carefree life. These champions of the old order, however, could not resist boasting that they were being paid for their efforts by Senator R. F. Pettigrew, who in turn was working on behalf of cattlemen who wanted the Lower Brulé Reservation thrown open to whites. The design became clear in April 1892, when Senator Pettigrew introduced legislation in the Senate to open Lower Brulé even though three-fourths of the Lower Brulé Indians had refused to sign a cession agreement. He pushed his bill through the Committee on Indian Affairs, and only the vigorous opposition of the Indian Rights Association prevented him from slipping it through the full Senate.[29]

Among the Sioux, the Ghost Dance religion had been dealt a shattering blow. Wounded Knee demonstrated that Ghost Shirts would not, as the apostles had promised, turn the bullets of the white man. The Government had moved to restore ration issues to former levels and to carry out the other recommendations of the Crook Commission, thus alleviating much of the distress that had made the religion so appealing. And Kicking Bear and Short Bull, apostles of the religion, had been removed from the reservation. Throughout the late winter and early spring of 1891, the Army remained alert for signs of trouble. There was some basis for concern. Travelers among the outlying settlements, especially on the Pine Ridge Reservation, reported that the Indians were restless and seemingly making ready for an out-

29. Welsh, *Civilization among the Sioux Indians* (Philadelphia, 1893), p. 21. IRA, *Eleventh Annual Report* (1893), p. 52. IRA, "Protest by the Executive Committee . . . against the Passage of Senator Pettigrew's Bill for Removal of the Lower Brule Indians to the Rosebud Reserve" (Philadelphia, Feb. 23, 1893).

break in the spring, the time originally prophesied for the millennium. But spring came and went without any difficulty, and gradually the Sioux discarded the religion that had promised so much.

The story was similar elsewhere. When the millennium failed to come, the other plains tribes either gave up the religion or merged it, shorn of the more spectacular features, with the rest of their religious beliefs. Until his death in 1932, Wovoka lived quietly among his people, the Paiutes, who continued to call him "Our Father." "Had Wovoka's religion a timelessness and a staying quality," concluded his biographer, "Sitting Bull and the dead of the Wounded Knee Massacre would have risen as its saints. But the Messiah himself, in setting positive dates for the great millennium, had signed a death warrant for the faith."[30]

Religion had failed to restore the old life. For the Indians of the West, there was now no choice but to submit to the new life.

30. Bailey, *Wovoka*, p. 200; see also Mooney, *Ghost-Dance*, p. 927.

Bibliography

1. Manuscript Material

McCormick, Maj. L. S., "Wounded Knee and Drexel Mission Fights," December 1904, in E. S. Luce Seventh Cavalry Collection. McCormick observed the two battles in which the Seventh Cavalry participated from the vantage of regimental adjutant. His military bias detracts only slightly from the value of his detailed account.

National Archives. All correspondence cited in the footnotes without source identification is in the National Archives. Consulted were Record Group (RG) 75, Records of the Bureau of Indian Affairs; RG 48, Records of the Office of the Secretary of the Interior; RG 107, Records of the Office of the Secretary of War; RG 94, Records of the Adjutant General's Office; and RG 98, Records of United States Army Commands. Especially valuable were the four drawers of Special Case 188, RG 75, containing Indian Bureau correspondence relating specifically to the Ghost Dance troubles; the transcript of testimony of the Wounded Knee court of inquiry; General Miles' Letters-Sent Field Book; the field messages from Carr and Brooke to Miles during the Pine Ridge campaign; and the reports of Inspector General Kent's investigations into the escape of Big Foot and the Drexel Mission fight. James Mooney used some of these records in writing his *Ghost-Dance,* but neither he nor any subsequent student systematically exploited the official documents in depth. They are the principal body of sources shaping the narrative and interpretations of this book.

Nebraska State Historical Society. The Judge Eli S. Ricker Collection consists of interviews with many actors in the history of the Sioux from about 1850 until the close of the century, recorded in pencil on ruled tablets. The largest share pertains to the Ghost Dance, for it was a comparatively recent event when Ricker pursued his investigations, and many participants were still living. Especially useful were the interviews with mixed-blood participants. Having lived with the Sioux and speaking their language, these men understood what was happening on the Indian side and, unlike their full-blood kinsmen, could relate it in terms that make sense to the white student. To anyone who has dealt very extensively with Indian testimony, their accounts are refreshingly coherent. Too, Judge Ricker was an intelligent, capable interviewer who could establish rapport with his subjects and knew which questions to ask. Even so, there is much fantasy in the Ricker interviews, and they must be carefully checked against contemporary documents and balanced against probabilities.

Order of Indian Wars, American Military Institute, Washington, D.C. Miscellaneous files.

Rhodes, Maj. Gen. Charles D., "Diary of the Brule-Sioux (Pine Ridge) Indian War," Manuscript, 1940, shelved in East Search Room, National Archives. Rhodes was a lieutenant in the 6th Cavalry in 1891. Although this regiment played a less active role in the campaign than the 7th and 9th, the diary contains some useful information.

2. GOVERNMENT PUBLICATIONS

Board of Indian Commissioners, *Annual Reports,* 1885–95. This was a quasi-official body formed in 1869 as a feature of Grant's Peace Policy. By 1880 the Board had lost much of its influence, but its reports contain interesting commentary, generally reflecting the attitudes of the reform organizations, on the course of Indian policy.

Commissioner of Indian Affairs, *Annual Reports,* 1880–92. The printed reports of the Commissioner reveal the policies pursued and advocated by Federal officials and also contain statistical data as well as the annual reports and other correspondence of the agents.

Congressional Record, 51st Cong., 1st sess., Vol. 22.

Densmore, Frances, *Teton Sioux Music,* Bureau of American Ethnology Bulletin 61, Washington, 1918. The author was one of the pioneer ethnologists to work among the Sioux. This study deals with cultural matters considerably broader than the title indicates and was valuable to this book chiefly for its material on the Sun Dance.

Dorsey, J. O., *A Study of Siouan Cults,* 11th Annual Report of the Bureau of American Ethnology, 1888–89, Washington, 1894. Another early ethnologist among the Sioux, Dorsey's study aids in understanding Sioux social organization.

Ewers, John C., *Teton Dakota Ethnology and History,* Berkeley, National Park Service, 1938. An excellent synthesis, with emphasis on material culture, by an outstanding ethnologist. This is a mimeographed report prepared mainly for reference by museum planners.

Kappler, Charles J., comp. and ed., *Indian Affairs, Laws and Treaties.* . . . Vol. 1–2: Senate Documents, 57th Cong., 1st sess., No. 452; Vol. 3: Senate Documents, 62d Cong., 2d sess., No. 719.

Mooney, James, *The Ghost-Dance Religion and the Sioux Outbreak of 1890,* 14th Annual Report of the Bureau of American Ethnology, 1892–93, Pt. II, Washington, 1896. This classic study has been evaluated in the text.

Otis, D. S., "History of the Allotment Policy," *Readjustment of Indian Affairs,* Hearings before the Committee on Indian Affairs, House of Representatives, 73d Cong., 2d sess., on H. R. 7902.

Richardson, James D., *A Compilation of Messages and Papers of the Presidents, 1789–1897,* 9 vols. Washington, 1898.

Royce, Charles C., comp., *Indian Land Cessions in the United States,* 18th Annual Report of the Bureau of American Ethnology, 1896–97, Washington, 1899. An exhaustive, definitive work indispensable for any student of Indian history.

Secretary of War, *Annual Reports,* 1890–92. The report for 1891 contains many official reports of the military activities on the Sioux reservations but omits some key documents.

Senate Documents, 50th Cong., 2d sess., No. 17. Correspondence and transcript of councils of the Sioux Commission of 1888.

Senate Documents, 51st Cong., 1st sess., No. 51. Correspondence and transcript of councils of the Sioux Commission of 1889.

Swanton, John R., *The Indian Tribes of North America,* Bureau of Ethnology Bulletin 145, Washington, 1952. Helpful reference study of linguistic and tribal classifications.

U.S. Statutes at Large, 51st Cong. (1889–91), Vol. 26.

War Department, *General Orders and Circulars,* 1890–91.

War Department, *Special Orders,* 1890–91.

3. NEWSPAPERS. 1890–91

Chicago Tribune

Nebraska State Journal (Lincoln)

New York Herald

Omaha *Daily Bee*

Sioux City Journal

Sioux Falls Argus-Leader

Washington *Evening Star*

4. PERIODICALS AND ARTICLES

Army and Navy Journal, 1890–91.

Arnold, Lt. Col. Frazer, "Ghost Dance and Wounded Knee," *Cavalry Journal, 43* (1934), 18–20. Reproduces Lieutenant Mann's letter to his brother written just after Wounded Knee, a vital document for understanding certain phases of the engagement.

Bourke, John G., "The Indian Messiah," *Nation* (Dec. 4, 1890), pp. 439–40.

Brininstool, E. A., "Buffaloing Buffalo Bill," *Hunter-Trader-Trapper* (April 1938). Popular account of Cody's mission to arrest Sitting Bull.

Colby, Brig. Gen. L. W., "The Sioux Indian War of 1890–'91," *Transactions and Reports of the Nebraska State Historical Society, 3* (1892), 144–90. Colby commanded the Nebraska militia in the Sioux campaign. This article is detailed and useful but inaccurate in many respects. It includes several letters of importance.

Colby, Brig. Gen. L. W., "Wanagi Olowan Kin (The Ghost Songs of the Dakotas)," *Proceedings and Collections of the Nebraska State Historical Society, 1*, 2d ser. (1895), 131–50. Reproduces translations of ghost songs.

Dawes, Henry L., "Have We Failed the Indian?" *Atlantic Monthly, 84* (1899), 280. Senator Dawes questions the means of executing the Dawes Severalty Act.

Dougherty, Capt. W. E., "The Recent Messiah Craze," *Journal of the Military Service Institution of the United States, 12* (1891), 576–78. Observations of an infantry officer at Pine Ridge during the outbreak.

Eastman, Elaine Goodale, "The Ghost Dance War and Wounded Knee Massacre of 1890–91," *Nebraska History, 26* (1945), 26–42.

Elaine Goodale taught school at Pine Ridge during the Ghost Dance troubles and later married the agency physician, Dr. Charles Eastman, a Santee Sioux. This article, which includes excerpts from her diary, is a valuable source despite its antimilitary tone.

Fechet, Maj. E. G., "The True Story of the Death of Sitting Bull," *Proceedings and Collections of the Nebraska State Historical Society*, 2d ser. 2 (1898), 179–89. Reprinted from *Cosmopolitan, 20* (1896), 493–501. A slightly different version appears in *South Dakota Historical Collections, 4* (1908), 493–501. Fechet led the troops in the Grand River affair. His lengthy account is detailed and accurate and indispensable to any account of the killing of Sitting Bull.

Finley, Mrs. James A., "The Messiah Superstition," *Journal of American Folk-Lore, 4* (1891), 66–68. Reprinted from *Essex County Mercury* (Salem, Mass.), Nov. 26, 1890. Eyewitness account of a Ghost Dance at Pine Ridge by the wife of the Wounded Knee postmaster.

Fitzgerald, Sister Mary Clement, "Bishop Marty and His Sioux Missions," *South Dakota Historical Collections, 20* (1940), 525–58.

Frank Leslie's Illustrated Newspaper, 1890–91.

Frink, Maurice M., "Died Here Innocent," *Outing* (February 1915), 549–54. Interesting article based on personal experience at Pine Ridge when Wounded Knee was still fresh in the minds of survivors.

Gibbon, Brig. Gen. John, "Transfer of Indian Bureau to War Department," *American Catholic Quarterly Review, 19* (1894), 244–59. Plea by a veteran Indian fighter for military responsibility for Indian affairs.

Godfrey, Maj. E. S., "Cavalry Fire Discipline," *Journal of the Military Service Institution of the United States, 19* (1896), 259. A technical article illustrated with personal experiences from Wounded Knee and other battles.

Goldfrank, Esther S., "Historic Change and Social Character: A Study of the Teton Dakota," *American Anthropologist, 45* (1943), 67–83.

Green, Charles L., "The Indian Reservation System of the Dakotas to 1889," *South Dakota Historical Collections, 14* (1928), 307–415. An excellent survey.

Green, Lt. L. D., "The Army and the Indian," *Harper's Weekly, 38* (May 19, 1894), 471. Army officers make good Indian agents and Indians benefit from serving in the Army.

Gresham, Lt. John C., "The Story of Wounded Knee," *Harper's*

Weekly, 35 (Feb. 7, 1891), 106–07. Good firsthand account by a participant.

Grinnell, George Bird, "Account of the Northern Cheyenne concerning the Messiah Superstition," *Journal of American Folk-Lore, 4* (1891), 62–67. Expert analysis by one of the best interpreters of Indian life and history.

Harper's Weekly, 1890–91.

Hawthorne, Lt. Harry L., "The Sioux Campaign of 1890–91," *Journal of the Military Service Institution of the United States, 19* (1896), 185–87. Hawthorne and Lt. W. P. Richardson (see below) carried on a warm but inconclusive debate in this periodical over the management of the Wounded Knee engagement.

Illustrated American, 1890–91.

Kelley, W. F., "The Indian Troubles and the Battle of Wounded Knee," *Transactions and Reports of the Nebraska State Historical Society, 4* (1892), 30–50. Excellent article by a newspaper reporter who covered the Pine Ridge campaign and participated in the battle of Wounded Knee.

Mattes, Merrill J., "The Enigma of Wounded Knee," *Plains Anthropologist, 5* (1960), 1–11. Good analysis of published evidence.

Mattison, Ray H., "The Indian Reservation System on the Upper Missouri, 1865–1890," *Nebraska History, 36* (1955), 141–72. Good survey.

Maus, Capt. Marion P., "The New Indian Messiah," *Harper's Weekly, 34* (Dec. 6, 1890), 944. A member of Miles' staff, Maus observed the Ghost Dance in October 1890 when the general visited Pine Ridge as a member of the Northern Cheyenne Commission.

Mekeel, Scudder, "A Short History of the Teton-Dakota," *North Dakota Historical Quarterly, 10* (1943), 137–205. Good survey.

Miles, Maj. Gen. Nelson A., "The Future of the Indian Question," *North American Review, 152* (1891), 1–11. A plea for his solution to the Indian question.

Mooney, James, "The Indian Ghost Dance," *Collections of the Nebraska State Historical Society, 16* (1911), 168–86. In this speech before the Nebraska State Historical Society, Mooney approached the topic in a more popular vein than in the Bureau of American Ethnology publication.

Moorehead, Warren K., "The Indian Messiah and the Ghost Dance," *American Antiquarian and Oriental Journal, 12* (1891),

161–67. An anthropologist's personal observations of the Sioux Ghost Dance.

Parker, Mrs. Z. A., "Ghost Dance at Pine Ridge," *Journal of American Folk-Lore, 4* (1891), 160–62. Reprinted from New York *Evening Post,* April 18, 1891. Eyewitness account of a Ghost Dance.

Philip, George, "James (Scotty) Philip," *South Dakota Historical Collections, 20* (1940), 358–406. Philip ranched in the ceded tract in 1890 and was visited by some Ghost Dancers.

Phillips, David Graham, "The Sioux Chiefs before the Secretary," *Harper's Weekly, 35* (Feb. 21, 1891), 142.

Phister, Lt. N. P., "The Indian Messiah," *American Anthropologist,* o.s. *4* (1891), 105–08. Account of the origins of the Ghost Dance religion among the Paiutes.

Remington, Frederic, "Chasing a Major-General," *Harper's Weekly, 34* (Dec. 6, 1890), 946–47. Remington accompanied Miles and the Northern Cheyenne Commission.

Remington, Frederic, "The Art of War and Newspaper Men," *Harper's Weekly, 34* (Dec. 6, 1890), 947.

Remington, Frederic, "Indians as Irregular Cavalry," *Harper's Weekly, 34* (Dec. 27, 1890), 1004–06.

Remington, Frederic, "The Sioux Outbreak in South Dakota," *Harper's Weekly, 35* (Jan. 24, 1891), 57–62. Excellent reportorial coverage of the Pine Ridge campaign.

Remington, Frederic, "Lieutenant Casey's Last Scout," *Harper's Weekly, 35* (Jan. 31, 1891), 85–91.

Richardson, Lt. W. P., "Some Observations upon the Sioux Campaign of 1890–91," *Journal of the Military Service Institution of the United States, 18* (1896), 512–31. See Hawthorne, H. L.

Robinson, Doane, "Some Sidelights on the Character of Sitting Bull," *Collections of the Nebraska State Historical Society, 16* (1911), 187–92.

Robinson, Doane, "The Education of Redcloud," *South Dakota Historical Collections, 12* (1924), 156–78. Details the conflict between Red Cloud and Agent McGillycuddy over organization of the Indian police force at Pine Ridge.

Schwatka, Lt. Frederick, "The Sun-Dance of the Sioux," *Century Magazine, 39* (1890), 753–59. Excellent eyewitness account of the last Sioux Sun Dance.

Scott, Brig. Gen. E. D., "Wounded Knee, a Look at the Record,"

Field Artillery Journal, 24 (1939), 5–24. Analysis of the Wounded Knee court of inquiry records with the aim of vindicating the Army.

Seymour, Charles G., "The Sioux Rebellion, the Final Review," *Harper's Weekly, 35* (Feb. 7, 1891), 106.

Smith, Marian W., "The War Complex of the Plains Indians," *Proceedings of the American Philosophical Society, 78* (1938), 425–64.

Sword, George, "The Story of the Ghost Dance," transl. Emma Sickels, *Folk-Lorist, 1* (1892–93), 28–31. Sword was the intelligent and able captain of the Pine Ridge police. This is an important source and also contains translations of some ghost songs.

Thayer, James B., "A People without Law," *Atlantic Monthly, 48* (1891), 540–51, 676–87. Plea for extension of U.S. law to the Indians.

Traub, Capt. Peter E., "The First Act of the Last Sioux Campaign," *Journal of the United States Cavalry Association, 15* (1905), 872–79. Traub was at Fort Yates in 1890 and here deals with the means by which Buffalo Bill's attempt to arrest Sitting Bull was thwarted.

Voget, Fred W., "The American Indian in Transition: Reformation and Accommodation," *American Anthropologist, 58* (1956), 249–63. Discussion of nativistic religious movements produced by culture conflict.

Walker, J. R., "The Sun Dance and Other Ceremonies of the Ogla-la Division of the Teton Dakota," *Anthropological Papers of the American Museum of Natural History, 16*, Pt. 2 (1917). Although modified in some respects by later investigations, this remains the most exhaustive and detailed study of Oglala religion.

Watson, Elmo Scott, "The Last Indian War, 1890–91—A Study of Newspaper Jingoism," *Journalism Quarterly, 20* (1943), 205–19. Excellent scholarly study by a leading journalistic historian.

Watson, Elmo Scott, "Pine Ridge, 1890–91," *Westerners Brand Book* (Denver, 1946), pp. 3–4. List of prominent people at Pine Ridge during the Ghost Dance trouble.

Watson, Julia S., "A Sketch of George H. Harries, Reporter of Wounded Knee," *New York Westerners Brand Book, 3* (1956), 73–76.

Wells, Philip F., "Ninety-six Years Among the Indians of the Northwest," *North Dakota History, 15* (1948), 265–312. Wells' contemporary testimony is far more valuable than this reminiscence.

Welsh, Herbert, "The Indian Question, Past and Present," *New England Magazine, 2* (1890), 257–66. Plea for the Indian policies advocated by the Indian Rights Association, of which Welsh was the influential corresponding secretary.

Welsh, Herbert, "The Meaning of the Dakota Outbreak," *Scribner's Magazine, 9* (1891), 429–52. Again, Welsh presents the Sioux troubles as the price of not following policies championed by the reform groups.

Wilson, G., "The Sioux War," *Nation, 52* (1891), 29–30.

Wissler, Clark, "Societies and Ceremonial Associations of the Oglala Division of the Teton-Dakota," *Anthropological Papers of the American Museum of Natural History, 11,* Pt. 2 (1916). The most valuable work on Oglala social organization.

Woodruff, K. Brent, "The Episcopal Mission to the Dakotas," *South Dakota Historical Collections, 20* (1940), 525–58.

5. Books and Pamphlets

Alexander, Hartley B., *The World's Rim* (Lincoln: University of Nebraska Press, 1933). Contains a perceptive if impressionistic treatment of the Ghost Dance against the backdrop of earlier movements of similar character.

Bailey, Paul, *Wovoka, the Indian Messiah* (Los Angeles: Westernlore Press, 1957). Although treating the Ghost Dance among the Sioux briefly and somewhat superficially, this biography of the founder of the religion is very well done and will continue to serve as the basic source.

Beyer, W. F., and Keydel, O. F., eds., *Deeds of Valor* (Detroit, 1907), Vol. 2. Contains Cpl. Paul Weinert's graphic story of his experiences at Wounded Knee.

Bland, Thomas A., *A Brief History of the Late Military Invasion of the Home of the Sioux* (Washington, National Indian Defense Association, 1891). This partisan defense of the Sioux in the Ghost Dance troubles contains some very valuable letters and interviews.

Bourke, John G., *On the Border with Crook* (New York, 1891). This classic of frontier history by General Crook's aide includes a few pages dealing with the general's role in the land cession of 1889.

Boyd, James P., *Recent Indian Wars* (Philadelphia, 1891). This is valuable chiefly as a compilation of press dispatches from Pine Ridge during the Ghost Dance outbreak.

Brady, Cyrus T., *Indian Fights and Fighters* (New York, 1904). Contains an appendix recounting Maj. Guy V. Henry's adventures in the Pine Ridge campaign.

Burdick, Usher L., ed., *My Friend the Indian, or Three Heretofore Unpublished Chapters of the Book Published under the Title of My Friend the Indian, by Major James McLaughlin* (Baltimore: Proof Press, 1936). McLaughlin's publishers rejected his final three chapters, containing much of interest to the story of the Ghost Dance at Standing Rock, and they were published in this pamphlet.

Campbell, Walter S. See Vestal, Stanley.

Carter, Lt. Col. W. H., *From Yorktown to Santiago with the Sixth U.S. Cavalry* (Baltimore, 1900). Carter was an officer of the 6th in the Pine Ridge campaign. His history of the regiment contains a graphic chapter on the role of this unit in the campaign.

Cook, James H., *Fifty Years on the Old Frontier* (New Haven: Yale University Press, 1923). A scout at Pine Ridge, Cook was a perceptive, literate observer who understood both white and Indian motivations.

Crook, George. See Schmitt, Martin F.

DeBarthe, Joe, *Life and Adventures of Frank Grouard* (Buffalo, Wyo., n.d.), 2d ed. ed. E. I. Stewart (Norman: University of Oklahoma Press, 1958). Grouard was one of the great frontier scouts, but his contribution regarding the Pine Ridge outbreak, in which he was a scout, is disappointing.

Dewey, M. E., *Historical Sketch of the Formation and Achievements of the Women's National Indian Association* (n.p., 1900).

Eastman, Charles A., *From Deep Woods to Civilization: Chapters in the Autobiography of an Indian* (Boston: Little, Brown & Co., 1920). Most of Eastman's writings on Indian history have been seriously questioned, but his account of the Ghost Dance at Pine Ridge, where he was agency physician, is an outstanding source generally corroborated by other evidence.

Eastman, Elaine Goodale, *Pratt, the Red Man's Moses* (Norman: University of Oklahoma Press, 1935). The standard biography of the founder of Carlisle Indian School portrays Pratt in the conventional image of the reform groups of the 1880s, in which the Sioux would hardly have concurred. A pioneer in Indian education herself, Mrs. Eastman questions none of the assumptions on which the education program was founded.

Farrow, Edward S., *Farrow's Military Encyclopedia: A Dictionary of Military Knowledge* (3 vols., New York, 1885).

Fiske, Frank Bennett, *Life and Death of Sitting Bull* (Fort Yates, N.D.: Pioneer-Arrow Press, 1933). Reared at Standing Rock, Fiske as a youth observed the events of 1890 and later obtained much information from participants. This book is a valuable source for the Standing Rock story.

Gessner, Robert, *Massacre: A Survey of Today's American Indian* (New York: Farrar & Co., 1931). The title is misleading. This is an intensely antimilitary and grossly inaccurate history of Wounded Knee that created a sensation when it was published.

Hodge, Frederick Webb., ed., *Handbook of American Indians North of Mexico* (2 vols. Washington, 1912). Still the richest storehouse of knowledge about the Indian.

Howe, M. A. DeWolfe, *The Life and Labors of Bishop Hare* (New York, 1911). Contains important material on the Episcopal missionary effort among the Sioux.

Hyde, George E., *Red Clouds' Folk: A History of the Oglala Sioux Indians* (Norman: University of Oklahoma Press, 1937; 2d ed. 1957). Hyde is one of the few historians who has mastered the techniques of exploiting Indian evidence, and, despite some faults, his Sioux trilogy will long stand as an example of Indian history at its best.

Hyde, George E., *A Sioux Chronicle* (Norman: University of Oklahoma Press, 1956). This deals with the first decade of the reservation period, 1878–91.

Hyde, George E., *Spotted Tail's Folk: A History of the Brulé Sioux* (Norman: University of Oklahoma Press, 1961).

Indian Rights Association, *Brief Statement of the Nature and Purpose of the Indian Rights Association, with a Summary of Its Work for the Year 1892* (Philadelphia, 1893).

Indian Rights Association, *Protest by the Executive Committee of the Indian Rights Association against the Passage of Senator Pettigrew's Bill for the Removal of the Lower Brule Indians to the Rosebud Reserve* (Philadelphia, 1893).

Indian Rights Association, *Annual Reports*, 1886–93. These are immensely valuable not only for revealing the conventional reform theories of the time but also for the many factual reports of the IRA investigators, who kept close watch on the activities at the Indian agencies.

Johnston, Sister Mary Antonio, *Federal Relations with the Great Sioux Indians of South Dakota, 1887–1933, with Particular Reference to Land Policy under the Dawes Act* (Washington: Catholic University of America Press, 1948). Despite bad organization and excessive footnoting, this is a basic study.

LaFarge, Oliver, ed., *The Changing Indian* (Norman: University of Oklahoma Press, 1942). Contributions by experts in Indian matters on the many problems confronted by the Indian as a result of conquest, official policy, and culture conflict.

Lake Mohonk Conference of Friends of the Indian and Other Dependent Peoples, *Annual Reports,* 1885–95. The reform groups met each year at Lake Mohonk, N.Y., to formulate policies to press upon Congress and the Government. The annual reports reveal reform philosophies and activities.

Leupp, Francis E., *Civil Service Reform Essential to a Successful Indian Administration* (Philadelphia, Indian Rights Association, 1895). Leupp, a realistic reformer, later became Commissioner of Indian Affairs.

Lindquist, G. E., *The Red Man in the United States* (New York: Doran, 1923).

Lowie, Robert H., *Primitive Religion* (New York: Boni and Liveright, 1924).

McGillycuddy, Julia B., *McGillycuddy: Agent* (Palo Alto: Stanford University Press, 1941). Laudatory biography of the stormy agent at Pine Ridge; generally good despite inaccuracies.

MacGregor, Gordon, *Warriors without Weapons: A Study of the Society and Personality Development of the Pine Ridge Sioux* (Chicago: University of Chicago Press, 1946). A team of field investigators gathered data for this excellent study of the impact of white ways upon the Sioux.

McGregor, James H., *The Wounded Knee Massacre from the Viewpoint of the Sioux* (Minneapolis: Lund Press, 1940). Although badly partisan and disorganized, this book contains many accounts by Indian participants. Few, however, are coherent enough to be useful.

McLaughlin, James, *My Friend the Indian* (Boston and New York: Houghton Mifflin Co., 1910). See also Burdick, Usher L. As well as presenting the point of view of the Standing Rock agent, this autobiography sets forth much important detail. Indispensable for understanding the death of Sitting Bull.

Miller, David H., *Ghost Dance* (New York: Duell, Sloan and Pearce, 1959). Uncritical reliance on Indian evidence, mostly obtained by the author himself, and superficial investigation of standard sources make this popular account of doubtful value.

Moorehead, Warren K., *The American Indian in the United States, 1850–1914* (Andover, Mass.: Andover Press, 1914). The author, an anthropologist, was at Pine Ridge in 1890–91.

Morgan, Thomas J., *The Present Phase of the Indian Question,* Boston Indian Citizenship Committee, Pub. 10 (Boston, 1891). Defense of Morgan's policies as Indian Commissioner.

Neihardt, John G., *Black Elk Speaks: Being a Life Story of a Holy Man of the Oglala Sioux* (New York: Morrow, 1932). Reminiscence of a Pine Ridge Sioux, which is factually weak.

Neihardt, John G., *Song of the Messiah: A Cycle of the West* (New York: Macmillan & Co., 1949). Neihardt sensitively catches the mood of the new religion as felt by the Sioux.

Priest, Loring B., *Uncle Sam's Stepchildren: The Reformation of the Indian Policy, 1865–1887* (New Brunswick: Rutgers University Press, 1942). The author of this standard history of Federal Indian policy tends in general to accept as desirable the goals toward which the reformers of the period were working, and also the means they advocated.

Robinson, Doane, *A History of the Dakota or Sioux Indians* (2d. ed. Minneapolis: Ross and Haines, 1956). Although poorly written, this pioneering history of the Sioux contains considerable information not found elsewhere.

Rodenbough, Theo. F., ed. *The Army of the United States* (New York, 1896).

Roosevelt, Theodore, *Report of the Hon. Theodore Roosevelt Made to the United States Civil Service Commission, upon a Visit to Certain Indian Reservations and Indian Schools in South Dakota, Nebraska, and Kansas* (Philadelphia, Indian Rights Association, 1893).

Russell, Don, *The Lives and Legends of Buffalo Bill* (Norman: University of Oklahoma Press, 1960). The definitive biography of the legendary scout.

Schell, Herbert S., *History of South Dakota* (Lincoln: University of Nebraska Press, 1961).

Schofield, Gen. John M., *Forty-six Years in the Army* (New York, 1897).

Schmeckebier, Laurence F., *The Office of Indian Affairs: Its History, Activities and Organization* (Baltimore: Johns Hopkins University Press, 1927). A thorough study of the Indian Bureau, past and present. The history of Indian policy is concise and accurate.

Schmitt, Martin F., ed., *General George Crook, His Autobiography* (Norman: University of Oklahoma Press, 1946). The excerpts from Crook's diary reveal much about the techniques by which the land agreement of 1889 was sold to the Sioux.

Secoy, Frank R., *Changing Military Patterns on the Great Plains,* American Ethnological Society, *Monographs,* 21 (New York, 1953).

Seymour, Flora Warren, *Indian Agents of the Old Frontier* (New York: Appleton-Century, 1941). Romanticized sketches of selected agents.

Seymour, Flora Warren, *The Story of the Sioux* (p.p. Girard, Kans., 1924). Popular and romanticized history.

Slattery, Charles L., *Felix Reville Brunot, 1820–1898* (New York, 1901). Laudatory biography of one of the leading reformers.

Smith, DeCost, *Red Indian Experiences* (London: Allen and Unwin, 1949).

Spindler, Will H., *Tragedy Strikes at Wounded Knee* (n.p., 1955).

Standing Bear, Luther, *My People the Sioux* (Boston: Houghton Mifflin Co., 1928). Another Indian reminiscence, interesting mainly for point of view.

Textor, Lucy, *Official Relations between the United States and the Sioux Indians* (Palo Alto, 1896). Standard authority.

Vestal, Stanley, ed., *New Sources of Indian History, 1850–1891* (Norman: University of Oklahoma Press, 1934). Reproduces unofficial documents that are vital to any study of the Sioux troubles of 1890–91.

Vestal, Stanley, *Sitting Bull: Champion of the Sioux* (Boston: Houghton Mifflin, 1932; 2d ed. Norman: University of Oklahoma Press, 1957). Writing under the pseudonym of Stanley Vestal, Walter S. Campbell gathered a great quantity of firsthand Indian testimony and wove it into several vividly written works of Sioux history. His work is significant, but must always be read in light of his uncritical reliance upon Indian evidence and uniform bias toward the Indian viewpoint.

Vestal, Stanley, *Warpath and Council Fire* (New York: Random House, 1948).

Welsh, Herbert, *The Appointment of a First-Rate Indian Agent by the New Administration* (Philadelphia, Indian Rights Association, 1893).

Welsh, Herbert, *Civilization among the Sioux Indians: Report of a Visit to Some of the Sioux Reservations of South Dakota and Ne-braska* (Philadelphia, Indian Rights Association, 1893).

Welsh, Herbert, *The Murrain of Spoils in the Indian Service* (Baltimore, National Civil Service Reform League, 1898).

Welsh, Herbert, *How to Bring the Indian to Citizenship and Citizenship to the Indian* (Philadelphia, Indian Rights Association, 1892).

Welsh, Herbert, *Allotment of Lands: Defense of the Dawes Indian Severalty Bill* (Philadelphia, Indian Rights Association, 1887).

Welsh, Herbert, *A Dangerous Assault upon the Integrity of the Civil Service Law in the Indian Service* (Philadelphia, Indian Rights Association, 1893).

Wissler, Clark, *Indian Cavalcade, or Life on the Old-Time Indian Reservations* (New York: Sheridan House, 1938). Wissler's residence at Pine Ridge in the early years of the twentieth century gave him an insight into the institutions of the reservation system and the process by which they broke down the old Indian life. Although presented in a popular vein, this book is invaluable to the student of the reservation system.

Wissler, Clark, *North American Indians of the Plains* (New York: American Museum of Natural History, 1934; 2d ed. 1948). Standard authority.

Index

Illustrations

1. Pine Ridge Agency about 1885: (1) boarding school, (2) council room and physician's office, (3) offices, (4) supply storehouse, (5) commissary, (6) police quarters, (7) employees' quarters, (8) agent's quarters, (9) interpreter's quarters, (10) stable and annuity issue center, (11) ice and meat house, (12) water works, (13) oil house, (14) Red Cloud's house.

2. The Crook Commission at Crow Creek Agency in July 1889. Seated left to righ
Gov. Charles Foster, William Warner, Maj. Gen. George Crook, Maj. Cyrus
Roberts, aide to Crook. Standing left to right: John A. Lott, stenographer; Wilso
messenger; John Warner, clerk; Jerome Miller, secretary.

3. Photographs of the Ghost Dance actually in progress are extremely rare. This one was taken on the Pine Ridge Reservation in December 1890 by A. G. Johnson of York, Neb.

4. American Horse (left) and Red Cloud at Pine Ridge Agency in January 1891.

5. Sitting Bull, as photographed by D. F. Barry shortly after his surrender in 1881.

6. Sgt. Red Tomahawk, Yanktonai Sioux policeman who shot Sitting Bull at Grand River on December 15, 1890. This photograph shows him as captain of Indian police about 1892.

7. Short Bull (left) and Kicking Bear, apostles of the Ghost Dance religion among the Sioux.

8. Troops from the "camp of observation" near the forks of Cheyenne River mingle with Miniconjou Ghost Dancers of Big Foot's band in the autumn of 1890.

9. Maj. Gen. Nelson A. Miles, as commander of the Division of the Missouri, directed the campaign against the Sioux Ghost Dancers in 1890–91. A distinguished Civil War general and Indian fighter, he later commanded the United States Army during the Spanish American War. This portrait was made about 1895.

10. Two Strike, boyhood friend of Spotted Tail, was one of the few genuine chiefs left among the Brulés in 1890. Although more than 70 years old and nearly senile, Two Strike led his people into the Ghost Dance ranks when troops appeared at Rosebud in November 1890. This picture was taken in Washington by Alexander Gardner 18 years earlier.

11. Little Wound, Oglala chief, was at first a powerful advocate of the Ghost Dance, but shortly after the appearance of troops at Pine Ridge he shifted his influence to the cause of peace. William Dinwiddie made this portrait in 1896.

12. Brig. Gen. John R. Brooke, commanding the Department of the Platte, exercised field command of the troops at Pine Ridge in 1890–91.

13. The officer corps of the Seventh U.S. Cavalry still contained veterans of the Little Bighorn when this picture was taken at Pine Ridge in January 1891, shortly after the Battle of Wounded Knee. Seated left to right: Capt. W.S. Edgerly, Capt. Henry J. Nowlan, unidentified, Capt. Charles A. Varnum, Col. James W. Forsyth, Maj. Samuel M. Whitside, Capt. Myles Moylan, Capt. Edward S. Godfrey, unidentified.

14. Troop of the Seventh Cavalry at Pine Ridge Agency in January 1891.

15. Part of Battery E, First U.S. Artillery, at Pine Ridge Agency in January 1891. Cpl. Paul H. Weinert is seated behind the Hotchkiss gun with which he drove the Sioux from the ravine "pocket" at Wounded Knee and thus won a Medal of Honor.

16. The field of Wounded Knee as it appeared during the burial of the dead. The body in the foreground is that of Yellow Bird, the medicine man who incited the young men of Big Foot's band to fight. This is a drawing executed by Mary Irvin Wright from an imperfect photograph for James Mooney's *Ghost-Dance*.

17. The dead of Big Foot's band were buried in a mass grave on top of the hill from which the artillery had fired during the battle. A civilian group did the work under contract. Infantrymen stood by to guard against attack by angry Sioux.

18. Two Strike, Crow Dog, and High Hawk, prominent leaders of the Brulé Sioux, at Pine Ridge Agency after the surrender in January 1891.

19. General Miles and staff viewing the Indian camp at Pine Ridge Agency on January 16, 1891, the day after the surrender.

20. The military camp at Pine Ridge Agency on the day of the grand review, January 21, 1891.

21. Buffalo Bill and Sioux leaders at Pine Ridge Agency in January 1891. Seated left to right: Thunder Hawk, American Horse, John A. McDonough (correspondent of the *New York World*), Young-Man-Afraid-of-His-Horses, Kicking Bear, Maj. John Burke (manager of Cody's Wild West show); standing left to right: Rocky Bear, Good Voice, Two Lance, J. C. Craiger, Two Strike, Buffalo Bill Cody, Crow Dog, High Hawk, Short Bull.

22. Plenty Horses murdered Lt. E. W. Casey to wipe out the stain of Carlisle Indian School and win the favor of his people. A court judged the crime an act of war and set him free. He is shown here at Fort Meade while awaiting trial in the spring of 1891.

23. Ghost Dancers imprisoned at Fort Sheridan, Ill., following the surrender, January 1891. Nos. 4 and 5 are Kicking Bear and Short Bull.

24. The Wounded Knee battlefield today, looking north. In the foreground is the ravine "pocket" from which the Sioux inflicted heavy casualties on the troops before artillery drove them out. The church stands on Cemetery Hill, from which the Hotchkiss guns raked the Indian village below (right, near windmill). The dead of Big Foot's band are buried in a common grave behind the church.